CENTER STAGE

Express Yourself in English

Lynn Bonesteel   **Samuela Eckstut-Didier**

Series Consultants

MaryAnn Florez

Sharon Seymour

PEARSON

Longman

Center Stage 4: Express Yourself in English

Pearson Education, 10 Bank Street, White Plains, NY 10606

Staff credits: The people who made up the *Center Stage 4* team, representing editorial, production, design, and manufacturing, are Elizabeth Carlson, Dave Dickey, Laura Le Dréan, Martha McGaughey, Gabriela Moya, Robert Ruvo, Julie Schmidt, and Kim Steiner.

Cover art: Gilbert Mayers / Superstock

Photo Credits: **page 3** © Gabe Palmer/Corbis; **page 4** (first) © Michael Ochs Archives/Corbis, (second) © Sunset Boulevard/Sygma/Corbis, (third) © John Springer Collection/Corbis, (fourth) © Paul Buck/epa/Corbis, (fifth) © Rufus F. Folkks/Corbis, (sixth) © Peter Foley/epa/Corbis; **page 5** © Corbis Sygma; **page 6** Royalty Free/GettyImages; **page 7** (first) © Dex Image/Corbis, (second) © ColorBlind Images/Blend Images/Corbis, (third) © Dex Image/Corbis, (fourth) © Russell Glenister/image100/Corbis; **page 8** image100/Royalty Free/Fotosearch; **page 9** © Jeremy Woodhouse/Blend Images/Corbis; **page 12** © Bettmann/Corbis; **page 13** © CinemaPhoto/Corbis; **page 14** Image State/Rights Managed/Fotosearch; **page 17** Stockbyte/GettyImages; **page 18** © image100/Corbis; **page 22** © Reuters/Corbis; **page 26** Rob Lewine/Corbis; **page 40** © Free Agents Limited/Corbis; **page 42** © Burstein Collection/Corbis; **page 45** (first) © image100/Corbis, (second) Photodisc Blue/GettyImages; **page 46** © dura lux/plainpicture/Corbis; **page 47** © Shannon Fagan/Corbis; **page 48** (first) © Tischenko Irina/ShutterStock, (second) oote boe/Alamy, (third) © JuniterImages/Brand X Pictures; **page 49** © Flirt/Corbis; **page 53** © Peter M. Wilson/Corbis; **page 54** © Phil Schermeister/Corbis; **page 59** Stockbyte/GettyImages; **page 63** © Stanley Fellerman/Corbis; **page 67** © Joseph McCullar/ShutterStock; **page 68** Westend 61/GettyImages; **page 70** © Peter Turnley/Corbis; **page 73** (first) Jose Fuste Raga/Corbis, (second) © Craig Lovell/Corbis; **page 74** (first) © Thierry Gouegnon/Reuters/Corbis, (second) © Oswaldo Rivas/Reuters/Corbis, (third) © Owen Franken/Corbis, (fourth) © Owen Franken/Corbis; **page 76** PhotoObjects.net/Fotosearch; **page 77** © Bohemian Nomad Picturemakers/Corbis; **page 78** © Rick Barrentine/Corbis; **page 79** © Owen Franken/Corbis; **page 80** Push/GettyImages; **page 81** (first) Natural Visions/Alamy, (second) Peter Ardito/Index Stock Imagery, (third) Dynamic Graphics Group/IT Stock Free/Alamy; **page 82** (first) © Judy Griesedieck/Corbis, (second) © Bettmann/Corbis; **page 84** © Adam Woolfitt/Corbis; **page 87** Robert Harding Picture Library Ltd/Alamy; **page 89** © Layne Kennedy/Corbis; **page 90** (first) Image Source/Alamy, (second) Phototake Inc./Alamy; **page 92** © pbnj productions/Brand X/Corbis; **page 96** www.CartoonStock.com; **page 106** (first) AGE/Rights Managed/Fotosearch, (second) NiKreationS/Alamy, (third) Motoring Picture Library/Alamy, (fourth) © Duomo/Corbis, (fifth) Donald C Landwehrle/GettyImages, (sixth) Bloom Works Inc./Alamy; **page 107** © Michael Price/Corbis; **page 108** Stockbyte/Corbis; **page 120** (first) Hugh Threlfall/Alamy, (second) Gabe Palmer/Alamy; **page 126** Arthur Rothstein/Corbis; **page 132** (first) Russ Merne/Alamy, (second) © James Leynse/Corbis, (third) Brian Peters/Masterfile; **page 136** ©Atlantide Phototravel/Corbis; page 138 © Andresr/Dreamstime.com; **page 143** © Stockbyte/Corbis; **page 147** (first) © Christophe Boisvieux/Corbis, (second) Ricky John Molloy/Corbis, (third) © Jose Luis Pelaez, Inc./Blend Images/Corbis, (fourth) © Tim Pannell/Corbis, (fifth) © Tanya Constantine/Brand X/Corbis, (sixth) George Doyle/GettyImages; **page 148** © Tom Stewart/Corbis; **page 150** © Paul Almasy/Corbis; **page 152** © Roy McMahon/Corbis; **page 155** © Cezar Perelles; **page 160** © Roy McMahon/Corbis; **page 166** © Ricardo Herrera; **page 171** © Bob Krist/Corbis; **page 172** Riser/GettyImages; **page 173** © MedioImages/Corbis; **page 174** (first) Digital Vision/GettyImages, (second) Richard Ross/GettyImages, (third) Photographers Choice/Royalty Free/Fotosearch; **page 176** RubberBall/Alamy; **page 179** Paul Simcock/GettyImages; **page 180** © Corbis; **page 185** Stockbyte/GettyImages; **page 194** © Heiko Prigge/zefa/Corbis; **page 199** Ryan McVay/GettyImages; **page 205** © Nation Wong/Corbis; **page 208** © Ashley Cooper/Corbis; **page 210** © Mark E. Gibson/Corbis; **page 218** © Dave Bartruff/Corbis; **page 222** © Vincent Laforet/Pool/Reuters/Corbis; **page 227** Glowimages/GettyImages; **page 228** (first) Jim West/Alamy, (second) © Reuters/Corbis; **page 231** (first) © Louis Schwartzberg/Corbis, (second) Jeremy Horner/Alamy, (third) © Paul Glendell/Alamy, (fourth) © Visions of America, LLC/Alamy; **page 232** © Brian Snyder/Reuters/Corbis; **page 234** Dynamic Graphics Group/Creatas/Alamy; **page 235** © Car Culture/Corbis; **page 236** (first) © Hulton-Deutsch Collection/Corbis, (second) © Bettmann/Corbis; **page 241** Digital Vision/GettyImages; **page 242** © Jose Luis Pelaez, Inc./Corbis; **page 245** Alexsander Jocic/Shutterstock; **page 247** © Atlantide Phototravel/Corbis; **page 248** www.CartoonStock.com; **page 249** © Car Culture/Corbis; **page 250** © Randy Faris/Corbis; **page 255** © Mika/zefa/Corbis; **page 256** © David H. Wells/Corbis; **page 269** © SGO/Image Point FR/Corbis; **page 270** © T. Hoenig/A.B./zefa/Corbis; **page 274** © Tina Chang/Veer/Corbis; **page 278** © Ariel Skelley/Corbis; **page 280** Stock Connection/Fotosearch; **page 293** (first) © Underwood & Underwood/Corbis, (second) © Bettmann/Corbis, (third) © Hulton-Deutsch Collection/Corbis, (fourth) © Hulton-Deutsch Collection/Corbis; **page 299** (first) © Bettmann/Corbis, (second) Hulton Archive/GettyImages, (third) Hulton Archive/GettyImages, (fourth) © Hulton-Deutsch Collection/Corbis

Text composition: 101 Studio

Text font: 12 Minion

Illustrations: A Corazón Abierto (Marcela Gómez), Steve Attoe, Laurie A. Conley, Debby Fisher, Marty Harris, John Kanzler, Luis Montiel, Francisco Morales, Chris Pavely, Mari Rodríguez, Roberto Sadí, John Schreiner, Steve Schulman, Gary Torrisi, Meryl Treatner

Library of Congress Cataloging-in-Publication Data
Frankel, Irene.
Center Stage.—1st ed.
    p. cm.
    Contents: 1. Beginning / Irene Frankel — 2. High beginning / Lynn Bonesteel and Samuela Eckstut-Didier — 3. Intermediate / Lynn Bonesteel and Samuela Eckstut-Didier — 4. High intermediate / Lynn Bonesteel and Samuela Eckstut-Didier.
    ISBN 0-13-170881-3 (student book : bk. 1 : alk. paper) — ISBN 0-13-187490-X (student book : bk. 2 : alk. paper) — ISBN 0-13-194778-8 (student book : bk. 3 : alk. paper) — ISBN 0-13-194784-2 (student book : bk. 4 : alk. paper) 1. English language--Textbooks for foreign speakers. 2. English language—Grammar—Problems, exercises, etc. 3. Vocabulary—Problems, exercises, etc. 4. Life skills—United States.   I. Bonesteel, Lynn. II. Eckstut-Didier, Samuela. III. Title. PE1128.F67425 2007
428.2'4—dc22

                                2006014957

ISBN: 0-13-194784-2
Printed in the United States of America
2 3 4 5 6 7 8 9 10—QWD—12 11 10 09 08

Acknowledgments

We would like to thank everyone at Pearson Longman for the time and effort they have put into seeing this project through. Specifically, we would like to thank our editors, Andrea Bryant, Robert Ruvo, Julie Schmidt, and Kim Steiner, for their attention to detail and their insights; to Rhea Banker, for her considerable contributions to the design and visual appeal of the series, and to Laura Le Dréan, for her commitment to every phase of this complex project. Most importantly, we are grateful to Claudia and Robert for their support and encouragement and for always reminding us of the other worlds out there.

Lynn Bonesteel and Sammi Eckstut-Didier,
authors of Student Books 2, 3, and 4

The publisher would like to extend special thanks to MaryAnn Florez and Sharon Seymour, our Series Consultants, and to the following individuals who reviewed the *Center Stage* program and whose comments were instrumental in shaping this series.

Ruth Afifi, Fresno Adult School, Fresno, CA; **Janet L. Barker**, Tarrant Community College, Fort Worth, TX; **Sarah Barnhardt**, Community College of Baltimore County, Baltimore, MD; **Janet Bryant**, Truman College, Chicago, IL; **Rachel Burns**, New England School of English, Cambridge, MA; **Debby Cargill**, Prince William County Public Schools, Manassas, VA; **Veronique Colas**, Los Angeles Technology Center, Los Angeles, CA; **Dave Coleman,** Belmont Community Adult School, Los Angeles, CA; **Eleanor Comegys**, Los Angeles Community Adult School, Los Angeles, CA; **Ludmila Ellis**, Dutchess Community College, Poughkeepsie, NY; **MaryAnn Florez**, Arlington Education & Employment Program, Arlington, VA; **Liz Flynn**, Centers for Education and Technology, San Diego, CA; **Gayle Forgey**, Garden Grove Unified School District, Lincoln Education Center, Garden Grove, CA; **Stephanie Garcia,** Gwinnett Technical College, Lawrenceville, GA; **Jennifer Gaudet**, Santa Ana College, Santa Ana, CA; **Sally Gearhart**, Santa Rosa Junior College, Santa Rosa, CA; **Jeanne Gibson**, Colorado State University, Pueblo, CO; **Anthony Halderman**, Cuesta College, San Luis Obispo, CA; **Cam Tu Huynh**, Banning Adult Learning Center, Los Angeles Unified School District, Los Angeles, CA; **Iordana Iordanova**, Triton College, River Grove, IL; **Mary Jane Jerde**, Price George's County Adult Education and Howard Community College, Bladensburg, MD; **Britt Johnson**, Albany Park Community Center, Chicago, IL; **Kathleen Krokar**, Truman College, Chicago, IL; **Xay Lee**, Fresno Adult School, Fresno, CA; **Sarah Lynn**, Somerville Community Adult Learning Experiences, Somerville, MA; **Ronna Magy**, Division of Adult and Career Education, LAUSD, Los Angeles, CA; **Dr. Suzanne Medina**, California State University, Carson, CA; **Dr. Diana Mora**, Fresno Adult School, Fresno, CA; **Jenny Moreno**, LAUSD, Los Angeles, CA; **Meg Morris**, Los Altos Adult Education, Mount View, CA; **John Nelson, Ph.D.**, Co-Director ESOL MA Program, University of Maryland, Baltimore County, MD; **Robert Osgood**, Westchester Community College, Valhalla, NY; **Judie Plumb**, Gwinnett Technical College, Lawrenceville, GA; **Barbara Pongsrikul**, Cesar Chavez Campus, San Diego, CA; **Dr. Yilin Sun**, Seattle Central Community College, Seattle, WA; **Alisa Takeuchi**, Garden Grove Adult Education, Chapman Education Center, Garden Grove, CA; **Garnet Templin-Imel**, Bellevue Community College, Bellevue, WA; **Lay Kuan Toh**, Westchester Community College, Valhalla, NY; **Marcos Valle**, Edmonds Community College, Edmonds, WA; **Carol van Duzer,** Center for Adult English Language Acquisition, Center for Applied Linguistics, Washington, DC; **Michele Volz,** Centennial Education Center, Santa Ana, CA; **Merari Weber**, Glendale Community College, Los Angeles, CA.

Scope and Sequence

Writing	Critical Thinking	CASAS	LAUSD Intermediate High	FL. Adult ESOL High Intermediate
Writing Skill: Use a logical sequence of ideas in a paragraph Prewriting: Use guided writing Writing: Write a paragraph about your favorite movie	Infer word meaning from context Draw conclusions Compare and contrast personal experiences Evaluate changes in society	0.1.2, 0.1.4, 0.2.1, 0.2.4, 2.6.1, 2.7.6, 7.2.1	A: Competencies: 2, 5a, 9, 44, 45 A: Grammar: 1, 4a, b, c, 23a B: Competencies: 1a, 5, 6a B: Grammar: 26a, b Language Skill Proficiencies (A and B): L: 1, 3, 5; S: 1, 6, 7; R: 1; W: 1, 5	5.05.01, 5.05.02, 5.15.01, 5.15.02, 5.15.07, 5.15.10, 5.15.13, 5.15.15, 5.16.01, 5.16.02, 5.16.03, 5.16.04, 5.16.06
Writing Skill: Use topic sentences Prewriting: Use a cluster Write a paragraph about a medical problem	Infer word meaning from context Hypothesize scenarios Draw logical conclusions Compare and contrast health scenarios Compare and contrast personal experiences and interests Support personal opinion with examples	0.1.2, 0.1.3, 0.1.4, 0.2.1, 0.2.4, 3.1.1, 3.1.3, 3.4.2, 3.5.2, 3.5.8, 7.1.1, 7.1.3, 7.2.6, 7.5.1, 7.5.2, 7.5.4, 8.3.2	A: Competencies: 5a, 8a, c; 9, 28, 30a, b A: Grammar: 1, 2a, 4a, b, c; 5, 23a, b, c B: Competencies: 1a, 5, 27, 41 B: Grammar: 26a, b Language Skill Proficiencies (A and B): L: 1, 2, 3, 5; S: 1, 2, 7; R: 1, 2; W: 1, 5	5.07.01, 5.15.01, 5.15.02, 5.15.07, 5.15.11, 5.15.13, 5.15.15
Writing Skill: Use time expressions and adverbs Prewriting: Write about pictures Write a paragraph about a crime	Infer word meaning from context Interpret and analyze charts Hypothesize scenarios Make predictions Classify and order information	0.1.2, 0.1.3, 2.7.3, 5.3.7, 5.3.8, 5.5.6, 6.7.1, 6.8.1, 7.2.1, 7.2.4, 7.2.5	A: Competencies: 5, 43, 45 A: Grammar: 1, 6, 21b, 23a, b, c B: Competencies: 5, 23a, b B: Grammar: 3, 4, 26a, b Language Skill Proficiencies (A and B): L: 1, 2, 3, 5; S: 1, 2, 3, 6, 7; R: 1, 7; W: 1, 5	5.05.01, 5.05.02, 5.05.05, 5.10.02, 5.15.01, 5.15.02, 5.15.03, 5.15.07, 5.15.08, 5.15.10, 5.15.13, 5.16.01, 5.16.02, 5.16.03, 5.16.04, 5.16.05, 5.16.06
Writing Skill: Use supporting sentences Prewriting: Use an outline Write a paragraph on a topic concerning a living situation	Infer word meaning from context Hypothesize scenarios Compare and contrast personal experiences Evaluate solutions Compare and contrast housing situations Classify information	0.1.2, 0.1.4, 0.1.6, 0.2.1, 1.4.1, 1.4.5, 1.4.7, 1.5.2, 7.2.1, 7.2.2, 7.2.3, 7.2.5, 7.2.6, 7.2.7	A: Competencies: 5a, b; 6, 9, 23, 24, 43 A: Grammar: 1, 15, 23a, b, c B: Competencies: 1, 5, 6a, b, d, 7, 8d, 19, 20 B: Grammar: 18a, b, c, 26a, b Language Skill Proficiencies (A and B): L: 1, 3, 4, 5; S: 1, 2, 3, 6, 7; R: 1, 7, 8; W: 1, 5	5.05.01, 5.05.02, 5.05.05, 5.11.01, 5.11.02, 5.11.04, 5.11.05, 5.15.01, 5.15.02, 5.15.03, 5.15.07, 5.15.08, 5.15.13, 5.15.15, 5.16.01, 5.16.02, 5.16.03, 5.16.04, 5.16.05, 5.16.06

Unit	Grammar	Listening	Speaking	Reading
5 **New on the Job** Page 58	Tag Questions *So / Too / Either / Neither* *Both . . . and /* *Either . . . or /* *Neither . . . nor*	Listen to an interview with a job candidate Listen to conversations about work situations Listen for intonation Listen for details	Ask and answer questions about a job interview Talk about similarities of people in your group Talk about the job performance of a new employee	Read an article about factors in job satisfaction Reading Skill: Scan headings
6 **Food** Page 72	Simple Present Passive Simple Past Passive Passive and Active	Listen to a conversation about food history and customs Listen to a report about foods used as medicine Listen for main topics	Talk about the preparation of foods in your country Ask and answer questions about food history Talk about foods and drinks from around the world Talk about how food is used as medicine	Understand steps in a process Read an article about a traditional feast Reading Skill: Visualize
7 **Safety** Page 86	Present Perfect Passive Passive with *Need(s) to* Present Progressive Passive	Listen to a conversation about repairs for a building Listen to a news report about safety problems Listen for details	Talk about health problems in a restaurant Talk about problems in your neighborhood Talk about safety problems in your home	Read notes Read an article about food safety problems Reading Skill: Make inferences
8 **Advertising** Page 100	Adjectives ending in *–ing* and *–ed* Adjectives with *so* and *such* Adjective Word Order	Listen to a radio advertisement for a hybrid car Listen to a radio report about advertisements Listen for details	Describe the benefits of a product or service Talk about why particular ads are effective or not Talk about ads with specific qualities	Read an article about the language of advertising Reading Skill: Identify the main idea from the introduction

Writing	Critical Thinking	CASAS	LAUSD Intermediate High	FL. Adult ESOL High Intermediate
Writing Skill: Use connectors to compare or contrast ideas Prewriting: Use a Venn diagram Write a paragraph comparing and contrasting two jobs	Infer word meaning from context Infer information not explicit in the text Compare and contrast past experiences Support personal opinion with reasoning	0.1.2, 0.1.4, 0.1.6, 0.2.1, 0.2.4, 4.1.5, 4.1.6, 4.1.7, 7.1.1	A: Competencies: 1a, b; 5a, b; 9, 34, 35b, c; 36, 38a, 39a, c; 40d, 43 A: Grammar: 1, 23a, b, c; 24 B: Competencies: 1a, 5a, 31a, b; 41 B: Grammar: 24, 25, 26a, b; 27 Language Skill Proficiencies (A and B): L: 1, 2, 3; S: 1, 2; R: 1, 2, 3, 4, 5, 6, 7; W: 1, 5	5.05.01, 5.05.02, 5.05.04, 5.05.05, 5.02.01, 5.05.01, 5.05.02, 5.05.05, 5.15.01, 5.15.02, 5.15.03, 5.15.04, 5.15.06, 5.15.07, 5.15.13, 5.15.15, 5.16.01, 5.16.02, 5.16.03, 5.16.04, 5.16.05, 5.16.06, 5.17.03
Writing Skill: Use transition words for steps in a process Prewriting: List steps Write a paragraph about preparing a feast or recipe	Infer word meaning from context Compare and contrast food Classify and order information Draw logical conclusions	0.1.2, 0.2.1, 1.3.8, 2.7.2, 7.2.1, 7.2.3	A: Competencies: 5, 8d, 28, 43 A: Grammar: 1, 11a, b; 23a, b, c B: Competencies: 8c, 27, 40, 41 B: Grammar: 11a, 18a, b, c, d; 26a, b Language Skill Proficiencies (A and B): L: 1, 3, 5; S: 1, 2, 6, 7; R: 1, 2, 3, 4, 5, 6, 7; W: 1, 5	5.05.01, 5.15.01, 5.15.02, 5.15.07, 5.15.13, 5.15.15, 5.16.01, 5.16.02, 5.16.03, 5.16.05, 5.16.06
Writing Skill: Write a letter of complaint Prewriting: Use a problem-solution diagram Write a letter of complaint	Infer word meaning from context Make predictions Hypothesize scenarios Compare and contrast neighborhoods Evaluate safety situations Infer information not explicit in the text Identify problems and propose solutions	0.1.2, 0.1.4, 0.2.1, 1.4.7, 1.4.8, 1.7.4, 2.7.3, 3.4.2, 3.4.9, 5.6.1, 7.2.1, 7.3.1, 7.3.2, 8.2.6	A: Competencies: 4, 5a, 8b, 9, 23, 32, 43, 44, 45 A: Grammar: 1, 2a, 11a, b; 15, 23a, b, c B: Competencies: 1a, 4, 5, 6c, 20 B: Grammar: 11a, b, c, d; 26a, b Language Skill Proficiencies (A and B): L: 1, 3, 5; S: 1, 2, 6, 7; R: 1, 2, 3; W: 5	5.02.01, 5.05.01, 5.05.02, 5.10.01, 5.11.01, 5.15.01, 5.15.02, 5.15.05, 5.15.06, 5.15.07, 5.15.16, 5.16.01, 5.16.02, 5.16.03, 5.16.04, 5.16.05, 5.16.06
Writing Skill: Identify off-topic sentences Prewriting: Use a cluster Write a paragraph about an ad you like or dislike	Infer word meaning from context Support personal opinions with examples Interpret advertisements	0.1.2, 0.1.3, 0.2.1, 0.2.4, 1.2.1, 1.2.5, 7.2.1, 7.2.2, 7.2.3, 7.2.4, 7.2.5, 7.2.7, 7.3.1	A: Competencies: 5a, 6, 9, 43, 44, 45 A: Grammar: 1, 4a, b; 15, 16, 17, 23a, b, c B: Competencies: 1a, 5, 6a, 7, 18, 41 B: Grammar: 17, 26a, b Language Skill Proficiencies (A and B): L: 1, 2, 3, 4, 5; S: 1, 2, 6, 7; R: 1, 2, 3, 6; W: 5	5.05.01, 5.05.02, 5.11.10, 5.15.01, 5.15.02, 5.15.05, 5.15.06, 5.15.07, 5.15.09, 5.15.15, 5.16.01, 5.16.02, 5.16.03, 5.16.04, 5.16.05, 5.16.06

Unit	Grammar	Listening	Speaking	Reading
9 **Gadgets** Page 114	Adjective Clauses Subject and Object Relative Pronouns Relative Pronouns as Objects of Prepositions	Listen to conversations between a salesman and customers Listen to the text of an e-mail about gadgets Listen for details	Describe and identify common classroom objects Describe groups of things in pictures Talk about a useful invention	Read advertisements Read an article about microwave ovens Reading Skill: Scan for details
10 **Shopping** Page 128	Noun Clauses: Question Words and *That* Noun Clauses: Indirect Questions Noun Clauses: *If / Whether*	Listen to conversations at a shopping mall Listen to a conversation between a customer and a sales associate Listen to a report about small businesses and superstores Listen for opinions	Share opinions about shopping Ask and answer questions about shopping where you live now	Read an article about online shopping Reading Skill: Recognize purpose
11 **Interviews** Page 142	Reported Speech: Statements Reported Speech: Information Questions Reported Speech: *Yes / No* Questions	Listen to a conversation about a job interview Listen to a conversation about a college interview Listen to conversations about two interviews Listen for details	Talk about problems with a roommate Talk about questions at job interviews Compare interviews at different colleges Talk about an interview that you have had	Read an email Read an article about job interview tips Reading Skill: Identify goals for reading
12 **Psychology and Personality** Page 156	Gerunds as Subjects Gerunds as Objects of Prepositions Gerunds as Objects of Verbs	Listen to a conversation about a personality quiz Listen to definitions of types of learners Listen to a lecture about learning styles Listen for details	Talk about the qualities of different types of learners Talk about personal experiences Talk about your experience as a language learner	Read advertisements Read an article about successful entrepreneurs Reading Skill: Improve reading speed

Writing	Critical Thinking	CASAS	LAUSD Intermediate High	FL. Adult ESOL High Intermediate
Writing Skill: Use signpost words Prewriting: Use a T-Chart Write a paragraph about a gadget or invention	Infer word meaning from context Interpret pictures Draw logical conclusions Support personal opinion with examples Develop arguments for or against an issue	0.1.2, 0.2.1, 0.2.4, 1.2.1, 1.2.5, 1.7.3, 3.4.1	A: Competencies: 1, 5a, 9, 43, 44, 45 A: Grammar: 1, 15, 22, 23a, b, c B: Competencies:1, 5, 6a, c; 41 B: Grammar: 23a, b; 26a, b Language Skill Proficiencies (A and B): L: 1, 3, 4, 5; S: 1, 2, 6, 7; R: 1, 2, 3, 5, 6, 7; W: 5	5.05.01, 5.05.02, 5.15.01, 5.15.02, 5.15.03, 5.15.05, 5.15.06, 5.15.07, 5.15.09, 5.15.15, 5.16.01, 5.16.02, 5.16.03, 5.16.05, 5.16.06
Writing Skill: Use concluding sentences Prewriting: Freewrite Write a paragraph about the dangers of a type of shopping	Infer word meaning from context Interpret illustrations Support personal opinions with examples Evaluate statements Compare and contrast stores	0.1.2, 0.1.4, 0.2.1, 0.2.4, 2.7.3, 4.1.6, 4.2.2, 4.8.1, 5.1.4, 5.1.6, 5.6.1, 5.6.2, 5.6.3, 7.2.1, 7.2.2, 7.2.4, 7.3.1, 7.3.2	A: Competencies: 5a, 9, 21a A: Grammar: 20a, b; 23a, b, c B: Competencies: 5, 6a, 8d, 40, 41 B: Grammar: 10a, 18a, b, d; 26a, b Language Skill Proficiencies (A and B): L: 1, 2, 3, 4, 5; S: 1, 2, 3, 6, 7; R: 1, 2, 3, 4, 5, 6, 7; W: 1, 5	5.05.01, 5.05.02, 5.05.05, 5.08.05, 5.10.01, 5.11.07, 5.15.01, 5.15.02, 5.15.03, 5.15.06
Writing Skill: Write a cover letter Prewriting: Complete a Y-Chart Write a cover letter	Infer word meaning from context Hypothesize scenarios Evaluate statements Compare and contrast interview experiences Classify and order information	0.1.2, 0.1.3, 0.1.4, 0.2.1, 0.2.3, 0.2.4, 2.5.5, 4.1.2, 4.1.5, 4.1.7, 4.1.8, 4.1.9, 4.4.1, 4.4.2, 4.4.5, 4.4.6, 4.6.1, 4.6.2, 4.7.3, 7.1.1, 7.2.1	A: Competencies: 1a, 4b, 5a, 9, 11b, 23, 24, 35b, c; 36, 40, 42, 44, 45 A: Grammar: 1, 20a, b; 23a, b, c B: Competencies: 1, 1a, 4, 5, 31 B: Grammar: 18a, b, c; 26a, b Language Skill Proficiencies (A and B): L: 1, 3, 4, 5; S: 1, 2, 3, 7; R: 1, 2, 3, 4, 6; W: 2, 5	5.01.04, 5.01.05, 5.02.01, 5.02.04, 5.03.01, 5.05.01, 5.05.02, 5.05.05, 5.14.01, 5.15.01, 5.15.02, 5.15.03, 5.15.05, 5.15.09, 5.15.11, 5.15.15, 5.15.16, 5.16.01, 5.16.02, 5.16.03, 5.16.05, 5.16.06
Writing Skill: Understand essay structure Prewriting: Use guided writing Write an essay about the skills and personality required for a particular job	Infer word meaning from context Evaluate statements Classify information Support personal opinions with examples Infer information not explicit in the text	0.1.2, 0.1.3, 0.1.4, 0.2.1, 0.2.4, 3.5.8, 7.2.1, 7.2.6, 7.4.3, 7.4.9, 7.5.1, 7.5.7	A: Competencies: 1a, 5a, 7c, 8a, 9, 42, 43, 44, 45 A: Grammar: 1, 12b,c; 15, 23a, b, c B: Competencies: 1a, 5, 6c, 35, 39, 41 B: Grammar: 26 a, b Language Skill Proficiencies: (A and B): L: 1, 3, 5; S: 1, 2, 3, 6; R: 1, 2, 3, 4, 6; W: 5	5.01.01, 5.05.01, 5.05.02, 5.05.05, 5.15.01, 5.15.02, 5.15.03, 5.15.06, 5.15.07, 5.15.09, 5.15.15, 5.15.18, 5.16.01, 5.16.02, 5.16.06

Unit	Grammar	Listening	Speaking	Reading
13 **Looking Back** Page 170	*Used to do and Be used to doing* Verb + Infinitive or Gerund Verb + Object + Infinitive	Listen to a conversation comparing life on a farm to life in the city Listen to a man describing his relationship with his parents when he was a teenager Listen to an interview about a bicultural childhood	Talk about an important change in your life Talk about what you were like as a child Talk about the kind of parent you are or would like to be Talk about your childhood	Read a story comparing two countries Read an article about schools in the 19th century Reading Skill: Use a dictionary
14 **Socializing** Page 184	Suggestions and Offers: *Let's / Let me / Why don't we / Why don't I* Preferences: *Would rather / Would prefer* Polite Requests: *Would you mind*	Listen to conversations about living in an apartment complex Listen to a lecture about polite language Listen to requests Listen to offers and suggestions	Ask and answer questions about what people prefer to do over the weekend Make and respond to requests for help Make and respond to suggestions and offers	Read an article about rules for polite behavior Reading Skill: Predict the topic from pictures
15 **On the Road** Page 198	*Should / Ought to / Had better* *Have to / Be supposed to / Can* *Had to / Was / Were supposed to*	Listen to a conversation about a road test for a driver´s license Listen to advice and warnings Listen to a report about advice for parents of teenage drivers Listen for details	Talk about good advice to give a new driver Talk about driving laws in different countries Talk about a driver´s obligations Act out a dialogue	Understand charts Read an article about driving safety Reading Skill: Evaluate arguments
16 **Natural Disasters** Page 212	*Should have* for Regrets about the Past *May have / Might have* for Past Possibility *Must have* for Logical Conclusions about the Past	Listen to a conversation about a home damaged by a hurricane Listen to regrets about the past Listen to a conversation about responses to an earthquake Listen to a TV program about a city damaged by a hurricane	Talk about a time you were not prepared for an important event Talk about what might have happened in dangerous situations	Read an article about Hurricane Katrina Reading Skill: Ask questions

Writing	Critical Thinking	CASAS	LAUSD Intermediate High	FL. Adult ESOL High Intermediate
Writing Skill: Write an introduction Prewriting: Freewrite Write an essay about a powerful memory	Infer word meaning from context Compare and contrast past experiences Hypothesize scenarios Evaluate changes in society	0.1.2, 0.1.3, 0.1.4, 0.1.6, 0.2.1, 0.2.4, 1.2.5, 1.7.3, 4.5.1, 7.2.1, 7.2.2, 7.2.3, 7.2.4, 7.2.5	A: Competencies: 1a, b; 2, 5, 7c, 9, 43, 44, 45 A: Grammar: 1, 3, 8a, b; 9a, b; 12b, c; 13a, b; 14, 15, 23a, b, c B: Competencies: 1a, 5, 7, 38, 41 B: Grammar: 2, 8, 12, 26a, b Language Skill Proficiencies (A and B): L: 1, 2, 3, 4, 5; S: 1, 2, 6, 7; R: 1, 2, 3, 4, 5, 6, 7; W: 5	5.05.01, 5.05.02, 5.05.03, 5.05.05, 5.14.01, 5.14.02, 5.15.01, 5.15.02, 5.15.03, 5.15.05, 5.15.06, 5.15.07, 5.15.09, 5.15.10, 5.15.11, 5.15.12, 5.15.15, 5.16.01, 5.16.02, 5.16.03, 5.16.04, 5.16.05, 5.16.06
Writing Skill: Write body paragraphs Prewriting: Use guided writing Write an essay comparing differences between two countries, two generations, etc.	Infer word meaning from context Compare and contrast preferences Hypothesize scenarios Interpret illustrations	0.1.2, 0.1.3, 0.1.4, 0.2.1, 0.2.4, 2.6.1, 2.7.2, 3.5.8, 7.3.2, 7.5.1, 7.5.2, 7.5.6, 8.1.3	A: Competencies: 5a, 7c, 8a, b; 44, 45 A: Grammar: 1, 15, 23a, b, c B: Competencies: 5a, 6, 8a, b; 44, 45 B: Grammar: 10b, c, d, 26a, b Language Skill Proficiencies (A and B): L: 1, 2, 3, 4, 5; S: 1, 2, 3, 6, 7; R: 1, 2, 3, 6; W: 5	5.05.01, 5.05.02, 5.05.04, 5.05.05, 5.15.01, 5.15.02, 5.15.03, 5.15.05, 5.15.06, 5.15.07, 5.15.09, 5.16.01, 5.16.02, 5.16.03, 5.16.04, 5.16.05, 5.16.06
Writing Skill: Write a problem and solution essay Prewriting: Use guided writing Write a problem and solution essay on a driving topic	Infer word meaning from context Interpret signs Compare and contrast driving rules Interpret charts Hypothesize scenarios Evaluate the quality of arguments Identify problems and propose solutions	0.1.1, 0.1.2, 0.1.3, 0.1.4, 0.2.1, 0.2.4, 1.9.1, 1.9.2, 1.9.8, 2.2.2, 2.7.3, 3.4.2, 7.2.1, 7.2.2, 7.2.3, 7.3.1, 7.3.2, 7.5.5	A: Competencies: 5a, 6, 7c, 9, 43, 44, 45 A: Grammar: 1, 7b, 8a, b; 9b, 10, 15, 23a, b, c B: Competencies: 1a, 5, 6a, c; 7, 41 B: Grammar: 7, 8, 26a, b Language Skill Proficiencies (A and B): L: 1, 2, 3, 4, 5; S: 1, 2, 3, 6, 7; R: 1, 2, 3, 4, 6; W: 5	5.05.01, 5.05.02, 5.05.05, 5.09.06, 5.15.01, 5.15.02, 5.15.03, 5.15.05, 5.15.06, 5.15.07, 5.15.09, 5.15.11, 5.16.01, 5.16.02, 5.16.03, 5.16.04, 5.16.05, 5.16.06
Writing Skill: Write a narrative essay Prewriting: Use guided writing Write a narrative essay on a chosen topic	Infer word meaning from context Compare and contrast personal experiences Interpret illustrations Hypothesize scenarios Draw logical conclusions	0.1.2, 0.1.4, 0.2.1, 0.2.4, 2.3.3, 2.7.3, 3.5.8, 3.5.9, 5.2.4, 5.7.1, 7.2.2, 7.2.4	A: Competencies: 5a, 8, 9, 27, 32, 43, 44, 45 A: Grammar: 1, 15, 23a, b, c B: Competencies: 1a, 5, 6a, c; 12, 23, 41 B: Grammar: 6a, b; 26a, b Language Skill Proficiencies (A and B): L: 1, 2, 3, 4, 5; S: 1, 2, 6, 7; R: 1, 2, 3, 4, 6; W: 5	5.05.01, 5.05.02, 5.05.05, 5.13.01, 5.15.01, 5.15.02, 5.15.05, 5.15.06, 5.15.07, 5.15.09, 5.15.15, 5.16.01, 5.16.02, 5.16.03, 5.16.04, 5.16.05, 5.16.06

Writing	Critical Thinking	CASAS	LAUSD Intermediate High	FL. Adult ESOL High Intermediate
Writing Skill: Support an opinion Prewriting: Use guided writing Write an opinion essay on a chosen topic	Infer word meaning from context Support personal opinions with reasoning Compare and contrast personal experiences Interpret photographs Compare and contrast opinions about politics	0.1.2, 0.1.4, 0.2.1, 0.2 .4, 2.7.3, 4.1.6, 4.2.2, 5.1.4, 5.1.6, 5.6.1, 5.6.2, 5.6.3, 7.2.1, 7.2.2, 7.2.4, 7.3.1, 7.3.2	A: Competencies: 1, 5a, b; 6, 7a, b, c; 9, 27, 43, 44, 45 A: Grammar: 1, 23a, b, c B: Competencies: 1a, 5, 6a, b, c; 7, 8a, 23, 41 B: Grammar: 22, 26a, b Language Skill Proficiencies (A and B): L: 1, 2, 3, 4, 5; S: 1, 2, 6, 7; R: 1, 2, 3, 5, 6, 7; W: 1, 5	5.05.01, 5.05.02, 5.12.04, 5.12.05, 5.15.01, 5.15.02, 5.15.05, 5.15.06, 5.15.07, 5.15.08, 5.15.09, 5.15.13, 5.15.15, 5.16.01, 5.16.02, 5.16.03, 5.16.04, 5.16.05, 5.16.06
Writing Skill: Write a contrast essay Prewriting: Use guided writing Write a contrast essay on a chosen topic	Infer word meaning from context Interpret charts Compare and contrast community services Interpret expressions Identify cause and effect	0.1.1, 0.1.2, 0.1.3, 0.2.1, 0.2.4, 1.3.1, 1.3.2, 1.3.3, 1.5.1, 1.5.2, 1.7.1, 1.8.3, 1.8.4, 1.9.5	A: Competencies: 1, 5a, 6, 8b, 9, 20, 43, 44, 45 A: Grammar: 1, 8a, 18a, b; 23a, b, c B: Competencies: 1a, 5, 6a, c; 7, 14, 17, 41 B: Grammar: 19, 26a, b Language Skill Proficiencies (A and B): L: 1, 3, 4, 5; S: 1, 2, 6, 7; R: 1, 2, 3, 5, 6, 7; W: 1, 5	5.05.01, 5.05.02, 5.08.02, 5.08.03, 5.08.04, 5.11.07. 5.15.01, 5.15.02, 5.15.05, 5.15.06, 5.15.07, 5.15.09, 5.15.11, 5.15.13, 5.15.15, 5.16.01 5.16.02, 5.16.03, 5.16.04, 5.16.05, 5.16.06
Writing Skill: Write Conclusions Prewriting: Use guided writing Write an essay about an important decision that someone made	Infer word meaning from context Interpret illustrations Compare and contrast past experiences Hypothesize scenarios Draw conclusions	0.1.1, 0.1.2, 0.1.3, 0.2.1, 0.2.4, 2.7.3, 3.5.7, 3.5.8, 3.5.9, 7.1.1, 7.5.1, 7.5.2, 7.5.7	A: Competencies: 1, 5, 8b, 9, 43, 44, 45 A: Grammar: 1, 23a, b, c B: Competencies: 1a, 5, 6a, c; 9a, b; 41 B: Grammar: 20, 26a,b Language Skill Proficiencies (A and B): L: 1, 2, 3, 4, 5; S: 1, 2, 6, 7; R: 1, 2, 3, 4, 5, 6, 7; W: 1, 4, 5	5.01.01, 5.05.01, 5.05.02, 5.05.03, 5.15.01, 5.15.02, 5.15.05, 5.15.06, 5.15.07, 5.15.09, 5.15.10, 5.15.11, 5.15.13, 5.15.15, 5.16.01, 5.16.02, 5.16.03, 5.16.04, 5.16.05, 5.16.06
Writing Skill: Choose a title Prewriting: Use guided writing Write an essay about a career	Infer word meaning from context Compare and contrast personal experiences Interpret illustrations Describe characters in a story	0.1.2, 0.2.1, 0.2.4, 2.5.5, 2.7.3, 3.5.8, 4.1.8, 7.1.1, 7.2.1, 7.3.1, 7.5.1, 7.5.2, 7.5.6	A: Competencies: 1, 5a, 9, 11, 42, 43, 44, 45 A: Grammar: 1, 23a, b, c B: Competencies: 1a, 5, 6a, 10, 35, 41 B: Grammar: 13, 26a, b Language Skill Proficiencies (A and B): L: 1, 2, 3, 4, 5; S: 1, 2, 6, 7; R: 1, 2, 3, 4, 5, 6, 7; W: 1, 4, 5	5.01.01, 5.05.01, 5.05.02, 5.14.01, 5.15.01, 5.15.02, 5.15.05, 5.15.06, 5.15.07, 5.15.09, 5.15.10, 5.15.11, 5.15.13, 5.15.15, 5.16.01, 5.16.02, 5.16.03, 5.16.04, 5.16.05, 5.16.06

To the Teacher

Center Stage is a four-level, four-skills course that supports student learning and achievement in everyday work and life situations. Practical language and timely topics motivate adult students to master grammar along with speaking, listening, reading, and writing skills.

Features

- *Grammar to Communicate* presents key grammar points with concise charts and abundant practice in real-life situations.

- **Communicative activities**, such as *Time to Talk*, promote opportunities for meaningful expression and active learning.

- Extensive **listening** practice helps students to succeed in their daily lives.

- *Reading* and *Writing* lessons develop essential academic skills and provide real-life models, tasks, and practice.

- *Review and Challenge* helps teachers to assess students' progress and meet the needs of multi-level classrooms.

- Easy-to-follow, **two-page lessons** give students a sense of accomplishment.

Additional Components

- The **Teacher's Edition** includes unit tests, multilevel strategies, learner persistence tips, expansion activities, culture, grammar and language notes, and answer keys.

- A **Teacher's Resource Disk**, in the back of the Teacher's Edition, offers numerous worksheets for supplementary grammar practice, supplementary vocabulary practice, graphic organizers, and learner persistence.

- **Color transparencies** provide an ideal resource for introducing, practicing, and reviewing vocabulary.

- The **Audio Program** contains recordings for all listening activities in the Student Book.

- The *ExamView® Assessment Suite* includes hundreds of test items, providing flexible, comprehensive assessment.

Unit Description

Each of the twenty units centers on a practical theme for the adult learner. A unit consists of 14 pages and is divided into the following lessons: *Vocabulary and Listening, Grammar to Communicate 1, Grammar to Communicate 2, Grammar to Communicate 3, Review and Challenge, Reading,* and *Writing*.

Each lesson is presented on two facing pages and provides clear, self-contained instruction taking approximately 45 to 60 minutes of class time. In some cases, the *Reading* and *Writing* lessons may take longer.

Vocabulary and Listening

Each unit opens with an eye-catching illustration that sets the context and presents high frequency, leveled vocabulary that is recycled in the unit and throughout the course. After hearing the new words, students listen to a dialogue related to the unit theme. In the dialogue, students hear the grammar for the unit before it is formally presented. Students listen for meaning and check their comprehension and inference skills in follow-up exercises.

Grammar to Communicate

Each unit has three *Grammar to Communicate* lessons that present target structures in concise charts. Students practice each language point through a variety of exercises that build from controlled to open-ended. Extensive meaningful practice leads students toward mastery.

> **Look Boxes.** *Grammar to Communicate* is often expanded with tips in *Look Boxes*. These tips provide information on usage, common errors, and vocabulary.

> **Time to Talk.** *Grammar to Communicate* culminates with a *Time to Talk* activity. This highly communicative activity gives students the chance to personalize what they have learned.

Review and Challenge

Review and Challenge helps students review the unit material, consolidate their knowledge, and extend their learning with a variety of expansion activities. *Review and Challenge* includes:

> **Grammar.** Students check their understanding of the three grammar lessons of the unit.

> **Dictation.** Students listen to and write five sentences that recycle the language of the unit, giving them the opportunity to check their aural comprehension.

> **Speaking.** Students engage in a speaking activity related to the unit theme. This allows for lively practice as well as reinforcement of instructional material.

> **Listening.** Students listen to realistic material, such as radio interviews and reports. Comprehension exercises check students' understanding of the main idea and details, as well as their ability to make inferences. The listening section ends with a *Time to Talk* activity that calls for students to demonstrate what they have learned as they actively apply the material to their own lives.

Reading

The reading lesson recycles the grammar and vocabulary that have been taught in the unit. In *Getting Ready to Read*, students practice skills such as predicting and skimming before moving on to the reading selection, which is usually a magazine-style article. The selection contains new vocabulary that is practiced on the facing page in *After You Read*. Following the vocabulary exercise are comprehension questions. A *Reading Skill* box explains the skill being practiced in the unit.

Writing

The writing lesson begins with a *Writing Skill* box that introduces a writing skill, such as using topic sentences. The writing skill is practiced in an exercise. Following the exercise is a model paragraph or model essay. On the facing page, students complete a *Prewriting* task, such as completing an outline, before they move on to the final writing assignment.

Beyond the Unit

There are a number of supplementary resources in the back of the book.

Grammar Notes

The grammar notes are a reference for many grammar points covered in the units. They provide helpful supplementary information and examples.

Charts

Information on a variety of usage and grammar points, including verbs and reported speech is summarized in a series of easy-to-use charts.

Partner Activities

This section includes material students will need to complete several of the *Time to Talk* activities.

Audioscript

The audioscript includes all the recorded material that is not on the student book page.

Standards and Assessments

Standards. Meeting national and state standards is critical to successful adult instruction. *Center Stage 4* clearly integrates material from key grammar and life skills standards. The Scope and Sequence on pages iv-xiii links each unit with the corresponding standards.

Assessment. *Center Stage* includes several assessment tools. Teachers have multiple opportunities for performance-based assessment on productive tasks using the 80 *Time to Talk* communicative activities. In addition, teachers can test student performance in the *Review and Challenge* section. Students have many opportunities for self-assessment in the *Review and Challenge* section.

The testing material for *Center Stage* includes end-of-unit tests found in the *Teacher's Edition*. In addition, the *ExamView® Assessment Suite* includes hundreds of test items for each Student Book.

About the Authors

Lynn Bonesteel has been teaching ESL since 1988. She is currently a full-time senior lecturer at the Center for English Language and Orientation Programs at Boston University Center for English Language and Orientation Programs (CELOP). Ms. Bonesteel is also the author of *Password 3: A Reading and Vocabulary Text*.

Samuela Eckstut-Didier has taught ESL and EFL for over twenty-five years in the United States, Greece, Italy, and England. She currently teaches at Boston University, Center for English Language and Orientation Programs (CELOP). She has authored or co-authored numerous texts for the teaching of English, notably *Strategic Reading 1, 2 and 3*; *What's in a Word? Reading and Vocabulary Building*; *Focus on Grammar Workbook*; *In the Real World*; *First Impressions*; *Beneath the Surface*; *Widely Read*; and *Finishing Touches*.

About the Series Consultants

MaryAnn Florez is the lead ESL Specialist for the Arlington Education and Employment Program (REEP) in Arlington, Virginia where she has program management, curriculum development, and teacher training responsibilities. She has worked with Fairfax County (VA) Adult ESOL and the National Center for ESL Literacy Education (NCLE), and has coordinated a volunteer adult ESL program in Northern Virginia. Ms. Florez has offered workshops throughout the U.S. in areas such as teaching beginning-level English language learners, incorporating technology in instruction, strategies for a multi-level classroom, and assessment. Her publications include a variety of research-to-practice briefs and articles on adult ESL education. Ms. Florez holds an M.Ed in Adult Education from George Mason University.

Sharon Seymour is an ESL instructor at City College of San Francisco where she has extensive experience teaching both noncredit adult ESL and credit ESL. She recently completed ten years as chair of the ESL Department at CCSF. She is also currently a co-researcher for a Center for Advancement of Adult Literacy Project on Exemplary Noncredit Community College ESL Programs. Ms. Seymour has been president of CATESOL and a member of the TESOL board of directors and has served both organizations in a variety of capacities. She has served on California Community College Chancellor's Office and California State Department of Education committees relating to ESL curriculum and assessment. Ms. Seymour holds an M.A. in TESOL from San Francisco State University.

Tour of the Program

Welcome to *Center Stage*

Center Stage is a four-level, four-skills course that supports student learning and achievement in everyday work and life situations. Practical language and timely topics motivate adult students to master grammar along with vocabulary, speaking, listening, reading, and writing skills.

Target grammar is clearly defined at the start of the unit.

Students **listen** for general comprehension and details in real life contexts.

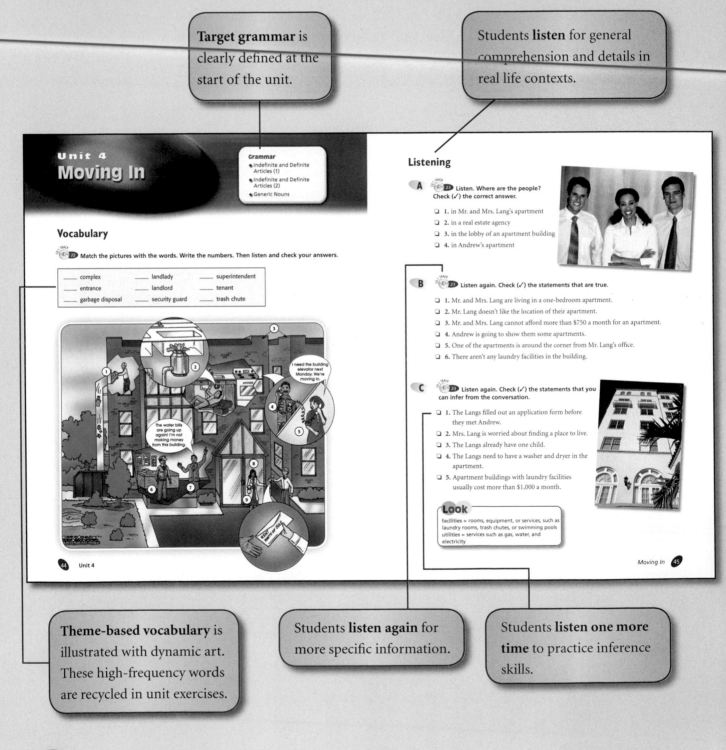

Theme-based vocabulary is illustrated with dynamic art. These high-frequency words are recycled in unit exercises.

Students **listen again** for more specific information.

Students **listen one more time** to practice inference skills.

Each unit has three **Grammar to Communicate** lessons that present the target grammar in a clear and concise chart followed by practice exercises.

Look Boxes expand on the *Grammar to Communicate* charts and include usage information, common errors, and vocabulary notes.

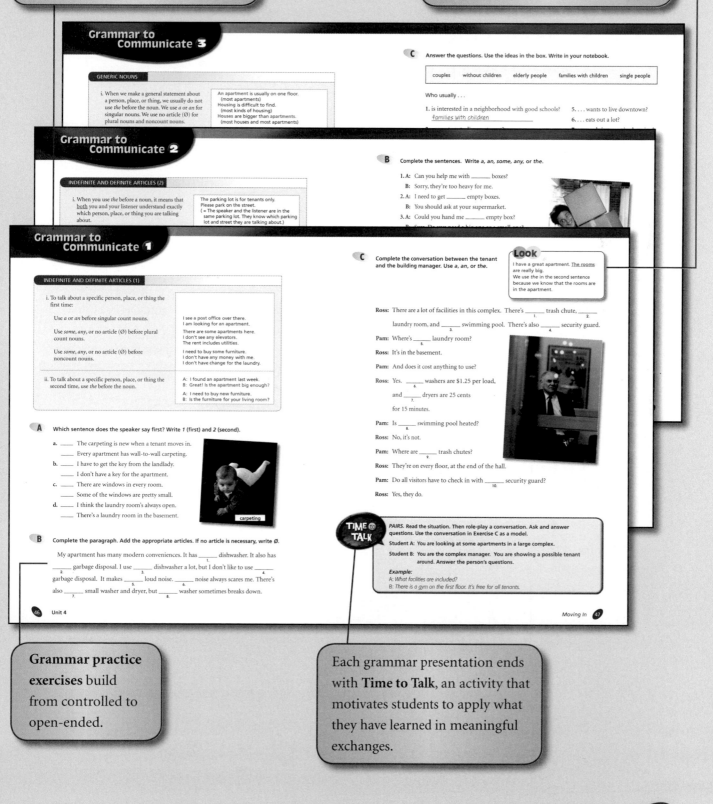

Grammar to Communicate 3

GENERIC NOUNS

i. When we make a general statement about a person, place, or thing, we usually do not use *the* before the noun. We use *a* or *an* for singular nouns. We use no article (Ø) for plural nouns and noncount nouns.

An apartment is usually on one floor. (most apartments)
Housing is difficult to find. (most kinds of housing)
Houses are bigger than apartments. (most houses and most apartments)

C Answer the questions. Use the ideas in the box. Write in your notebook.

| couples | without children | elderly people | families with children | single people |

Who usually . . .

1. is interested in a neighborhood with good schools?   5. . . . wants to live downtown?
   families with children   6. . . . eats out a lot?

Grammar to Communicate 2

INDEFINITE AND DEFINITE ARTICLES (2)

i. When you use *the* before a noun, it means that <u>both</u> you and your listener understand exactly which person, place, or thing you are talking about.

The parking lot is for tenants only.
Please park on the street.
(= The speaker and the listener are in the same parking lot. They know which parking lot and street they are talking about.)

B Complete the sentences. Write *a, an, some, any,* or *the.*

1. A: Can you help me with _____ boxes?
   B: Sorry, they're too heavy for me.
2. A: I need to get _____ empty boxes.
   B: You should ask at your supermarket.
3. A: Could you hand me _____ empty box?

Grammar to Communicate 1

INDEFINITE AND DEFINITE ARTICLES (1)

i. To talk about a specific person, place, or thing the first time:

Use *a* or *an* before singular count nouns.

Use *some, any,* or no article (Ø) before plural count nouns.

Use *some, any,* or no article (Ø) before noncount nouns.

I see a post office over there.
I am looking for an apartment.
There are some apartments here.
I don't see any elevators.
The rent includes utilities.
I need to buy some furniture.
I don't have any money with me.
I don't have change for the laundry.

ii. To talk about a specific person, place, or thing the second time, use *the* before the noun.

A: I found an apartment last week.
B: Great! Is the apartment big enough?
A: I need to buy new furniture.
B: Is the furniture for your living room?

A Which sentence does the speaker say first? Write *1* (first) and *2* (second).

a. _____ The carpeting is new when a tenant moves in.
   _____ Every apartment has wall-to-wall carpeting.
b. _____ I have to get the key from the landlady.
   _____ I don't have a key for the apartment.
c. _____ There are windows in every room.
   _____ Some of the windows are pretty small.
d. _____ I think the laundry room's always open.
   _____ There's a laundry room in the basement.

carpeting

B Complete the paragraph. Add the appropriate articles. If no article is necessary, write Ø.

My apartment has many modern conveniences. It has _____ dishwasher. It also has
_____ garbage disposal. I use _____ dishwasher a lot, but I don't like to use _____
garbage disposal. It makes _____ loud noise. _____ noise always scares me. There's
also _____ small washer and dryer, but _____ washer sometimes breaks down.

C Complete the conversation between the tenant and the building manager. Use *a, an,* or *the.*

Look
I have a great apartment. The rooms are really big.
We use *the* in the second sentence because we know that the rooms are in the apartment.

Ross: There are a lot of facilities in this complex. There's _____ trash chute, _____
laundry room, and _____ swimming pool. There's also _____ security guard.

Pam: Where's _____ laundry room?

Ross: It's in the basement.

Pam: And does it cost anything to use?

Ross: Yes. _____ washers are $1.25 per load,
and _____ dryers are 25 cents
for 15 minutes.

Pam: Is _____ swimming pool heated?

Ross: No, it's not.

Pam: Where are _____ trash chutes?

Ross: They're on every floor, at the end of the hall.

Pam: Do all visitors have to check in with _____ security guard?

Ross: Yes, they do.

TIME to TALK
PAIRS. Read the situation. Then role-play a conversation. Ask and answer questions. Use the conversation in Exercise C as a model.
Student A: You are looking at some apartments in a large complex.
Student B: You are the complex manager. You are showing a possible tenant around. Answer the person's questions.
Example:
A: *What facilities are included?*
B: *There is a gym on the first floor. It's free for all tenants.*

46 Unit 4

Moving In 47

Grammar practice exercises build from controlled to open-ended.

Each grammar presentation ends with **Time to Talk**, an activity that motivates students to apply what they have learned in meaningful exchanges.

Review and Challenge reviews, consolidates, and extends the *Grammar to Communicate* lessons.

Challenging **listening exercises** give students practice with more advanced listening skills.

Getting Ready to Read prepares students for the reading tasks.

After You Read exercises practice vocabulary, comprehension, and inferencing.

Reading features high-interest texts and practices essential reading skills.

The **Reading Skill** box gives clear, concise explanations on the reading skills students will use.

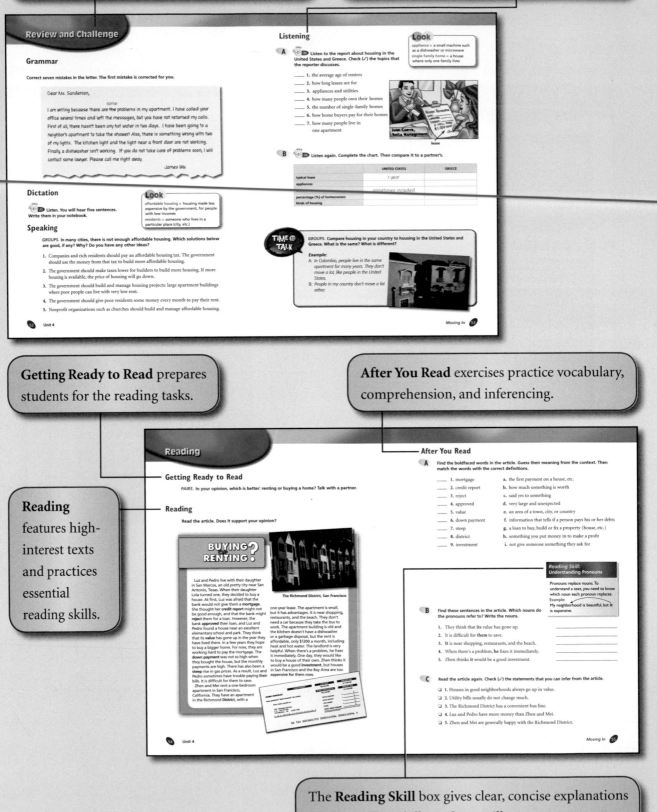

The **Writing Skill** gives clear, concise explanations of the writing skills students will be using in this section.

Prewriting features charts, graphic organizers, and guided writing. In **Writing**, students use what they have learned to write a paragraph, letter, or short essay.

Students practice using the **Writing Skill** with a subsequent exercise.

The **Model Paragraph** or **Model Essay** gives students a realistic sample to follow.

Writing

Writing Skill: Using Supporting Sentences

In a paragraph, the topic sentence is followed by **supporting sentences**. These sentences contain details such as examples, facts, or descriptions that make the topic sentence clear or support the opinion in the topic sentence.

Read each topic sentence. Check (✓) the sentences that would be good supporting sentences.

1. There are many advantages to living in hot places.
   ☐ a. It is possible to swim year-round in outdoor pools.
   ☐ b. Many mosquitoes and other insects enjoy a warm climate.
   ☐ c. You can grow fruit trees like lemon trees and orange trees in your backyard.
   ☐ d. The warm beaches are beautiful, but you must be careful to avoid sunburns.

2. There are several disadvantages to living on an island.
   ☐ a. Some groceries, such as lettuce, cost more than they do on the mainland.
   ☐ b. Many tourists come to visit, so the beaches can be crowded.
   ☐ c. There are beautiful volcanoes, and hiking to the top of them is exciting.
   ☐ d. Although there is often a lot of rain, the climate is mild and pleasant.

Read the model paragraph. Then complete the tasks.

Living in Cold Climates

There are several advantages to living in very cold climates. First, cold areas like Montreal, Canada, have great winter sports like ice hockey, skiing, and ice-skating. Also, in a cold climate, all four seasons are beautiful to see—for example, there are deep red and gold leaves on the trees in the fall, and snow-capped mountains in the winter. Finally, in a very cold climate, during most months you can build a fire in your fireplace and enjoy the quiet and beauty of a bright fire.

1. Circle the topic sentence.
2. Underline the supporting sentences.
3. What are the writer's three supporting ideas? Write them in your own words:
   a. _____
   b. _____
   c. _____

Unit 4

Prewriting: Using an Outline

A You are going to write a paragraph about a living situation. Choose one from the box.

living alone	living in an older house
living in an apartment	living in a warm climate
living in a cold climate	living with a large family
living in a large city	living with parents

B Look at the outline the writer used for the model paragraph. Then complete your own outline on the topic you chose.

Topic Sentence: _There are several advantages to living in very cold climates._

A. _winter sports_
B. _four seasons are beautiful_
C. _quiet and beauty of a fire_

Topic Sentence: _____

A. _____
B. _____
C. _____

Writing

Write a paragraph on the topic you chose. Use the model paragraph and your outline to help you. Make sure your topic sentence gives your opinion and has three supporting points. Write in your notebook.

Moving In

Beyond the Unit

Grammar Notes expand on the *Grammar to Communicate* presentations.

A variety of **Charts** provide additional support.

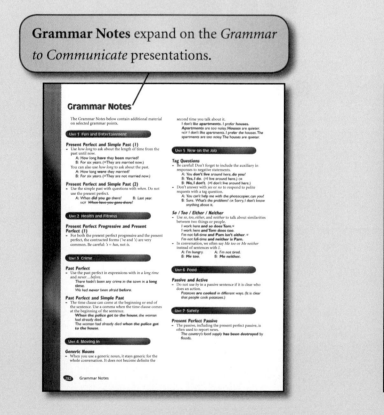

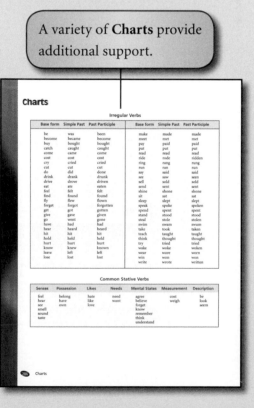

Teaching Support

The *Center Stage Teacher's Edition* features learning goals, learner persistence tips, step-by-step teaching notes, expansion activities, multilevel strategies, unit tests, and answer keys. The accompanying **Teacher's Resource Disk** includes supplementary grammar and vocabulary exercises, learner persistence worksheets, and graphic organizers.

Learner persistence tips introduce techniques to engage and retain students and help teachers adapt to a variety of student needs.

A variety of **teaching notes** provide step-by-step instruction and additional support.

Multilevel strategies maximize flexibility for every classroom.

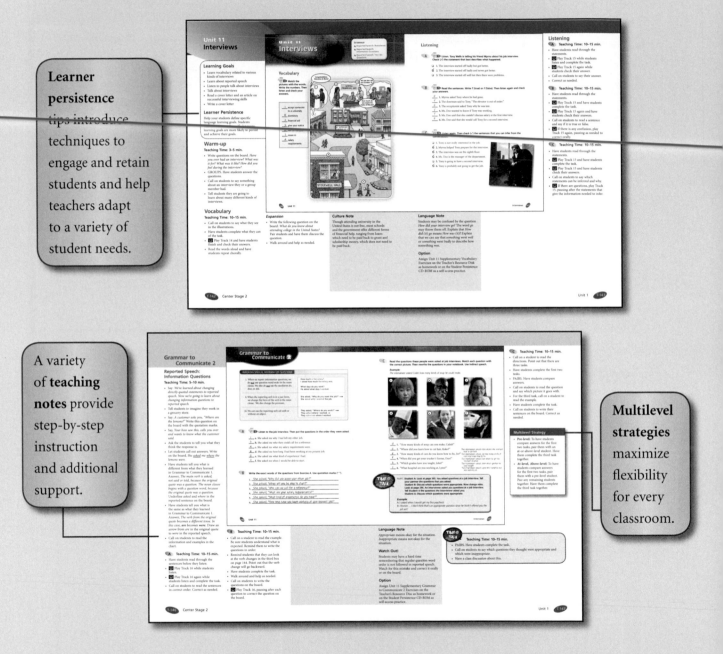

The complete *Center Stage* program

- Audio program
- *ExamView® Assessment Suite*
- Transparencies
- Companion Website

CENTER STAGE

4

Express Yourself in English

Unit 1
Fun and Entertainment

Grammar
- Present Perfect
- Present Perfect and Simple Past (1)
- Present Perfect and Simple Past (2)

Vocabulary

CD 1 TRACK

2 Match the pictures with the words. Write the numbers. Then listen and check your answers.

_____ appear in a movie	_____ direct	_____ perform in a play	_____ win an award
_____ be in a competition	_____ get a part	_____ try out for	

Marilyn Monroe Becomes a Star . . .

Marilyn, you will play Rose.

Marilyn, you'll read the part of Rose.

1947

1952

MARILYN MONROE starring as Rose

niagara

I want to stay out here and think about things.

You're acting funny tonight, Anna.

1953

1956

1960

Listening

 A 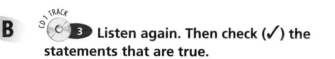 Listen. What does the boy want the girl to do? Check (✓) the correct answer.

❏ **1.** To try out for a dance competition
❏ **2.** To try out for the school play
❏ **3.** To teach him how to dance
❏ **4.** To dance with him in the school play

B Listen again. Then check (✓) the statements that are true.

❏ **1.** Tina tried out for the school play last year.
❏ **2.** Tina hasn't tried out for this year's school play.
❏ **3.** Tina has performed a lot.
❏ **4.** Bruce and Tina have been in several dance competitions.
❏ **5.** Tina danced with Bruce at last year's graduation.
❏ **6.** So far, Bruce has not learned how to dance.

> **Look**
> **play** = a story that is written to be performed by actors, especially in a theater

C Listen again. Check (✓) the statements that you can infer from the conversation.

❏ **1.** Bruce and Tina are good friends.
❏ **2.** Bruce has already tried out for the school play.
❏ **3.** This is Bruce and Tina's last year of high school.
❏ **4.** Bruce will not dance with Tina at graduation.
❏ **5.** Tina and Bruce will be in the school play together.

Grammar to Communicate 1

PRESENT PERFECT

i. Use the present perfect for an action or a state that began in the past and continues in the present. The action or state may or may not continue in the future.	They **have been** married for three years. (= They got married three years ago. They are married now.)
ii. Use the present perfect when you say that something happened in the past, but you do not say when it happened.	Sam **has gotten** a part in the movie. (= Sam tried out for the part and got it, but we don't know when.)
iii. Use the simple past for actions that are complete and cannot happen again. Do not use the present perfect.	Laurence Olivier **appeared** in many plays. (= Laurence Olivier is dead. He can't appear in other plays.)

A **Complete the sentences. Circle the correct name.**

Louis Armstrong, 1901–1971, jazz musician

Marilyn Monroe, 1926–1962, actress

Orson Welles, 1915–1985, actor, movie director

Melanie Griffith, 1957– _____ , actress, with Antonio Banderas 1960– _____ , actor

Ang Lee 1954– _____ , movie director

Shakira, 1977– _____ , singer

1. **Orson Welles /Antonio Banderas** appeared in many movies.

2. **Louis Armstrong / Shakira** has performed in public a lot.

3. **Orson Welles / Ang Lee** has directed many movies in his career.

4. **Marilyn Monroe / Melanie Griffith** has performed in many countries.

5. **Marilyn Monroe / Melanie Griffith** didn't use her real name.

B Complete the sentences. Write the correct form of the verbs. Use the present perfect or the simple past.

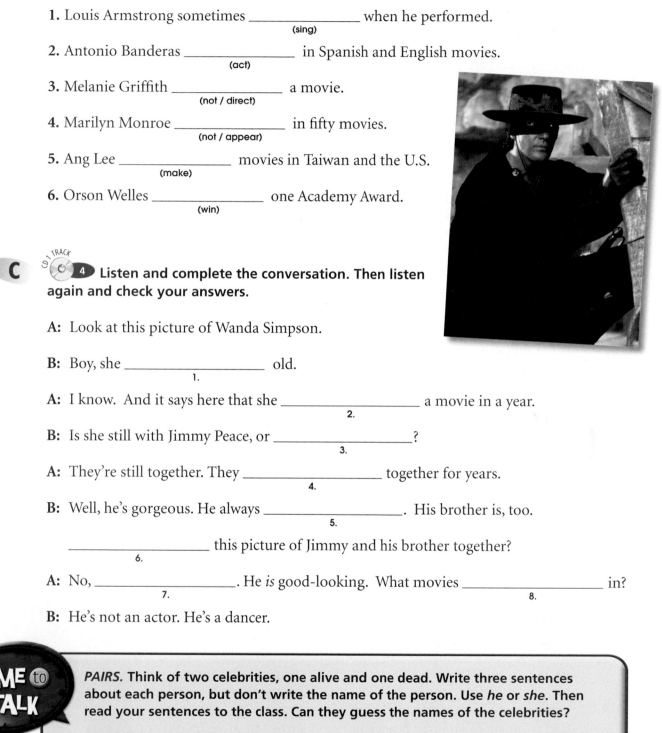

1. Louis Armstrong sometimes _____ when he performed.
   (sing)

2. Antonio Banderas _____ in Spanish and English movies.
   (act)

3. Melanie Griffith _____ a movie.
   (not / direct)

4. Marilyn Monroe _____ in fifty movies.
   (not / appear)

5. Ang Lee _____ movies in Taiwan and the U.S.
   (make)

6. Orson Welles _____ one Academy Award.
   (win)

C CD 1 TRACK **4** Listen and complete the conversation. Then listen again and check your answers.

A: Look at this picture of Wanda Simpson.

B: Boy, she _____ old.
   1.

A: I know. And it says here that she _____ a movie in a year.
   2.

B: Is she still with Jimmy Peace, or _____?
   3.

A: They're still together. They _____ together for years.
   4.

B: Well, he's gorgeous. He always _____. His brother is, too.
   5.

_____ this picture of Jimmy and his brother together?
6.

A: No, _____. He *is* good-looking. What movies _____ in?
   7.   8.

B: He's not an actor. He's a dancer.

TIME to TALK

PAIRS. Think of two celebrities, one alive and one dead. Write three sentences about each person, but don't write the name of the person. Use *he* or *she*. Then read your sentences to the class. Can they guess the names of the celebrities?

Example:
Student: *She has recorded many albums. She's American, but she has lived in London for a while.*
    Class: *Is it Madonna?*

Grammar to Communicate 2

PRESENT PERFECT AND SIMPLE PAST (1)

i. Use the present perfect for an action or a state that began in the past and continues in the present.	We **have been** in the band for a long time. (= We joined the band a long time ago, and we are still in the band.)
Use the simple past for an action or a state that began and finished in the past.	We **were** in the band in high school. (= We are not in the band anymore.)
ii. Use *for* to say the period of time. Use *since* to say when something began. *Since* can also start a time clause.	We **have known** each other **for** a few years. We **have known** each other **since** 1998. We have been friends <u>since we were 16.</u> time clause

A Match the sentences on the left with the sentences on the right. Write the correct letter.

__b__ **1.** Ben played in a band for three years.

_____ **2.** Tom has played in a band for five years.

        a. He practices every day.

        b. He quit two weeks ago.

_____ **3.** Martha and Tina were dance partners for six months.

_____ **4.** Pat and Kim have been dance partners for two months.

        a. They weren't very good.

        b. They have won twice.

_____ **5.** Max and Mia have been in acting school for a year.

_____ **6.** Lisa and Paul went to the same acting school.

        a. They graduated in June.

        b. They are learning a lot.

B Write sentences with the words. Use the present perfect and simple past. Write in your notebook.

1. I / know how to dance / since / I / be / a small child
    I have known how to dance since I was a small child.

2. I / compete / in dance competitions / since / I / be / 8 years old

3. My dance partner and I / not / know each other/ for very long

4. We / win / a lot of awards / since / we / start dancing together

5. We / not / lose / any competitions / since / we / become / partners

C Complete the sentences. Use the present perfect and the simple past.

1. Hana opened a café in Oakland a few years ago. Before that, she worked at a café in Ventura from 1995 to 2005.

   <u>Hana has owned a café in Oakland</u> _____ for a few years.
   (own)
   <u>Hana worked at a café in Ventura</u> _____ for ten years.
   (work)

2. James is a professional soccer player. He joined a soccer team two years ago. Before that, he worked as a waiter from 2002 to 2006.

   _____ for two years.
   (play on a soccer team)
   _____ for several years.
   (work as a waiter)

3. Yoko and Hiro met each other in college in 2003. They played in a band from 2003 to 2007.

   _____ since 2003.
   (know)
   _____ for four years.
   (play in a band)

4. Tony is a singer in Las Vegas. He got a part in a show in 2000. Before that, he had a job as a music teacher from 1994 to 2000.

   _____ for many years.
   (be in the show)
   _____ for six years.
   (teach)

> **Look**
>
> **show** = a performance in movies, TV, radio, Broadway, etc.

TIME to TALK

PAIRS. **Talk about how long you have enjoyed your favorite activities, or how long you have liked your favorite artist, musician, actor, or athlete.**

Example:
A: *My favorite music is Salsa, and I love to dance.*
B: *How long have you liked Salsa music?*

Grammar to Communicate 3

i. Use the present perfect when you talk about an action or event that happened in the past, but you do not say when it happened.

Use the simple past for an action or event that happened at a specific time in the past.

> **Have** you ever **won** any championships?
> (= Sometime before now, but I'm not asking you when.)
>
> **Did** you **win** the championship last year?
> (= I'm asking you about last year.)

ii. *Up to now, so far,* and *in the past* + [time period] are common time expressions with the present perfect.

> **Up to now** we've won two championships.
> **So far** we haven't lost any games.
> We haven't lost any games **in the past six months**.

A CD 1 TRACK 5 **Listen. Three people are talking about what they have done in the past year. Complete the sentences.**

1. **Miranda:** I _____ how to dance.

2. **Steve:** I _____ much time for fun.

3. **Steve:** I _____ my own business a few months ago.

4. **Robert:** Since I joined my team, we _____ two championships.

championship

B **Complete the sentences. Use the simple past or the present perfect.**

Miranda: Since I _____ taking dance classes, I _____ how to dance to
           1. (start)   2. (learn)

all different kinds of music. Last month, the instructor _____ us two
                      3. (teach)

new dances.

Steve: Actually, I _____ two businesses over the years. I _____ my
           4. (have)   5. (open)

first business, a small restaurant, with my brother in 1995. We _____
                      6. (not / do)

well and _____ the restaurant two years later.
       7. (close)

C Complete the sentences. Circle the correct time expression.

1. I've been to only one concert **two days ago / on Monday / so far.**

2. We haven't won a championship **for two years / in 2006 / two years ago.**

3. She appeared in a play **a long time ago / so far / up to now.**

4. I've won two awards **in the past year / last month / when I was in high school.**

5. He got his first part in a show **since he was 18 / so far / when he was 18.**

D Complete the conversations. Use the present perfect or the simple past of the verbs in the box. Some verbs are used more than once. Then read the conversations with a partner.

1. **A:** I like to go out dancing.

   B: How many times ___have you gone___ dancing this month?

   A: Just once.

   B: Who ___taught___ you how to dance?

be	play
buy	see
go	teach

2. **A:** I love movies.

   B: What movies _____ recently?

   A: None. I've been too busy.

   B: What _____ the last movie you saw?

3. **A:** I love to collect cars.

   B: How many cars _____ ?

   A: Just one.

   B: When _____ it?

4. **A:** I love sports.

   B: _____ you ever _____ on a team?

   A: Yeah. Years ago.

   B: What sport _____ ?

TIME to TALK

GROUPS. Talk about the fun or interesting things that you have done in your life, and the things that you have not done yet but would like to do.

Example:

A: *I've watched concerts on TV, but I've never been to a live concert . . .*

Review and Challenge

Grammar

Correct the e-mail. There are seven mistakes. The first one is corrected for you.

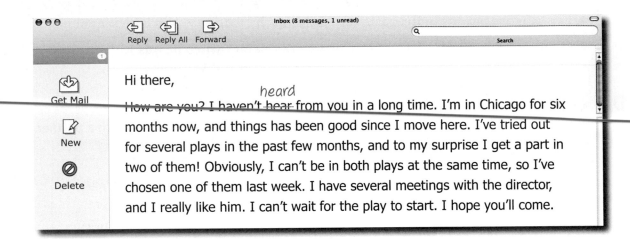

Hi there,

How are you? I haven't ~~hear~~ *heard* from you in a long time. I'm in Chicago for six months now, and things has been good since I move here. I've tried out for several plays in the past few months, and to my surprise I get a part in two of them! Obviously, I can't be in both plays at the same time, so I've chosen one of them last week. I have several meetings with the director, and I really like him. I can't wait for the play to start. I hope you'll come.

Dictation

6 Listen. You will hear five sentences. Write them in your notebook.

Speaking

CLASS. Walk around the class and ask and answer questions. Complete the chart.

Example:

You: *Did you go to a baseball game last year?*
Anita: *No, I didn't. I don't like baseball.*
You: *Have you ever been to a baseball game?*
Anita: *Yes, I have. My father took me to a lot of games when I was young.*

FIND SOMEONE WHO...	NAME	FIND SOMEONE WHO...	NAME
went to a baseball game last year.		has never been to a baseball game.	
won an award in school.		has won several awards.	
met someone famous last year.		has gotten a famous person's autograph.	
was in the high school band.		has been in a band for a while.	
lost a game last week.		has won a championship.	
went to a concert last year.		has never been to a concert.	
went dancing last night.		has gone dancing this month.	

Listening

A **7** Listen to the radio report. Check (✓) the main idea of the report.

❏ **1.** why Hollywood movies are getting better and better

❏ **2.** why many people have stopped going to the movies

❏ **3.** why Hollywood movies have become so expensive to make

B **7** Check (✓) the sentences that are true, according to the report. Then listen again and check your answers.

❏ **1.** Movie ticket prices have fallen since 2001.

❏ **2.** People have gotten bored with Hollywood movies.

❏ **3.** People have a lot of entertainment choices today.

❏ **4.** People love to go to the movies on Saturday nights.

❏ **5.** People have less free time today than they did in the past.

❏ **6.** The cost of DVD players and widescreen TVs is too high.

❏ **7.** Movie theaters have become very uncomfortable.

TIME to TALK

GROUPS. Discuss the questions.

1. Have you gone to the movies recently? When was the last time you went? What movie did you see? How much was the ticket?

2. Have Hollywood movies gotten better or worse? Explain.

3. In your opinion, which is better: watching a movie at home or in a movie theater? Why?

4. In the future, will there still be movie theaters? Why or why not?

Reading

Getting Ready to Read

How are movies today different from movies in the 1920s and 1930s? Write in your notebook.

Reading

Read the article. What are the differences between movies now and movies in the 1920s and 1930s? Are they the same differences you wrote?

In the early days of Hollywood, during the 1920s and 1930s, movie theaters were very large, often with a thousand seats or more. This was because movie theaters **attracted** large **audiences**. The largest movie theater, Radio City Music Hall in New York City, opened in 1932 with almost 6,000 seats. The movie theaters of the time looked like **palaces**, with gold ceilings, red velvet curtains, and paintings on the walls. A trip to the movies was special and exciting. Television was only beginning. It was no competition for the excitement of the movie theater.

Now things are different. The movie **industry** has a difficult time making a **profit** because fewer people go to the movies. To attract more people, movie theaters have changed. Movie palaces have been replaced with multiplex theaters. These can show more movies at a time.

Because movie theaters do not attract as many people, the movie industry has looked for other ways to make money. One solution is blockbuster movies. Blockbusters have many **special effects** and the most popular movie stars. They often have large indoor or outdoor **sets** and unusual costumes. Blockbusters attract large audiences because they offer an experience that people cannot have at home on TV.

The movie industry also makes a profit in other ways. Today movies make the most money when they **come out on** DVD or television. Also, the movie industry makes money by selling **merchandise** based on popular movie **characters**. Movie merchandise such as toys, games, and clothing is very profitable. Finally, the movie industry has started to make money through the Internet; more people are paying to watch movies on their computer screens. The days of 1,000-seat movie palaces are far in the past, but the movie industry lives on.

After You Read

A Find the boldfaced words in the article and guess their meaning from the context. Then match the words with the correct definitions.

_____ 1. attracted   **a.** become available on

_____ 2. audiences   **b.** special lighting, sound, or animation

_____ 3. palaces   **c.** groups of people who watch a performance

_____ 4. industry   **d.** locations where movies are made

_____ 5. profit   **e.** things that are for sale in stores

_____ 6. special effects   **f.** were interesting to

_____ 7. sets   **g.** people in plays, books, or movies

_____ 8. come out on   **h.** beautiful buildings where kings and queens lived

_____ 9. merchandise   **i.** a type of business

_____10. characters   **j.** money made from doing business

The Wizard of Oz, 1939, was one of the first movies made in color, and had special effects.

> **Reading Skill:**
> **Guessing from Context**
>
> Often, you do not need to use a dictionary to understand the meaning of a new word in a text. You can guess the meaning from the **context** (the words and sentences before and after the new word.)

B Read the article again. Write *T* (true) or *F* (false) for each statement.

_____ 1. In the early days of Hollywood, television was more popular than movies.

_____ 2. When the movie industry started, theaters used to play several movies at one time.

_____ 3. The audiences for blockbusters are often larger than those for other movies.

_____ 4. Movie theaters make more money than DVDs for the movie industry.

_____ 5. Movie merchandise makes profits for the movie industry.

_____ 6. The movie industry can't make money when people watch movies on the Internet.

Writing

When you write a paragraph, you should organize the ideas in a logical order. Think about what the reader needs to know first, second, and so on.

A Put the sentences in logical order. Write the numbers. Then compare your answers with a partner. Do you have the same order?

_____ On its way from Southampton, England, to New York, the ship hit an iceberg and sank in the Atlantic Ocean.

__6__ This movie is powerful because the sinking of the *Titanic* looks very real.

__1__ My favorite movie is *Titanic*, about the famous luxury passenger ship *Titanic*.

_____ These people could not survive the freezing water because they were not in lifeboats.

_____ They were not in lifeboats because they were traveling in the third-class section of the ship.

_____ 500 people escaped in lifeboats and were rescued, but 1,200 more died.

B Read the model paragraph. Then answer the question.

My Favorite Movie: *Psycho*

My favorite movie is the horror movie *Psycho*. It was directed by Alfred Hitchcock in 1960. A woman steals a large amount of money from her boss. She runs away to meet her boyfriend. On the way, she stops her car at a lonely motel. In the most famous scene, an unknown person murders the young woman in the shower. We do not see the murder. We imagine it through the sound of the music and water and blood swirling down in the bathtub. This film has become a classic because it is so suspenseful—you never know what will happen next.

Where does the writer give an opinion?

a. at the beginning of the paragraph

b. in the middle of the paragraph

Prewriting: Using Guided Writing

Answer the questions.

1. What is your favorite movie?

_____

2. What type of movie is it?

_____

_____

3. Where and when does the story take place?

_____

_____

_____

4. What is the story about? What happens first, second, next?

_____

_____

_____

_____

_____

5. Why do you like this movie?

_____

_____

_____

_____

Writing

Write a paragraph about your favorite movie. Use the model paragraph and your notes to help you. Write in your notebook.

Vocabulary

D 1 TRACK

Match the pictures with the words. Write the numbers. Then listen and check your answers.

_____ act up	_____ chicken pox	_____ have a good appetite	_____ injury	_____ vitamins
_____ arthritis	_____ diabetes	_____ have trouble sleeping	_____ painkillers	

Listening

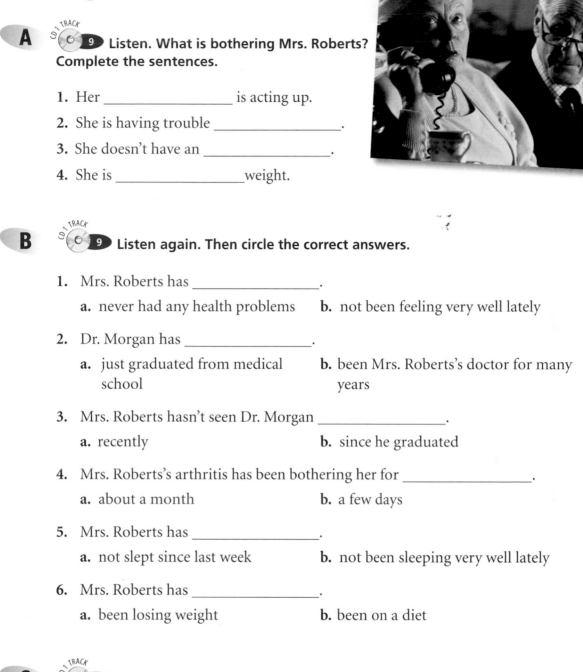

A 🔊 TRACK 9 **Listen. What is bothering Mrs. Roberts? Complete the sentences.**

1. Her _____ is acting up.
2. She is having trouble _____.
3. She doesn't have an _____.
4. She is _____ weight.

B 🔊 TRACK 9 **Listen again. Then circle the correct answers.**

1. Mrs. Roberts has _____.
   a. never had any health problems   **b.** not been feeling very well lately

2. Dr. Morgan has _____.
   a. just graduated from medical school   **b.** been Mrs. Roberts's doctor for many years

3. Mrs. Roberts hasn't seen Dr. Morgan _____.
   a. recently   **b.** since he graduated

4. Mrs. Roberts's arthritis has been bothering her for _____.
   a. about a month   **b.** a few days

5. Mrs. Roberts has _____.
   a. not slept since last week   **b.** not been sleeping very well lately

6. Mrs. Roberts has _____.
   a. been losing weight   **b.** been on a diet

C 🔊 TRACK 9 **Listen again. Check (✓) the statements that you can infer from the conversation.**

❏ **1.** The secretary and Mrs. Roberts know each other.
❏ **2.** Mrs. Roberts is upset when the secretary doesn't recognize her name.
❏ **3.** The secretary does not believe that Mrs. Roberts is really sick.
❏ **4.** Mrs. Roberts calls the doctor's office a lot.
❏ **5.** Mrs. Roberts has never been to Dr. Morgan's new office.
❏ **6.** Mrs. Roberts doesn't like things to change.

Grammar to Communicate 1

PRESENT PERFECT PROGRESSIVE

i. Use the present perfect progressive to show that an action began in the past and is continuing in the present.	A: I **have been feeling** sick lately. B: How long **has** this **been going on**? A: For about a week. C: I **haven't been feeling** well either.
ii. Use the present perfect progressive to show that an action began in the past and ended very recently.	Dana **has been crying**. Her eyes are red. (= She just stopped crying a minute ago.)
iii. With some verbs (*work*, *live*, *teach*) you can use the present perfect progressive or the present perfect. The meaning is the same.	They **have been living** there for years. (= They **have lived** there for years.)

A CD 1 TRACK 10 Read the sentences. Listen and put them in correct order. Write *1* (first sentence), *2* (second sentence), and so on. Then listen again and check your answers.

_____ **a.** And have you been exercising?

_____ **b.** I've been dieting for about a month.

_____ **c.** And what have you been eating?

_____ **d.** How long have you been dieting?

_____ **e.** Yes. I've been working out every day.

_____ **f.** I've been trying to eat healthy food.

_____ **g.** I've been eating a lot of vegetables, and I haven't been having dessert.

PAIRS. Where are the people in the conversation? Who are they?

B Complete the conversations. Use the present perfect progressive. Add *not* where necessary.

1. **A:** Jack, what's the matter?
   B: I don't know. I ___haven't been feeling___ well.
                                      (feel)

2. **A:** Hey, Jen. You look good.
   B: Thanks. I' _____ my weight.
                         (watch)

3. **A:** Why is Ken coughing so much?
   B: He _____ his asthma medication.
                  (take)

4. **A:** You look tired, Becky.
   B: I know. I _____ enough sleep.
                        (got)

5. **A:** You've lost weight.
   B: Really? Maybe it's because I _____ a lot of tennis.
                                              (play)

6. **A:** Why do you need a prescription for painkillers?

   B: My back _____.
                       (act up)

7. **A:** Are you and your wife getting more exercise these days?

   B: Yes. For the past month we _____ for long walks every day.
                                        (go)

C   **Answer the questions. Use the present perfect progressive and the verbs in the box. More than one answer is possible.**

cry	exercise	feel	practice	run	sleep	wait

1. Julia didn't go to work yesterday or today. Why?

   She hasn't been feeling well. _____

2. Two patients in a doctor's office are looking at their watches. They look angry. Why?

   _____

3. Steve and Lori know their little boy is not well. How do they know that?

   _____

4. Mark looked tired last week, and he looks tired this week. What's the matter with him?

   _____

5. Ann's legs hurt. Why?

   _____

TIME to TALK

PAIRS. Talk about your health lately. How have you been feeling? What have and haven't you been doing? Use the words in the box and your own ideas.

Example:
I haven't been taking care of myself. I've been working too hard. . .

eat a lot of junk food
get enough sleep
get in shape
spend a lot of time outdoors
take care of yourself
watch your weight

Grammar to Communicate 2

i. Use the present perfect progressive for activities that are *not* complete.	He **has been writing** a letter to the doctor. (= The letter is not finished.)
Use the present perfect for activities that are complete.	He **has written** a letter to the doctor. (= The letter is finished.)
ii. Use the present perfect progressive for an activity completed very recently.	They **have been working out**. They're still wearing their gym clothes.
Use the present perfect for an activity completed sometime before now.	They **have worked out** today.
iii. Do not use the progressive form with stative verbs. (See the list on page 286.)	I **have known** him for two years. NOT: I've been knowing him for two years.

A CD 1 TRACK 11 **Listen and complete the statements.**

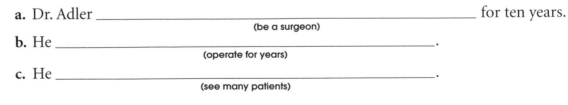

1. Ella _____ to the doctor for half an hour.

2. Ella _____ to the doctor.

3. He _____ an article about diabetes.

4. He _____ several articles about diabetes.

5. The surgeon _____ on many patients today.

operate

PAIRS. Talk about the situations above. Say, "This is happening now," or "This is finished."

B Write sentences with the present perfect or the present perfect progressive.

1. Dr. Adler became a surgeon ten years ago. He operates on patients almost every day.

   a. Dr. Adler _____ for ten years.
      (be a surgeon)

   b. He _____.
      (operate for years)

   c. He _____.
      (see many patients)

2. Chris woke up yesterday feeling sick and still feels bad.

   a. Chris _____.
      (cough a lot)

   b. She _____.
      (sleep all day today)

C 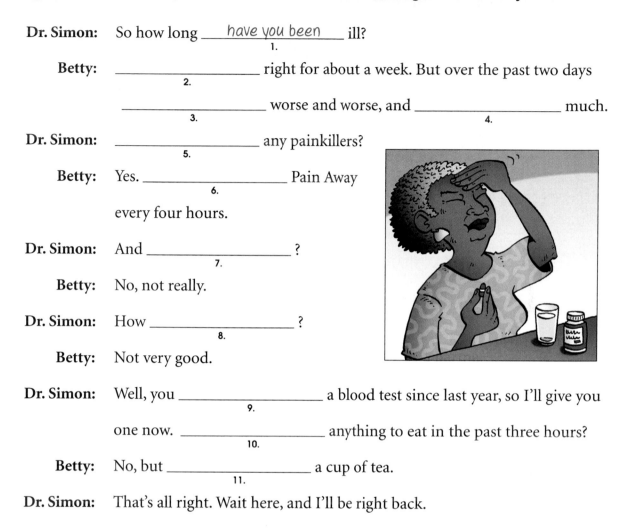 **12** **Listen and complete the conversation. Then listen again and check your answers.**

Dr. Simon: So how long _____have you been_____ ill?
                                    1.

Betty: _____ right for about a week. But over the past two days
                    2.

        _____ worse and worse, and _____ much.
                    3.   4.

Dr. Simon: _____ any painkillers?
                    5.

Betty: Yes. _____ Pain Away
                        6.

        every four hours.

Dr. Simon: And _____ ?
                        7.

Betty: No, not really.

Dr. Simon: How _____ ?
                        8.

Betty: Not very good.

Dr. Simon: Well, you _____ a blood test since last year, so I'll give you
                            9.

        one now. _____ anything to eat in the past three hours?
                        10.

Betty: No, but _____ a cup of tea.
                        11.

Dr. Simon: That's all right. Wait here, and I'll be right back.

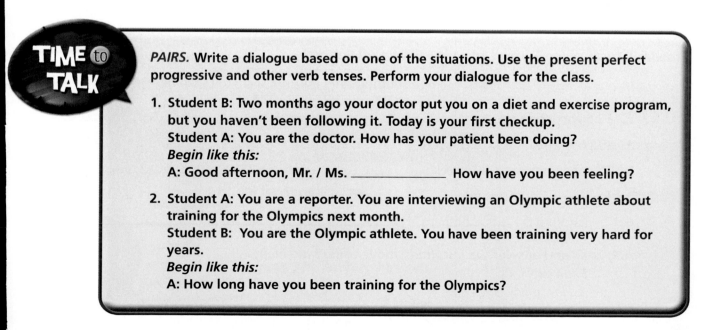

TIME to TALK

PAIRS. **Write a dialogue based on one of the situations. Use the present perfect progressive and other verb tenses. Perform your dialogue for the class.**

1. **Student B: Two months ago your doctor put you on a diet and exercise program, but you haven't been following it. Today is your first checkup.**
   Student A: You are the doctor. How has your patient been doing?
   Begin like this:
   A: Good afternoon, Mr. / Ms. _____ How have you been feeling?

2. **Student A: You are a reporter. You are interviewing an Olympic athlete about training for the Olympics next month.**
   Student B: You are the Olympic athlete. You have been training very hard for years.
   Begin like this:
   A: How long have you been training for the Olympics?

Grammar to Communicate 3

PRESENT PERFECT PROGRESSIVE AND PRESENT PERFECT (2)

i. Use the present perfect progressive to talk about *how long*.	I've been playing soccer **for five years.** A: **How long** has he been running? B: For two hours.
ii. Use the present perfect to emphasize *how much, how many,* or *how far.*	I've played **three soccer games** this month. A: **How many times has she played this** week? B: **Three times.** A: **How far** has he run? B: **12 miles.**

A   **Circle the correct words to complete the sentences.**

1. The two teams have played **one game / for half an hour**.

2. The two teams have been playing **one game / for an hour**.

3. Bonnie has been swimming **sixty laps / for an hour**.

4. Bonnie has swum **sixty laps / for an hour**.

5. Tony has been running **for thirty minutes / 4 miles**.

6. Tony has run **for thirty minutes / 4 miles**.

B   **Write sentences. Tell how many times these things have happened.**

1. I / go for a walk / this week
   I've gone for several walks this week. OR
   I haven't gone for a walk this week.

2. I / have / coffee today _____

3. I / go to the gym / this month _____

4. I / take vitamins / this week _____

5. I / have a cold / this year _____

6. I / play sports / this month _____

PAIRS. Ask and answer the questions above using *how many*.
   Example:
   A: *How many times have you gone for a walk this week?*
   B: *Several times. I've gone on three walks this week.*

C   Check (✓) the things that you do or that happen regularly.

- ❏ drink coffee
- ❏ drive to school/work
- ❏ have trouble sleeping
- ❏ have trouble waking up early

- ❏ play _____
      (sport)
- ❏ smoke
- ❏ take vitamins
- ❏ walk to school / work

- ❏ watch my weight
- ❏ wear glasses
- ❏ work out

PAIRS. Show your list to your partner, and look at your partner's list. Write questions with *How long...?* in your notebook. Then ask and answer the questions.

Example:
☑ have trouble sleeping
A: *How long have you been having trouble sleeping?*
B: *For a few days.*

ON YOUR OWN. Complete the chart with information about yourself.

	YOU		YOUR PARTNER	
	Yes	No	Yes	No
1. I've joined a health club.				
2. I've thought about joining a health club.				
3. I play _____ (sport)				
4. I've won a championship.				
5. I've had a sports injury.				
6. I've had the measles / mumps / chicken pox.				
7. I've broken my _____ (part of the body)				
8. I've been in a car accident.				

PAIRS. Now ask your partner the questions above and complete the chart. Use appropriate tenses. Start your questions with expressions like: *Have you ever . . .? How long . . .? How old were you when . . .? What happened?*

Example:
A: *Do you play any sports?*
B: *Yes, I play soccer.*
A: *How long have you been playing?*
B: *For more than twenty years.*
A: *That's a long time. How old were you when you started playing?*
B: *I was about four years old.*

Grammar

Correct the conversation. There are nine mistakes. The first one is corrected for you.

Craig: Hi, Adam. I ~~haven't been seeing~~ *haven't seen* you for a long time. How have you been?

Adam: I'm tired because I've studied a lot. Luckily the semester ends in a week. ~~What about you?~~ ~~What you been doing lately?~~

Craig: Well, I've been tried to get into shape for the marathon next month. I've been working out every day for the past four months.

Adam: That sounds tough. You've been going to a gym?

Craig: Yes, I go. And Clara have been going, too.

Adam: So you two are still together. That's great. Is she going to run in the marathon?

Craig: Of course. She been running for years. She's been running in several marathons.

Dictation

🎧 **13** **Listen. You will hear five sentences. Write them in your notebook.**

Speaking

GROUPS. **Look at the health and fitness items in the box. Have they been growing more popular in your country? Have you ever tried any of the activities or visited any of the places?**

aerobics	health / sports clubs	low fat food
day spas	herbal supplements	yoga

Example:
A: *Have day spas been growing more popular in your country?*
B: *Yes. A lot of day spas have been opening in the big cities.*
C: *Have you ever visited one?*
B: *No, I haven't. They're very expensive.*

Listening

A *PAIRS.* Talk about the health trends in the box. Do you think they have been going up or down?

average life expectancy	child mortality rate
cancer rate	number of smokers

Look

life expectancy = how long a person is expected to live
mortality rate = the number of deaths during a period of time among a group of people
trend = the way a situation develops or changes over time

B 🔊 **14** Listen. A reporter talks about recent trends in public health worldwide. Check (✓) the correct columns.

WORLDWIDE	↑ (GO UP = INCREASE = RISE)	↓ (GO DOWN = DECREASE = FALL)
average life expectancy		
cancer rate		
child mortality rate		
number of smokers		

C 🔊 **14** Read the sentences. Write *T* (true) or *F* (false). If you are not sure, write *?* Then listen again and check your answers.

_____ **1.** In some countries, men's life expectancy has been going down in recent years.

_____ **2.** The child mortality rate has gone down in all countries since 1990.

_____ **3.** As the world population has been getting older, cancer rates have been going up.

_____ **4.** In richer countries, the number of male smokers has been going up.

_____ **5.** In richer countries, the number of female smokers has been increasing.

TIME to TALK

GROUPS. Answer the questions.

1. Why do you think that life expectancy has been going down in some parts of the world?

2. Why do you think life expectancy rates are different for men and women?

3. There are more elderly people now than in the past. What problems can this cause for governments and families?

4. What are possible reasons for different smoking rates for men and women?

Reading

Getting Ready to Read

Have you ever had back pain or do you know someone who has? What are some causes and possible treatments? Write in your notebook.

Reading Skill:
Using What You Already Know

Before you read, think about the topic of the text. What do you already know about the topic? That information will help you understand the text.

Reading

Read the article. Does it mention the treatments you wrote about?

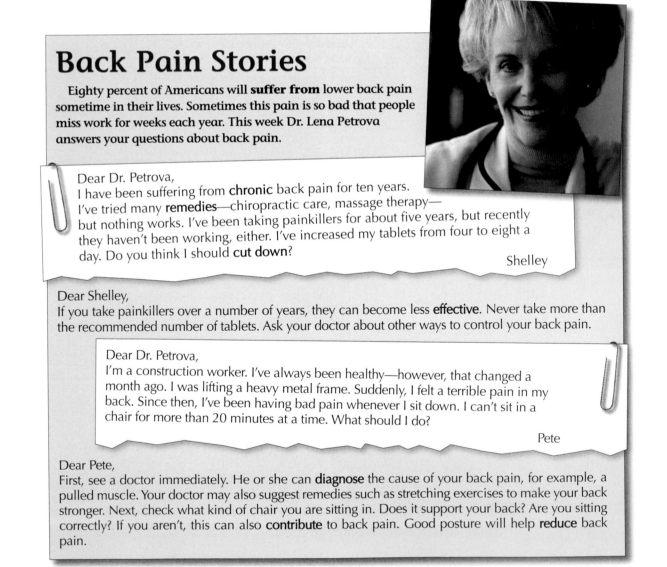

Back Pain Stories

Eighty percent of Americans will **suffer from** lower back pain sometime in their lives. Sometimes this pain is so bad that people miss work for weeks each year. This week Dr. Lena Petrova answers your questions about back pain.

Dear Dr. Petrova,
I have been suffering from **chronic** back pain for ten years. I've tried many **remedies**—chiropractic care, massage therapy— but nothing works. I've been taking painkillers for about five years, but recently they haven't been working, either. I've increased my tablets from four to eight a day. Do you think I should **cut down**?

Shelley

Dear Shelley,
If you take painkillers over a number of years, they can become less **effective**. Never take more than the recommended number of tablets. Ask your doctor about other ways to control your back pain.

Dear Dr. Petrova,
I'm a construction worker. I've always been healthy—however, that changed a month ago. I was lifting a heavy metal frame. Suddenly, I felt a terrible pain in my back. Since then, I've been having bad pain whenever I sit down. I can't sit in a chair for more than 20 minutes at a time. What should I do?

Pete

Dear Pete,
First, see a doctor immediately. He or she can **diagnose** the cause of your back pain, for example, a pulled muscle. Your doctor may also suggest remedies such as stretching exercises to make your back stronger. Next, check what kind of chair you are sitting in. Does it support your back? Are you sitting correctly? If you aren't, this can also **contribute** to back pain. Good posture will help **reduce** back pain.

After You Read

A Find the boldfaced words in the article. Guess their meaning from the context. Then circle the best meaning.

1. suffer from
   a. have pain from
   b. know about

2. chronic
   a. over a long period of time
   b. over a short period of time

3. remedies
   a. prescriptions
   b. treatments

4. cut down
   a. to remove something
   b. to do less of something

5. effective
   a. important
   b. useful

6. diagnose
   a. take a test
   b. recognize an illness

7. support
   a. hold up
   b. carry

8. contribute
   a. add to something
   b. give money

9. reduce
   a. decrease
   b. find

B Write *T* (true) or *F* (false) for each statement.

_____ 1. Many people are absent from work because of back pain.

_____ 2. Painkillers usually work well after many years of everyday use.

_____ 3. Lifting something very heavy can cause a sudden back injury.

_____ 4. If you have back problems, it can be painful to sit for a long time.

_____ 5. A good chair with support helps reduce back pain.

_____ 6. Exercise doesn't help back pain.

Writing

A paragraph has one main idea. The main idea is usually stated in the first or second sentence. This is called the **topic sentence**.

A   **Read the paragraph. Circle the best topic sentence.**

In the past, doctors sometimes did not know exactly what was wrong when children were sick. _____
For example, doctors now have a very good test for Strep throat. Strep throat is a common illness in children that is caused by a bacteria. Most sore throats are caused by viruses and go away without medicine. A Strep throat is more serious and causes fever, difficulty swallowing, and red and white patches in the throat. Now when children have a sore throat, doctors can test them quickly to see if they have the Strep bacteria. Doctors use a rapid Strep test, which gives results in about 5 minutes. If a child tests positive, she or he can take medicine immediately. This means the child will have less pain and will get well faster.

a. Now it is easier for doctors to diagnose many of children's illnesses.

b. Now doctors understand children's symptoms.

c. These days, children get sick less often.

B   **Read the model paragraph. Circle the topic sentence.**

Cold Remedies

There are several remedies for a cold. One remedy is to take aspirin every four hours. Aspirin can reduce a fever and stop headaches. You can also use over-the-counter cold remedies. Some people prefer natural remedies such as drinking hot water with honey and lemon. This is good if you have a sore throat and a cough. You can also gargle with warm saltwater for a sore throat. Another type of remedy is herbal tea. However, the best way to stop a cold is to have a healthy diet and get plenty of sleep at night.

Prewriting: Using a Cluster

A Choose a problem from the box.

arthritis	bad breath	heartburn	snoring

B Look at the cluster the writer used for her paragraph about cold remedies. Then complete your own.

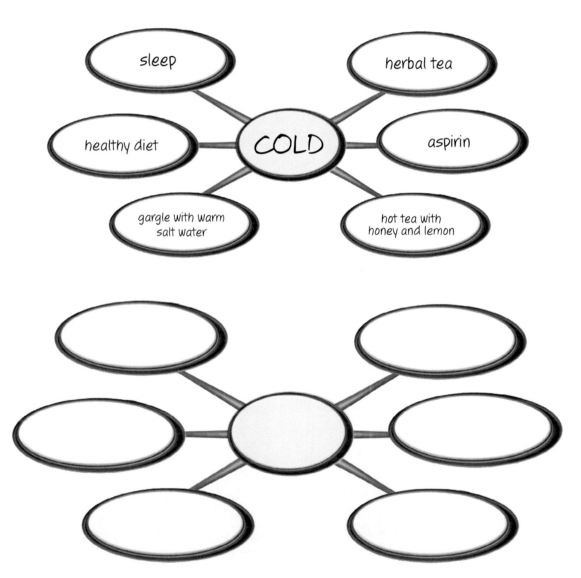

Writing

 Write a paragraph about the problem you chose. Describe the problem and suggest remedies. Use the model paragraph and your cluster to help you. Write in your notebook.

Unit 3
Crime

Vocabulary

Match the pictures with the words. Write the numbers. Then listen and check your answers.

_____ break-in
_____ detective
_____ investigate
_____ investigation
_____ murder
_____ question
_____ robbers
_____ robbery
_____ suspect
_____ victim
_____ witness

 Unit 3

Listening

A **16** Listen. Why is the detective interviewing Ms. Snodgrass? What happened? Check (✓) the correct answer.

❏ **1.** Ms. Snodgrass lost her dog, and she called the police for help.

❏ **2.** Ms. Snodgrass's friend Bernie called the police when she didn't answer the phone.

❏ **3.** Someone killed Ms. Snodgrass's dog.

❏ **4.** There was a crime near Ms. Snodgrass's house.

B **17** Read each pair of sentences. Then listen and circle the letter of the sentence that you hear in each pair.

1. a. Well, I've been shopping all day, so I'm tired.

   b. Well, I had been shopping all day, so I was tired.

2. a. What time did you get home from shopping?

   b. What time had you gotten home from shopping?

3. a. She hadn't eaten, so I fed her.

   b. She didn't want to eat, but I fed her.

4. a. He'd been away, and we hadn't talked in a while.

   b. He's been away, so we haven't talked in a while.

5. a. I hadn't looked at the clock.

   b. I didn't look at the clock.

6. a. Well, we had just started our walk when we heard a scream.

   b. Well, we were just walking along when we heard a scream.

Olivia Snodgrass

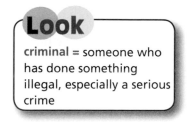

Look

criminal = someone who has done something illegal, especially a serious crime

C **18** Listen again. Check (✓) the statements that you can infer from the conversation.

❏ **1.** Ms. Snodgrass is a criminal.

❏ **2.** Ms. Snodgrass is a witness in an investigation.

❏ **3.** Ms. Snodgrass is a suspect in an investigation.

❏ **4.** The detective does not believe everything that Ms. Snodgrass says.

❏ **5.** Ms. Snodgrass loves her dog, Fluffy.

❏ **6.** Ms. Snodgrass usually takes Fluffy for a walk in the evening.

PAST PERFECT

i. Use the past perfect to talk about an event that happened before another event.	The police went to the robber's house, but he **had left several** hours before.
ii. The form of the past perfect is *had* or *had not* + past participle.	The robber **had taken** all of the money. He **had not told** anyone where he was going.
iii. The contracted forms of the past perfect are *'d* (*I'd, you'd, he'd*, etc.) and *hadn't*.	**He'd taken** all of the money. He **hadn't told** anyone where he was going.

A Circle the correct verbs.

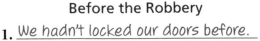

First Bank Robbery in Melrose

Melrose, Friday In the city of Melrose, the first bank robbery in local history occurred yesterday afternoon at the First N...

Robber in Jail

Melrose, Friday For the first time in years, Melrose police investigated the First National Union Bank robbery occurred yesterday afternoon on Main

1. There **hadn't been / had been** a bank robbery in Melrose before.

2. Melrose **had always been / had never been** a safe place to live.

3. The Melrose police **had done / hadn't done** investigations in a long time.

4. By Sunday, the police **had already caught / hadn't caught** the robber.

5. Bank managers **had worried / hadn't worried** about robberies before Friday.

B After the bank robbery in Melrose, people started to worry more about crime. Write sentences with the past perfect and *before*.

Before the Robbery	After the Robbery
1. _We hadn't locked our doors before._	1. We locked our doors all the time.
2. _____	2. We didn't leave a key under our doormat.
3. _____	3. We thought about getting an alarm.
4. _____	4. We called the police several times.
5. _____	5. We hid our jewelry.

C Look at the crime statistics. Then complete the sentences with the words in the box. Use the past perfect.

get a lot worse	not be much crime
get much better	not change
go up a little	start to go down

Look

Use *by* for an action that happened before a certain time.

> **By** the end of last year, there had been ten murders.

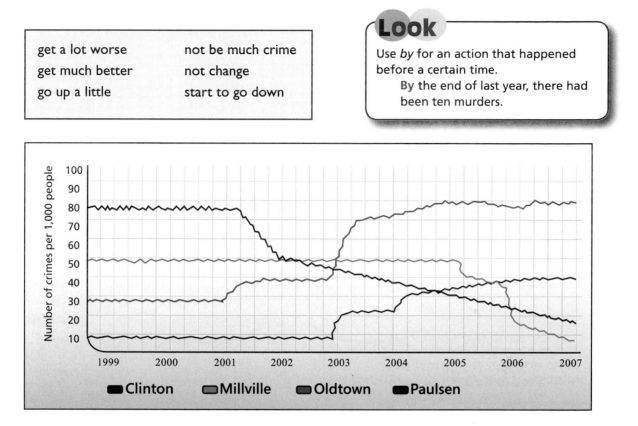

Number of crimes per 1,000 people

100
90
80
70
60
50
40
30
20
10

1999 2000 2001 2002 2003 2004 2005 2006 2007

■Clinton ▭Millville ▭Oldtown ■Paulsen

1. By 2002, the crime rate in Clinton _____

2. By 2003, the crime rate in Paulsen _____

3. By 2004, the number of crimes in Oldtown _____

4. Before 2005, the rate of crime in Millville _____

5. Before 2006, there _____ in Paulsen.

6. By 2006, the crime rate in Millville _____

TIME to TALK

PAIRS. Do this role-play. Then perform your role play for the class.

Student A: You are a police officer in the Melrose Police Department. You are investigating a bank robbery that happened yesterday.

Student B: You are a Melrose resident. You had just entered the bank yesterday when the robber came in. Tell the officer what happened.

Example:
A: *Please tell me everything that you saw and heard.*
B: *Well, it was exactly 1:00. I'm sure of the time, because I had just left work.*

Grammar to Communicate 2

PAST PERFECT AND SIMPLE PAST

i. When two past events happened at different times, use the past perfect with the first event. Use the simple past with the second event.

By the time the police **arrived**, the thief **had gotten** away.
              second event   first event

ii. When two past events happened at about the same time, use the simple past for both events.

When I got home, the police **called**.
(= The police called as soon as I got home.)

A   CD 1 TRACK 19   **Listen and complete the sentences with the correct verb forms.**

1. As soon as I _____ the door, I knew someone _____ in the house.

2. I _____ out every part of the house when the police _____.

3. My neighbors and I _____ because there _____ a break-in in the neighborhood in years.

4. By the time the police _____ the thief, he _____ into three more houses in the neighborhood.

PAIRS. **Talk about each sentence. Which event happened first?**

B   **Write sentences. Put the words in the correct order.**

1. because / She / a few break-ins / didn't want to leave / there had been / her car on the street

    _____

2. on the classroom wall / was angry / someone / The principal / because / had written

    _____

3. her keys in the car, / someone / so / Debbie / stole it / had left

    _____

4. his driver's license, / The criminal / so / knew his name / had dropped / the police

    _____

5. some jewelry / The security guard / had taken / stopped the woman / she / because

    _____

C **Complete the story. Write the past perfect or the simple past of the verbs. Use the simple past when the past perfect is not possible.**

Before last year, Mrs. Rogers _____ a very lucky woman. She

1. (be)

_____ about crime because she _____ a victim.

2. (never / worry)   3. (never / be)

She _____ the doors of her house. She _____

4. (never / lock)   5. (always / leave)

her car unlocked with the keys inside. She _____ out of her house

6.(always / go)

wearing expensive jewelry and carrying a lot of cash. Unfortunately, Mrs. Rogers's luck

_____ last year. By the end of the year, she _____

7. (run out)   8. (be)

the victim of a pickpocket, a burglar, and a car thief. Three months later, she

_____ to a new house in a new neighborhood.

9. (move)

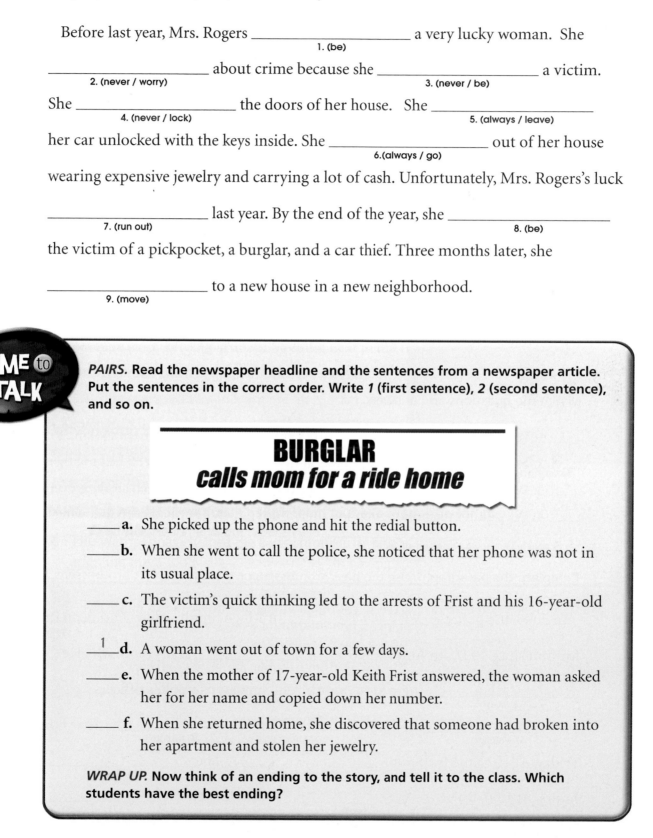

TIME to TALK

PAIRS. **Read the newspaper headline and the sentences from a newspaper article. Put the sentences in the correct order. Write *1* (first sentence), *2* (second sentence), and so on.**

BURGLAR
calls mom for a ride home

_____**a.** She picked up the phone and hit the redial button.

_____**b.** When she went to call the police, she noticed that her phone was not in its usual place.

_____**c.** The victim's quick thinking led to the arrests of Frist and his 16-year-old girlfriend.

__1__**d.** A woman went out of town for a few days.

_____**e.** When the mother of 17-year-old Keith Frist answered, the woman asked her for her name and copied down her number.

_____**f.** When she returned home, she discovered that someone had broken into her apartment and stolen her jewelry.

WRAP UP. **Now think of an ending to the story, and tell it to the class. Which students have the best ending?**

Grammar to Communicate 3

PAST PERFECT PROGRESSIVE

i. The form of the past perfect progressive is *had been* or *had not been* followed by the present participle.	**I had been waiting** for over an hour. I was angry. We **hadn't been talking** for very long. All of a sudden he got angry and left.
ii. Use the past perfect progressive to talk about an action in the past that continued for a period of time before another event in the past.	Officer Diaz **had been working** for the Miami Police Department for twenty years when she retired. (= She worked for twenty years. Then she retired.)
iii. Use the past progressive to stress that an activity was in progress when something else happened.	**I was thinking** about calling the police when they called me. (= At the moment when the police called me, I was thinking about calling them.)

A **Match the questions and answers.**

_____ 1. Why did Joe have a lot of electronics at home?   **a.** They had been looking for the wrong man.

_____ 2. How did the police know Joe was at home?   **b.** She had been helping them.

_____ 3. Why didn't the police arrest Joe's girlfriend?   **c.** He had been stealing from stores.

_____ 4. Why didn't the police catch Joe right away?   **d.** They had been following him.

B **Complete the paragraph. Use the past progressive or the past perfect progressive.**

In 2006, the police ___were looking___ for Ringo Smith. They ___had been looking___
          1. (look)   2. (look)

for him since 1997. In June, Ringo _____ at his mother's. He
                                                3. (live)

_____ there for a month. On Sunday, two police officers
     4. (live)

_____ Mrs. Smith's home. They _____ her home since
     5. (watch)   6. (watch)

Friday. At 10 P.M., Mrs. Smith _____. She _____ for two
                                          7. (sleep)   8. (sleep)

hours. At 1:00, Ringo _____ for his lawyer. He _____ for
                              9. (wait)   10. (wait)

three hours.

C Al Snodgrass was murdered last Sunday. Detective Jenkes thinks the murder happened at about 9 P.M. Complete the sentences about the six suspects. Use the correct verb forms.

Biff Brow, Al's son-in-law

Margo, Al's wife

Olivia, Al's sister

Carrie, Al's daughter

Anna Sasin, Al's secretary

Rob Banks, Al's business partner

1. Anna found her boss dead in his garage at 10 P.M. Somebody _____ him
   (kill)
   with a knife.

2. Earlier that day, Al and his son-in-law, Biff, _____ for a while. But by 9:00,
   (argue)
   Biff _____.
   (already / leave)

3. Margo _____ well all day, so she _____ to bed early.
   (not feel)   (go)

4. Olivia _____ her dog for a walk when she heard Anna scream. Earlier that
   (just / take)
   day, Olivia _____ for something in her brother's office.
   (look)

5. Al's daughter, Carrie, _____ tennis all evening on Sunday.
   (play)

6. Rob and Al had _____ business partners since they were young, but
   (be)

   _____ for several years.
   (not / get along)

TIME to TALK

GROUPS. Turn to page 290. Act out the investigation of the murder. Follow the instructions.

Review and Challenge

Grammar

Find the mistake in each sentence. Circle the letter and correct the mistake.

1. I <u>had</u> been <u>wait</u> for the police <u>for a long time</u> when they finally <u>came</u>.
      A   B   C   D

2. There <u>had been</u> a robbery at the school yesterday <u>when</u> everyone <u>had</u> <u>already</u> gone home.
          A   B   C   D

3. <u>By the time</u> the police <u>started</u> questioning people, many witnesses <u>left</u>.
      A   B   C   D

4. We <u>hadn't</u> <u>been knowing</u> our neighbors for very long <u>when</u> the police <u>arrested</u> them.
        A   B   C   D

5. Last week <u>was</u> my first time at a police station; I <u>had</u> never <u>go</u> to one <u>before</u>.
           A   B   C   D

Dictation

CD 1 TRACK **20** Listen. You will hear five sentences. Write them in your notebook.

Speaking

ON YOUR OWN. **Read a newspaper article about a crime. Make sure you understand what happened. Look in your dictionary or ask your teacher for help with new words.**

PAIRS. **Tell your partner about the crime that you read about. Do not look at the article. Then change roles and listen to your partner's story. Ask questions if you don't understand something.**

Example:
A: *Yesterday, there was a carjacking on Center Street.*
B: *Excuse me, a car what?*
A: *A carjacking. That's when someone tells you to get out of your car. Then they drive away in your car. So a woman was in her car. A man walked up to her . . .*

Listening

A **21** Listen to the news report about a bank robbery. Put the pictures in the correct order. Write *1* (first event that happened) and *5* (last event).

_____ a.

_____ b.

_____ c.

_____ d.

_____ e.

B **21** Listen again. What mistakes did the robber make? Make a list in your notebook. Then compare your list to a classmate's list.

TIME to TALK

GROUPS. Sit in a circle. Retell the story from the listening. Follow the steps.

Step 1: One student in the group starts the story.

Step 2: The student on his or her right continues the story.

Step 3: Continue until the end. Correct each other's mistakes.

Example:
A: *A man in Virginia robbed a bank.*
B: *He went into the bank and handed the teller a note....*

Reading

Getting Ready to Read

The *Mona Lisa* painting was stolen in 1911. Why would someone steal a painting? How could they steal it? Write in your notebook.

Reading

What new facts does the article tell you about the *Mona Lisa*? Talk with a partner.

THE THEFT OF THE MONA LISA

One of the most famous paintings in the world hangs in the Louvre Art Museum in Paris. It is the *Mona Lisa*, a small painting of a woman with a **mysterious** smile, painted by Leonardo da Vinci in the 16th century. Today the painting is protected by **bulletproof** glass and security alarms, but this was not always the case. In fact, the *Mona Lisa* was once the victim of a famous art **theft**.

The year was 1911. Vincenzo Peruggia was a worker in the Louvre. On August 20, after he had finished work, Peruggia hid in a closet in the museum. Later that night, he took down the famous painting, hid it under his coat, and walked out of the museum.

The next day, museum workers saw that the painting was **missing**, but they thought that it had been taken to the photography studio. Two days after the theft, they realized it had been stolen and called the police. The police **carried out** a full investigation, but there were no witnesses.

Detectives had been investigating for two years, when finally, on December 10, 1913, Peruggia tried to sell the *Mona Lisa* to an **art dealer** in Florence, Italy. Police immediately arrested Peruggia, and he was sent to prison.

Why did Peruggia steal the *Mona Lisa* and why did he wait two years before trying to sell it? Peruggia said that he had stolen the painting so he could return it to its home country, Italy. But the police **uncovered** another story. Eduardo de Valfierno, a man from Argentina, had paid Peruggia to steal the *Mona Lisa*. Before the theft, Valfierno had made six copies of the *Mona Lisa* and sent the **forgeries** to different countries where buyers were already waiting. Right after the theft, the copies were delivered to their buyers. Each buyer thought that he had the **original**.

The *Mona Lisa* was **eventually** returned to the Louvre, where it remains to this day.

After You Read

 A   **Find the boldfaced words from the article and guess their meaning from the context. Then complete the sentences with the words.**

1. The two men planned the robbery for a long time before they _____ the crime.

2. I bought several paintings from that _____ in Paris.

3. He told me that the paintings were by Picasso, but I think they are _____.

4. Thieves can't break the glass by shooting at it because it's _____.

5. If something is not where it should be and you can't find it, it is _____.

6. We don't know much about Vera; she is quiet and _____.

7. That painting is a copy; it is not the _____.

8. After a long investigation, the police finally _____ the truth.

9. It took a long time, but _____ the police found the murderer.

10. The _____ of the Mona Lisa shocked people in France.

B   **Put the events of the story in the correct order. Write _1_ (first event), _2_ (second event), and so on.**

_____ **a.** Peruggia tried to sell the *Mona Lisa*.

_____ **b.** Museum workers reported the theft to the police.

_____ **c.** Valfierno sent copies of the *Mona Lisa* to buyers in different countries.

_____ **d.** The police arrested Peruggia.

_____ **e.** Peruggia stole the *Mona Lisa*.

> **Reading Skill:**
> **Understanding Narrative Organization**
>
> A **narrative** is a story. The narrative is often told in time order to make it easy to understand. Sometimes, however, writers tell a story out of sequence, to make it more exciting.

C   **Check (✓) the statements that you can infer from the article.**

❏ 1. It is easier to steal the *Mona Lisa* today than it was in 1911.

❏ 2. The theft of the *Mona Lisa* was an inside job.

❏ 3. There was a big demand for the *Mona Lisa* on the black market.

❏ 4. The *Mona Lisa* is not a mysterious painting.

❏ 5. Peruggia has probably committed crimes before he stole the *Mona Lisa*.

>
> **inside job** = crime committed by people who know or work for the victim
> **black market** = buying and selling things illegally

Writing

Writing Skill: Using Time Expressions and Adverbs

A narrative uses time expressions and adverbs to make the time order clear.
Example: **On August 21, 1911** the *Mona Lisa* was stolen from the Louvre. It was finally found **two years later.**

A Read the model paragraph. Underline four time expressions.

The Scream

On August 31, 2006, police officers recovered *The Scream*, a famous painting by Edward Munch. It had been stolen two years before from an Oslo museum. Two men walked into the Munch Museum on a quiet Sunday morning and stole the work in front of terrified tourists. This was not the only copy of *The Scream*. Munch had painted two copies. The other painting had been stolen eight years before from Oslo's National Gallery. Police recovered it several months later, when they pretended to be art buyers. Many people think that criminals took the painting in order to sell it on the black market. *The Scream* is worth about $81 million dollars.

B Complete the paragraphs with the words in the box.

After	finally	for two years	immediately	in 1954	That night	then

On January 17, 1950, a famous robbery took place. It was called the Brinks robbery. _____ , four men broke into a money depository in Boston, Massachusetts. They were called "The Brinks Gang." They had been watching the building and planning the robbery _____. They had stolen the keys and made copies of them. They used their keys to enter the building and _____ tied up the employees. The robbers _____ took the money and escaped. _____ the robbery, the police followed many tips, but they could not find the Brinks Gang.

Then, _____, a member of the gang told the police about the Brinks robbery. The police _____ caught all the gang and found most, but not all, of the money. The gang had stolen over $275 million.

Prewriting: Writing About Pictures

Look at the pictures about a crime. In your notebook, write a sentence or two that describes each picture.

Writing

Write a paragraph about the crime above. Make up a story. Use time expressions and adverbs. Use the past perfect where appropriate. Use the model paragraph to help you. Write in your notebook.

Unit 4
Moving In

Grammar
- Indefinite and Definite Articles (1)
- Indefinite and Definite Articles (2)
- Generic Nouns

Vocabulary

CD 1 TRACK 22 **Match the pictures with the words. Write the numbers. Then listen and check your answers.**

_____ complex	_____ landlady	_____ superintendent
_____ entrance	_____ landlord	_____ tenant
_____ garbage disposal	_____ security guard	_____ trash chute

Listening

A 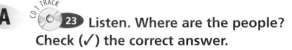 **23 Listen. Where are the people? Check (✓) the correct answer.**

❏ **1.** in Mr. and Mrs. Lang's apartment

❏ **2.** in a real estate agency

❏ **3.** in the lobby of an apartment building

❏ **4.** in Andrew's apartment

B **23 Listen again. Check (✓) the statements that are true.**

❏ **1.** Mr. and Mrs. Lang are living in a one-bedroom apartment.

❏ **2.** Mr. Lang doesn't like the location of their apartment.

❏ **3.** Mr. and Mrs. Lang cannot afford more than $750 a month for an apartment.

❏ **4.** Andrew is going to show them some apartments.

❏ **5.** One of the apartments is around the corner from Mr. Lang's office.

❏ **6.** There aren't any laundry facilities in the building.

C **23 Listen again. Check (✓) the statements that you can infer from the conversation.**

❏ **1.** The Langs filled out an application form before they met Andrew.

❏ **2.** Mrs. Lang is worried about finding a place to live.

❏ **3.** The Langs already have one child.

❏ **4.** The Langs need to have a washer and dryer in the apartment.

❏ **5.** Apartment buildings with laundry facilities usually cost more than $1,000 a month.

> ## Look
>
> **facilities** = rooms, equipment, or services, such as laundry rooms, trash chutes, or swimming pools
> **utilities** = services such as gas, water, and electricity

Grammar to Communicate 1

i. To talk about a specific person, place, or thing the first time:

Use *a* or *an* before singular count nouns.

Use *some, any*, or no article (Ø) before plural count nouns.

Use *some, any*, or no article (Ø) before noncount nouns.

I see **a post office** over there.
I am looking for **an apartment**.

There are **some apartments** here.
I don't see **any elevators**.
The rent includes **utilities**.

I need to buy **some furniture**.
I don't have **any money** with me.
I don't have **change** for the laundry.

ii. To talk about a specific person, place, or thing the second time, use *the* before the noun.

A: I found **an apartment** last week.
B: Great! Is **the apartment** big enough?

A: I need to buy **new furniture**.
B: Is **the furniture** for your living room?

A Which sentence does the speaker say first? Write *1* (first) and *2* (second).

a. _____ The carpeting is new when a tenant moves in.

_____ Every apartment has wall-to-wall carpeting.

b. _____ I have to get the key from the landlady.

_____ I don't have a key for the apartment.

c. _____ There are windows in every room.

_____ Some of the windows are pretty small.

d. _____ I think the laundry room's always open.

_____ There's a laundry room in the basement.

carpeting

B Complete the paragraph. Add the appropriate articles. If no article is necessary, write Ø.

My apartment has many modern conveniences. It has _____ dishwasher. It also has
1.

_____ garbage disposal. I use _____ dishwasher a lot, but I don't like to use _____
2.   3.   4.

garbage disposal. It makes _____ loud noise. _____ noise always scares me. There's
5.   6.

also _____ small washer and dryer, but _____ washer sometimes breaks down.
7.   8.

C Complete the conversation between the tenant and the building manager. Use *a*, *an*, or *the*.

> **Look**
>
> I have a great apartment. <u>The rooms</u> are really big.
> We use *the* in the second sentence because we know that the rooms are in the apartment.

Ross: There are a lot of facilities in this complex. There's _____ trash chute, _____
1.   2.

laundry room, and _____ swimming pool. There's also _____ security guard.
3.   4.

Pam: Where's _____ laundry room?
5.

Ross: It's in the basement.

Pam: And does it cost anything to use?

Ross: Yes. _____ washers are $1.25 per load,
6.

and _____ dryers are 25 cents
7.

for 15 minutes.

Pam: Is _____ swimming pool heated?
8.

Ross: No, it's not.

Pam: Where are _____ trash chutes?
9.

Ross: They're on every floor, at the end of the hall.

Pam: Do all visitors have to check in with _____ security guard?
10.

Ross: Yes, they do.

PAIRS. **Read the situation. Then role-play a conversation. Ask and answer questions. Use the conversation in Exercise C as a model.**

Student A: You are looking at some apartments in a large complex.

Student B: You are the complex manager. You are showing a possible tenant around. Answer the person's questions.

Example:
A: *What facilities are included?*
B: *There is a gym on the first floor. It's free for all tenants.*

Grammar to Communicate 2

INDEFINITE AND DEFINITE ARTICLES (2)

i. When you use *the* before a noun, it means that <u>both</u> you and your listener understand exactly which person, place, or thing you are talking about.	**The** parking lot is for tenants only. Please park on **the** street. (= The speaker and the listener are in the same parking lot. They know which parking lot and street they are talking about.)
ii. If <u>either</u> you or your listener does not know about the particular person, place, or thing, use *a / an*, *some*, or *any*. Do not use *the*.	There is **a** parking lot for tenants. (= The speaker knows about the parking lot, but the listener does not.)

A Read the conversations. Circle the true statement about each conversation.

light bulb

curtains

hammer

1. **Lou:** What is <u>the landlord's</u> name?
   Ann: I don't remember.
   a. There is one landlord.
   b. There is more than one landlord.

2. **Ann:** <u>The garbage disposal</u> isn't working.
   Bob: I'll have a look.
   a. There is one garbage disposal.
   b. There is more than one garbage disposal.

3. **Ann:** The lamp isn't working.
   Lisa: Yes, it is. Just give me a <u>light bulb</u>.
   a. The lamp needs a special light bulb.
   b. Lisa knows that Ann has some light bulbs.

4. **Ann:** Oh, no! People can see in the window.
   Tom: You should put up <u>some curtains</u>.
   a. Tom is looking at some curtains.
   b. Tom is not talking about any specific curtains.

5. **Ann:** Can you fix this door?
   Nick: Yeah. Just give me <u>the hammer</u>.
   a. Ann and Nick are in the same room.
   b. Ann doesn't have a hammer. She needs to go and buy one.

B Complete the sentences. Write *a, an, some, any,* or *the.*

1. **A:** Can you help me with _____ boxes?

   B: Sorry, they're too heavy for me.

2. **A:** I need to get _____ empty boxes.

   B: You should ask at your supermarket.

3. **A:** Could you hand me _____ empty box?

   B: Sure. Do you need a big one or a small one?

4. **A:** Uh-oh. I didn't buy _____ soap.

   B: I'll go and get you some.

5. **A:** I have a lot of things. I'm going to call

   _____ moving company.

   B: Oh, don't do that. Phil and I will help you.

6. **A:** Look inside _____ cabinets. They're really dirty.

   B: Ooh…you're right. Don't put the dishes in yet.

7. **A:** I'm going to buy _____ new towels. I don't want to pack my old ones.

   B: Well, don't throw them away. I'll take them.

C Steve is complaining to his landlord about his new apartment. Write his sentences.

1. _____
   (kitchen sink / not work)

2. _____
   (carpets / dirty)

3. _____
   (windows / not open)

4. _____
   (not have / smoke detector)

5. _____
   (there / strange noise)

6. _____
   (difficult to open / front door)

TIME to TALK

PAIRS. **Ask and answer questions about the place where you live now. Talk about positive and negative things. Use the vocabulary from the unit and your own ideas.**

Example:
A: *I'm not happy with my apartment.*
B: *Why not?*
A: *First of all, there aren't any smoke detectors.*

GENERIC NOUNS

i. When we make a general statement about a person, place, or thing, we usually do not use *the* before the noun. We use *a* or *an* for singular nouns. We use no article (Ø) for plural nouns and noncount nouns.

An apartment is usually on one floor.
  (most apartments)
Housing is difficult to find.
  (most kinds of housing)
Houses are bigger than **apartments**.
  (most houses and most apartments)

ii. When both the speaker and the listener know the specific person, place, or thing, use *the* before the noun.

~~The apartment~~ on Water Street is too small for us.
(There is one apartment. Both the speaker and listener have seen it.)

A  **24 Listen and complete the sentences. Then check (✓) the sentences that are true about you.**

> **Look**
>
> housing = the houses or apartments that people live in

- ❏ 1. _____ are great, but other things are more important.

- ❏ 2. _____ is important. We don't have a car.

- ❏ 3. _____ is important. I live alone.

- ❏ 4. _____ is important. I like to walk outside.

- ❏ 5. _____ are not very important to us. We don't have kids.

- ❏ 6. _____ are not very important. We hardly ever eat out.

B   **Rewrite the sentences. Make the boldfaced words plural and change the verb forms.**

1. A **studio apartment** doesn't have a separate bedroom.
   <u>Studio apartments don't have a separate bedroom.</u>

2. A **lease** is often for a year.
   _____

3. A **tenant** pays rent.
   _____

4. An **apartment complex** has several buildings with many apartments.
   _____

5. A **superintendent** takes care of an apartment building.
   _____

C Answer the questions. Use the ideas in the box. Write in your notebook.

| couples | without children | elderly people | families with children | single people |

Who usually . . .

1. is interested in a neighborhood with good schools?
   families with children

2. . . . rents a studio apartment?

3. . . . needs a big house?

4. . . . wants to live near a good hospital?

5. . . . wants to live downtown?

6. . . . eats out a lot?

7. . . . needs inexpensive housing?

D Complete the sentences with *a, an,* or *the.* If no article is necessary, write Ø. Capitalize letters where necessary.

1. __Ø__ *A* apartments are expensive in Cambridge.

2. I live in _____ brick apartment building next to the train station on Winter Street.

3. Overbrook has _____ good public transportation.

4. _____ best restaurants in town are on Market Street.

5. Kensington is _____ pretty place to live.

6. _____ crime isn't a problem in Somerville.

7. _____ expensive housing in my city is far away from downtown.

PAIRS. Repeat the sentences. Change them to make them true for you.
   Example: Apartments are expensive in _____ .
   (Write the name of a place in your area.)

TIME to TALK

ON YOUR OWN. When you are looking for a place to live, how important are these things to you? Write *1* (very important) and *2* (not very important).

_____ convenient location   _____ laundry facilities   _____ privacy

_____ friendly neighbors   _____ low price   _____ quiet location

_____ green space   _____ parking   _____ safety

PAIRS. Talk about what is and isn't important to you, and explain why.

Example:
A: *Green space is very important to me. I like to live near parks.*
B: *I like green spaces too, but a convenient location is more important.*

Review and Challenge

Grammar

Correct seven mistakes in the letter. The first mistake is corrected for you.

Dear Ms. Sanderson,

                                                     some

I am writing because there are ~~the problems in my apartment~~. I have called your office several times and left ~~the~~ messages, but you have not returned my calls. First of all, there hasn't been any hot water in two days. I have been going to a neighbor's apartment to take ~~the~~ shower! Also, there is something wrong with two of my lights. The kitchen light and the light near ~~a~~ front door are not working. Finally, ~~a~~ dishwasher isn't working. If you do not take care of problems soon, I will contact ~~some~~ lawyer. Please call me right away.

                                                   James Wu

Dictation

25 **Listen. You will hear five sentences. Write them in your notebook.**

Speaking

> **Look**
>
> **affordable housing** = housing made less expensive by the government, for people with low incomes
>
> **residents** = someone who lives in a particular place (city, etc.)

GROUPS. **In many cities, there is not enough affordable housing. Which solutions below are good, if any? Why? Do you have any other ideas?**

1. Companies and rich residents should pay an affordable housing tax. The government should use the money from that tax to build more affordable housing.

2. The government should make taxes lower for builders to build more housing. If more housing is available, the price of housing will go down.

3. The government should build and manage housing projects: large apartment buildings where poor people can live with very low rent.

4. The government should give poor residents some money every month to pay their rent.

5. Nonprofit organizations such as churches should build and manage affordable housing.

Listening

Look

appliance = a small machine such as a dishwasher or microwave

single family home = a house where only one family lives

A **26** Listen to the report about housing in the United States and Greece. Check (✓) the topics that the reporter discusses.

_____ 1. the average age of renters

_____ 2. how long leases are for

_____ 3. appliances and utilities

_____ 4. how many people own their homes

_____ 5. the number of single-family homes

_____ 6. how home buyers pay for their homes

_____ 7. how many people live in one apartment

Juan Cueva, Bella Management

lease

B **26** Listen again. Complete the chart. Then compare it to a partner's.

	UNITED STATES	GREECE
typical lease	1 year	
appliances		
utilities	sometimes included	
percentage (%) of homeowners		
kinds of housing		

TIME to TALK

GROUPS. Compare housing in your country to housing in the United States and Greece. What is the same? What is different?

Example:

A: _In Colombia, people live in the same apartment for many years. They don't move a lot, like people in the United States._

B: _People in my country don't move a lot either._

Moving In 53

Reading

Getting Ready to Read

PAIRS. In your opinion, which is better: renting or buying a home? Talk with a partner.

Reading

Read the article. Does it support your opinion?

BUYING OR RENTING?

The Richmond District, San Francisco

Luz and Pedro live with their daughter in San Marcos, an old pretty city near San Antonio, Texas. When their daughter Lola turned one, they decided to buy a house. At first, Luz was afraid that the bank would not give them a **mortgage**. She thought her **credit report** might not be good enough, and that the bank might **reject** them for a loan. However, the bank **approved** their loan, and Luz and Pedro found a house near an excellent elementary school and park. They think that its **value** has gone up in the year they have lived there. In a few years they hope to buy a bigger home. For now, they are working hard to pay the mortgage. The **down payment** was not so high when they bought the house, but the monthly payments are high. There has also been a **steep** rise in gas prices. As a result, Luz and Pedro sometimes have trouble paying their bills. It is difficult for them to save.

Zhen and Mei rent a one-bedroom apartment in San Francisco, California. They have an apartment in the Richmond **District**, with a one-year lease. The apartment is small, but it has advantages. It is near shopping, restaurants, and the beach. They don't need a car because they take the bus to work. The apartment building is old and the kitchen doesn't have a dishwasher or a garbage disposal, but the rent is affordable, only $1200 a month, including heat and hot water. The landlord is very helpful. When there's a problem, he fixes it immediately. One day, they would like to buy a house of their own. Zhen thinks it would be a good **investment**, but houses in San Francisco and the Bay Area are too expensive for them now.

| LOAN NUMBER | DUE DATE 01/01/07 | AMOUNT DUE $ 1120.46 |
| | IF NOT RECEIVED BY 01/16/07 | AMOUNT DUE $ 1142.86 |

PEDRO GONZÁLEZ
Have questions? Need answers? Go online!

Make checks payable to:

PHH Mortgage Services
P. O. BOX 371458
PITTSBURGH, PA 15250-7458

EXTRA PRINCIPAL +
EXTRA ESCROW +
LATE CHARGE +
OTHER +
TOTAL CHECK AMOUNT =

PAYMENTS IN EXCESS OF FUNDS DUE, UNLESS DESIGNATED, WILL BE APPLIED TO UNPAID LATE CHARGES AND THEN TO PRINCIPAL

00 954 0023801723 0000114286 0000112046 4

After You Read

A Find the boldfaced words in the article. Guess their meaning from the context. Then match the words with the correct definitions.

_____ **1.** mortgage   **a.** the first payment on a house, etc.

_____ **2.** credit report   **b.** how much something is worth

_____ **3.** reject   **c.** said yes to something

_____ **4.** approved   **d.** very large and unexpected

_____ **5.** value   **e.** an area of a town, city, or country

_____ **6.** down payment   **f.** information that tells if a person pays his or her debts

_____ **7.** steep   **g.** a loan to buy, build or fix a property (house, etc.)

_____ **8.** district   **h.** something you put money in to make a profit

_____ **9.** investment   **i.** not give someone something they ask for

> **Reading Skill:**
> **Understanding Pronouns**
>
> Pronouns replace nouns. To understand a text, you need to know which noun each pronoun replaces.
> Example:
> My neighborhood is beautiful, but **it** is expensive.

B Find these sentences in the article. Which nouns do the pronouns refer to? Write the nouns.

1. They think that **its** value has gone up.   _____

2. It is difficult for **them** to save.   _____

3. **It** is near shopping, restaurants, and the beach.   _____

4. When there's a problem, **he** fixes it immediately.   _____

5. Zhen thinks **it** would be a good investment.   _____

C Read the article again. Check (✓) the statements that you can infer from the article.

❏ **1.** Houses in good neighborhoods always go up in value.

❏ **2.** Utility bills usually do not change much.

❏ **3.** The Richmond District has a convenient bus line.

❏ **4.** Luz and Pedro have more money than Zhen and Mei.

❏ **5.** Zhen and Mei are generally happy with the Richmond District.

Writing

Read each topic sentence. Check (✓) the sentences that would be good supporting sentences.

1. There are many advantages to living in hot places.

   ❏ **a.** It is possible to swim year-round in outdoor pools.

   ❏ **b.** Many mosquitoes and other insects enjoy a warm climate.

   ❏ **c.** You can grow fruit trees like lemon trees and orange trees in your backyard.

   ❏ **d.** The warm beaches are beautiful, but you must be careful to avoid sunburns.

2. There are several disadvantages to living on an island.

   ❏ **a.** Some groceries, such as lettuce, cost more than they do on the mainland.

   ❏ **b.** Many tourists come to visit, so the beaches can be crowded.

   ❏ **c.** There are beautiful volcanoes, and hiking to the top of them is exciting.

   ❏ **d.** Although there is often a lot of rain, the climate is mild and pleasant.

Read the model paragraph. Then complete the tasks.

Living in Cold Climates

There are several advantages to living in very cold climates. First, cold areas like Montreal, Canada, have great winter sports like ice hockey, skiing, and ice-skating. Also, in a cold climate, all four seasons are beautiful to see—for example, there are deep red and gold leaves on the trees in the fall, and snow-capped mountains in the winter. Finally, in a very cold climate, during most months you can build a fire in your fireplace and enjoy the quiet and beauty of a bright fire.

1. Circle the topic sentence.
2. Underline the supporting sentences.
3. What are the writer's three supporting ideas? Write them in your own words:

   a. _____

   b. _____

   c. _____

Prewriting: Using an Outline

 A   You are going to write a paragraph about a living situation. Choose one from the box.

living alone	living in an older house
living in an apartment	living in a warm climate
living in a cold climate	living with a large family
living in a large city	living with parents

B   Look at the outline the writer used for the model paragraph. Then complete your own outline on the topic you chose.

Topic Sentence: _There are several advantages to living in very cold climates._

A. _winter sports_

B. _four seasons are beautiful_

C. _quiet and beauty of a fire_

Topic Sentence: _____

A. _____

B. _____

C. _____

Writing

Write a paragraph on the topic you chose. Use the model paragraph and your outline to help you. Make sure your topic sentence gives your opinion and has three supporting points. Write in your notebook.

Unit 5
New on the Job

Grammar
- Tag Questions
- So / Too / Either / Neither
- Both. . .and / Either. . . or / Neither. . . nor

Vocabulary

27 Complete the sentences with the words in the boxes. Then listen and check your answers.

are from around here	move up	offer
personality	qualifications	references

We have openings in both the Main Street and Bank Street offices. I think you have the right _____ for the job—a diploma and two years experience in real estate. You also have the right _____—I can see that you're friendly. You _____ too, so you know the town. You'll start out as an apartment rental agent. If you're successful, you will _____ to the sales department. However, I can't _____ you the job until I check your _____. Can you give me the names of two people?

am familiar with	cubicle	get a promotion
job performance	policies	

All new employees work on this floor. When they _____, they get an office with a window. This is your _____. You can put pictures on the wall if you want. And here is information about the company _____ on health insurance and vacation. I _____ the policies, so ask me if you have any questions. In June, your supervisors will talk to you about your _____. If they like your work, they will offer you a permanent position.

Listening

A **28** **Listen to the conversation. What is happening? Check (✓) the letter of the correct answer.**

❑ **a.** Mr. Torres and Ms. Bauer are interviewing Mr. Wilson for a position as a manager.

❑ **b.** Mr. Torres and Ms. Bauer are thinking about giving Mr. Wilson a promotion.

❑ **c.** Mr. Torres and Ms. Bauer are interviewing Mr. Wilson for a job at Townsend.

B **28** **Read the sentences. Then listen again. Who said each sentence? Write *T* (Mr. Torres), *B* (Ms. Bauer), or *W* (Mr. Wilson).**

_____ **1.** "You're familiar with the policies at Townsend, aren't you?"

_____ **2.** "Neither am I."

_____ **3.** "I felt that I was ready to move up, and so did my boss."

_____ **4.** "Grace, you don't have any other questions, do you?"

_____ **5.** "We'll make our decision either this week or next."

_____ **6.** "Neither Ms. Bauer nor I will be in the office tomorrow."

_____ **7.** "You know your way out, don't you?"

_____ **8.** "I did, too. And he's got both the qualifications and the personality we need."

C **28** **Listen again. Then check (✓) the sentences that you can infer from the conversation.**

❑ **1.** Earlier in the interview, Mr. Wilson was probably talking about his education and other work experience.

❑ **2.** Mr. Torres and Ms. Bauer both worked at Townsend in the past.

❑ **3.** Mr. Wilson did not bring a list of references with him to the interview.

❑ **4.** They will probably offer Mr. Wilson the job.

Grammar to Communicate 1

TAG QUESTIONS

i. Tag questions come at the end of a statement.

   If the statement is affirmative, the tag question is negative.

   If the statement is negative, the tag question is affirmative.

> You **are** new here, **aren't you**?
>
> You **were not** here last month, **were you**?

ii. If the verb is not *be*, use the auxiliary in the tag question.

> You **started** last week, **didn't you**?
> You don't **live** near here, **do you**?
> I'll **have** Saturdays off, **won't I**?

iii. The meaning of a tag question changes when your intonation* rises or falls.

   When you check that information is correct, your intonation rises.

   When you think the listener will agree with you, your intonation falls.

> We have a meeting today, don't we?
> (= I want to be sure we have a meeting.)
>
> It's warm today, isn't it? (= I think you're going to agree that it's warm.)

iv. When you make a polite request, your intonation rises. The statement is negative and the tag is affirmative.

> You couldn't lend me $20 dollars, could you?
> (= Could you lend me $20?)

 A **29** **Listen. Check (✓) the correct column.**

> **Look**
>
> *intonation = the way your voice changes (rises or falls) in order to give meaning to your words

	THE SPEAKER IS CHECKING INFORMATION.	THE SPEAKER EXPECTS YOU TO AGREE.
1. She has the right qualifications, doesn't she?		
2. His performance hasn't improved, has it?		
3. You're familiar with our policies, aren't you?		
4. It was quiet here last week, wasn't it?		
5. You're not from around here, are you?		
6. You didn't check her references, did you?		

PAIRS. Practice asking and answering the questions. Use the correct intonation.

B   Complete the questions that were asked at job interviews. Write tag questions.

1. You're not afraid to climb a ladder, _____

2. You're familiar with this phone system, _____

3. You've taken a patient's blood pressure before, _____

4. You used a cash register at your last job, _____

5. You don't have any allergies to animals, _____

PAIRS. Guess the job that each question was asked for.

C   Read the questions. Rewrite them as tag questions.

1. Excuse me. Have you seen my cell phone?
    <u>Excuse me. You haven't seen my cell phone, have you?</u>

2. Will you talk to the boss for me?

_____

3. Can you drop me off at the train station?

_____

4. Could you show me how to use the photocopier?

_____

5. Did you take my report home yesterday?

_____

PAIRS. Practice making and responding to the requests above.

Look

Look at the answers to polite requests with tag questions.

A: You don't have time to help, do you?
B: Sure. OR **No, sorry.**

TIME to TALK

PAIRS. **Think of a job. Write five tag questions to ask someone who is interviewing for that job. Read your questions to the class. Can they guess the job?**

Example:

     A: *You can drive, can't you?*
Class: *You're interviewing someone for a job as a driver, aren't you?*
     B: *No, we're not. Here's another question. You've had experience with children, haven't you?*
Class: *Oh, you're interviewing for a school bus driver, aren't you?*

Grammar to Communicate 2

SO / TOO / EITHER / NEITHER

i. We use *so* and *too* in <u>affirmative</u> responses to show that two people have something in common. *So* and *too* use different word order.

> A: I work here.
> B: **So do I.** (= I do, **too.**)
>
> A: I'm sick today
> B: **So am I.** (= I am, **too.**)

ii. We use *either* and *neither* in negative responses to show that two people have something in common. *Either* and *neither* use different word order.

> A: I didn't work last week.
> B: **Neither did I.** (= I didn't either.)
>
> A: I wasn't at work last Monday.
> B: **Neither was I** (= I wasn't either.)

A Match the statements on the left with the responses on the right. Write the correct letter.

_____ 1. I'm new here.

_____ 2. I don't know anyone's name yet.

_____ 3. I'm not very good with names.

_____ 4. I haven't met everybody in the office yet.

_____ 5. My supervisor has a great personality.

_____ 6. I hope to move up quickly.

_____ 7. I didn't like my old job.

_____ 8. I worked for a big company before.

a. Neither am I.

b. So does mine.

c. I did, too.

d. Neither do I.

e. I do, too.

f. I didn't either.

g. So am I.

h. I haven't either.

B Complete the sentences. Use *either, neither, so,* or *too.*

1. **A:** I'm not from around here.

   B: _____ am I.

2. **A:** I grew up in Belmont.

   B: _____ did I!

3. **A:** I didn't go to Belmont High.

   B: I didn't _____.

4. **A:** I went to Belmont Tech.

   B: I did, _____.

5. **A:** I didn't like Belmont Tech very much.

   B: _____ did I.

6. **A:** I graduated in 2001.

   B: _____ did I.

7. **A:** Amazing. I haven't met anyone from home since I got here!

   B: _____ have I.

C Two new employees are complaining. Write the responses.

1. **A:** I don't get a long vacation. (neither)
   B: _Neither do I._

2. **A:** I'm working too many hours. (so)
   B: _____

3. **A:** I haven't had a break today. (either)
   B: _____

4. **A:** My last paycheck wasn't right. (neither)
   B: _____

5. **A:** My cubicle is too small. (so)
   B: _____

6. **A:** I don't like my boss. (neither)
   B: _____

7. **A:** I need more money. (too)
   B: _____

8. **A:** I didn't get Sunday off. (either)
   B: _____

D Complete the sentences with true information.

1. When I was a child, I wanted to be _____

2. I got my first job _____

3. I believe that most people work because _____

4. I think that the best hours to work are _____

5. I want to retire when _____

PAIRS. Tell each other your sentences. Respond with *either, neither, so,* or *too* when you have something in common.

Example:
A: *When I was a child, I wanted to be a detective.*
B: *I did, too.*

TIME to TALK

GROUPS. Find similarities with your group members. Each person says something about him or herself. Members of the group who have the same thing in common answer with *either, neither, so,* or *too.*

Example:
  You: *I've never had a part-time job.*
 Tina: *Neither have I.*
 Ming: *I haven't either.*

WRAP-UP. Continue for fifteen minutes. Then one group member tells the class your group's similarities. The group with the most similarities wins.

Grammar to Communicate 3

i. Use *both…and* to connect two similar ideas in one sentence.	We'll discuss **both** salary **and** hours at the interview. (= We'll discuss salary. We'll discuss hours, too.)
ii. Use *either…or* to talk about a choice between two possibilities.	You need **either** a bachelor's degree **or** five years of experience. (= You don't need both.)
iii. Use *neither…nor* to connect two negative ideas. Always use an <u>affirmative</u> verb with *neither…nor*.	You <u>have</u> **neither** the experience **nor** the skills for the job. (= You don't have the experience or the skills.)
iv. When *both…and* connects two singular subjects, the verb is plural.	Both the **director** and the **manager** <u>are</u> women.
When *either…or* and *neither…nor* connect two singular subjects, the verb is <u>singular</u>.	Either **Mr. Tan** or **Ms. Ko** <u>is</u> going to interview you. Neither the **cook** nor the **waiter** <u>is</u> working hard enough.

A Complete the sentences. Use *both . . . and, either . . . or,* or *neither . . . nor.*

1. You can work _____ thirty hours a week _____ forty hours a week.

2. We can offer you _____ more money _____ more hours, but not both.

3. We have received _____ your résumé _____ your references. Did you send them?

4. You'll hear from _____ my secretary _____ my assistant next week.

5. There are positions for _____ cooks _____ waiters. Which interests you?

B Complete the sentences. Circle the correct form of the verb.

1. Neither the mailroom nor the office **is / are** open after 8 P.M.

2. Both the director and his assistant **has / have** their offices on the sixth floor.

3. Either the front door or back door **is / are** open on the weekend, but never both doors.

4. Both the fax machine and the photocopier **is / are** at the end of the hall.

5. This is a restricted area. Neither the mailman nor the cleaning person **is / are** allowed here.

C A boss is unhappy with a worker. Rewrite the boss's sentences with *neither...nor*.

1. You shouldn't touch the register or the computer. I told you that when you started here.
   You should touch neither the register nor the computer.

2. You can't use the photocopier or the printer for your personal business.
   _____

3. The coffee isn't for you or your friend. It's for the clients.
   _____

4. Employees don't wear jeans or sneakers in this office. It's the company policy.
   _____

5. You have not improved your job performance or your behavior.
   _____

D Combine the sentences. Use *both...and, either...or,* or *neither...nor* and the underlined words. Write in your notebook.

Look

We often use *neither...nor* in a formal situation.

Sandra's boss told her:

1. <u>Your child</u> isn't allowed in the office. <u>Your friend</u> isn't allowed in the office.
   Neither your child nor your friend is allowed in the office.

2. You have to work late on <u>Fridays</u>. You have to work late on <u>Saturdays</u>.

3. You can have <u>a half hour for lunch</u>. You can have <u>an hour for lunch</u>.

Peter's boss told him:

4. You can work from <u>9 to 5</u>. You can work from <u>11 to 7</u>.

5. In <u>September</u> you have to work six days a week. In <u>May</u> you have to work six days a week.

6. <u>The phone</u> is not for personal use. <u>The fax</u> is not for personal use.

PAIRS. Which work enviroment would you prefer?

TIME to TALK

PAIRS. Do a role-play. Use the sentences in Exercise C and your own ideas.
Student A: You are a new employee. You think you are doing a good job.
Student B: You are the boss. You are unhappy with the new employee.

Example:
A: *I like both the work and the people here.*
B: *Hmmm...I'm glad you do, but there have been some complaints.*
   First of all, you need to wear either a suit or a sports jacket.

Review and Challenge

Grammar

Find the mistake in each sentence. Circle the letter and correct the mistake.

1. Neither the bookstore nor the restaurant have any openings.
   A   B   C   D

2. You read both the vacation and the sick-time policies, you didn't?
      A   B   C   D

3. They are going to offer you either a full-time job and a part-time job, aren't they?
         A   B   C   D

4. You don't go to meetings both in the morning and afternoon, don't you?
             A   B   C   D

5. I can do it either on the phone or by e-mail, and Lucy can so.
     A   B   C   D

Dictation

 30 Listen. You will hear five sentences. Write them in your notebook.

Speaking

GROUPS. Walk around the classroom. Ask and answer tag questions. Complete the chart with the names of your classmates.

NAME	
	likes his or her job.
	expects to get a promotion.
	is familiar with computers.
	has had several jobs.

NAME	
	wants to change careers.
	isn't working these days.
	won't ever retire.
	doesn't want to be a manager.

Example:
A: *You like your job, don't you?*
B: *Yes, I do. I love it. How about you?*
A: *I like my job, too.*

PAIRS. Summarize the information in your chart. Use *both... and* and *neither...nor*.

Example:
Both Pepe and Jenny like their jobs.

Listening

A **31** Listen to the three conversations. Match the conversation with the situation.

_____ **1.** Conversation 1   **a.** A boss is talking to an employee about his work performance.

_____ **2.** Conversation 2   **b.** A man is leaving work to get something to eat.

_____ **3.** Conversation 3   **c.** Two co-workers are meeting each other for the first time.

B **31** Listen again. Check (✓) the true statements. Then listen again and check your answers.

Conversation 1

_____ **1.** The company has a lot of employees.

_____ **2.** The man doesn't have time to help the woman.

_____ **3.** The woman's air conditioner is broken.

Conversation 2

_____ **1.** The woman wants something to eat.

_____ **2.** The man has forgotten about the meeting.

_____ **3.** The meeting is important.

Conversation 3

_____ **1.** The man's wife has a job.

_____ **2.** The woman does not like children.

_____ **3.** The man's children are in day care.

air conditioner

TIME to TALK

GROUPS. Discuss the statements. Which do you agree with?

1. Neither employees nor employers should discuss their personal lives at work.

2. If you want to move up quickly, it is a good idea to spend time with your boss and co-workers after work.

3. Your success at work does not depend on either your co-workers or your boss. It depends on how hard you work.

4. To have a happy life, you need to enjoy both your work and your family.

5. Successful business people are either very lucky or very smart.

Reading

Getting Ready to Read

Which things below are important to you in a job? Write *1* (very important) or *2* (somewhat important). Compare your answers with a partner's.

_____ chances for promotion   _____ friendly co-workers   _____ good hours

_____ convenient location   _____ good pay and benefits   _____ job satisfaction

Reading

Read the article. Then scan the headings. Which heading mentions money?

Reading Skill:
Scanning Headings

To find specific information quickly, look first at any **headings** in a text.

Choosing the Right Job

What is most important to you in a job—for example, a high salary? job satisfaction? What **aspect** of your job do you enjoy most—for example, working on projects with others? Being creative? Making decisions? If you are looking for a new job, think about these **factors**:

Salary and Benefits
  Money is often the main reason for changing jobs. But how much money is enough? Try to **estimate** how much you need to pay your bills and still save every month. Also, salary is important, but so are benefits. Find out what kind of health insurance plan is available.

Location
  How long will it take to get to work, and how much will it cost? **Commuting** for hours by car, bus, or train can add stress to your working day.

Environment
  Does the job have any health **risks**? If so, what safety equipment is **provided**? Is the working space large or small? Does it seem like a good place to work?

Career Advancement
  Are there training opportunities? Does the company give promotions and allow employees to **take on** new responsibilities?

Both training and promotion are opportunities to increase your future salary.

Working Hours
  Do you sometimes need to leave work early? You may be able to share a job or find a job that has **flexible** hours. Will you have to work **overtime**? You may not want the position if you have to work long hours.

Management
  Who will you report to? Does this person seem helpful and supportive? Can this person make fair decisions and give you clear direction? It is important to have a boss who is both a kind person and a good manager.

  Finally, neither money nor **prestige** is enough to make most people happy. Of course, most people would like a large salary and a high position, but it's important to like the work you do. Is this job one that you will enjoy?

After You Read

A   **Find the boldfaced words in the article and guess their meaning from the context. Then complete the sentences with the words.**

1. My cousin likes being a scientist because people respect her and her job has

    _____.

2. This job requires a lot of travel, so a company car is _____.

3. The managers _____ that sales will increase by 10 percent this year.

4. Ed has to work sixty hours a week at the station. That's a lot of _____.

5. Peter is so tired of _____ for two hours every day, he's thinking about finding a job closer to his apartment.

6. This kind of construction work has certain _____. We try to be safe, but sometimes there are accidents.

7. Raphael has been doing a good job as a cashier, and now we think he's ready to _____ other tasks at the store.

8. I need to be at home for my children at 4:00. Luckily, my job has _____ hours.

9. There are two _____ that make this a good job for me: the benefits and salary.

10. One _____ of this job is difficult, and that is heavy lifting.

B   *PAIRS.* **Read the situations. Which job factor is most important to the speaker? Look back at the headings in the article. Tell your partner.**

1. I have to pick up my daughter from daycare at 4 P.M.

2. I don't have a car, and the bus is expensive.

3. I go to the doctor quite often, and I take several kinds of medication.

4. I am allergic to dust.

5. I want to get a better salary in the future.

Grammar
- Simple Present Passive
- Simple Past Passive
- Passive and Active

Vocabulary

Match the pictures with the words. Write the numbers. Then listen and check your answers.

_____ boil

_____ broil

_____ consume

_____ create

_____ cultivate

_____ fry

_____ invent

_____ marinate

_____ steam

Very nice food! What should I call this?

Sugar Swan by Chef Jan

Fourth Earl of Sandwich, 1762

MUSTARD

SOY SAUCE

ONION

Listening

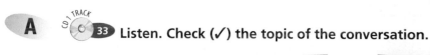

A **33** **Listen. Check (✓) the topic of the conversation.**

pyramids   a sacred cow in India

❏ recipes from around the world   ❏ the most unusual food in the world

❏ interesting facts about foods   ❏ food in India and Egypt

❏ how food is cooked in different countries

B **33** **Listen again. Complete the sentences with the words in the box. (Be careful! There are two extra answers.)**

Egypt	Europe	India	the Middle East	money	Pork	Seafood

1. Beef is not eaten in many parts of _____.

2. _____ is not eaten in many parts of the world.

3. Bread was used to pay workers in _____.

4. Salt and pepper were also used as _____.

5. Coffee was first introduced to _____ by the Dutch.

C **33** **Listen again. Check (✓) the statements that you can infer from the conversation.**

❏ 1. There aren't many cows in India.

❏ 2. Ben is surprised that Angela knows so much about food.

❏ 3. Angela has traveled to many different countries.

❏ 4. A long time ago, there weren't any coffee plants in Europe.

❏ 5. Most people incorrectly believe that tomatoes are a vegetable.

Grammar to Communicate 1

SIMPLE PRESENT PASSIVE

i. We sometimes use passive sentences. The object in an active sentence becomes the subject in a passive sentence.

ACTIVE: People grow tea in warm climates.

                              object

PASSIVE: Tea is grown in warm climates.

             subject

ii. The form of the simple present passive is *am, is,* or *are* + past participle.

ACTIVE: People sometimes serve tea with milk.

PASSIVE: Tea is sometimes served with milk.

A   Look at the photos. Then underline the passive verbs in the chart on page 75.

The bean pod is removed from the tree.

The bean pod is opened.

The beans are fermented and dried.

The beans are cleaned and bagged.

STEP	
1	The bean pods are cut from the tree and the pods are opened.
2	The pulp is removed and fermented.
3	The pulp is dried in the hot sun.
4	The dried beans are separated from the pulp.
5	The beans are bagged and sent to the manufacturer.
6	At the manufacturer, the beans are cleaned and roasted.

PAIRS. What sweet food is made from this process?

B   Complete the sentences. Use the passive form.

1. Steamed food _____ above boiling water.
   (place)

2. Sautéed food _____ in very little oil.
   (fry)

3. Stir-fried vegetables _____ very quickly in a small amount of oil.
   (fry)

4. Roasted food _____ in hot dry air, usually in an oven.
   (bake)

5. Cakes _____; chickens _____.
   (bake)   (roast)

6. Broiled steaks _____ directly to heat.
   (expose)

C   Make passive sentences. Add *not* where necessary.

1. water / boil   Water is boiled.   5. pizza / bake   _____

2. bread / bake   _____   6. peanuts / roast   _____

3. french fries / fry   _____   7. cookies / broil   _____

4. ice cream / marinate   _____   8. pasta / fry   _____

TIME to TALK

GROUPS. Talk about how five or more kinds of food are prepared, served, and eaten in your country. Use the words in the box and your own ideas.

bake	broil	marinate	sauté	serve hot	steam
boil	fry	roast	serve cold	serve raw	stir-fry

Example:
A: *In Ecuador, raw fish is marinated in lime juice and served cold with tomatoes, onions, and peppers. It isn't cooked. The dish is called* ceviche.

Grammar to Communicate 2

SIMPLE PAST PASSIVE	
i. The form of the simple past passive is *was* or *were* + past participle.	Ice cream **was invented** in Italy in the 17th century. The first bottles of Coca-Cola® **were sold** in 1886.
ii. The subject in an active sentence becomes the agent in a passive sentence. The agent does the action. Use *by* with an agent.	ACTIVE: **Marco Polo** brought pasta to Italy. *(subject)* PASSIVE: Pasta was brought to Italy **by** Marco Polo. *(agent)*

A Complete the sentences. Write *was, wasn't, were,* or *weren't*.

1. Food _____ first canned in the 20th century.

2. Pepsi® _____ invented by a pharmacist.

3. Pasta _____ created by Italian chefs.

4. The first cookbook _____ written in 1940.

5. Tomatoes _____ eaten until the 1700s in England.

6. The first sandwiches _____ eaten in England by the Fourth Earl of Sandwich.

canned soup

PAIRS. Do you have the same answers? Look on page 299 for the correct answers.

B Write sentences with the passive.

1. Rice / first cultivate / in China / over 4,000 years ago

_____

2. Frozen vegetables / sell / for the first time in 1930

_____

3. Chocolate / first / consume / as a drink / by the Mayans and Aztecs

_____

4. The first modern chocolate bar / make / in England / in 1847

_____

5. Potato chips / invent / in 1853 / in Saratoga, New York / by George Scrum

_____

C   **Rewrite the sentences with the passive. Use *by* when necessary.**

fertilize

> ## Look
>
> Use *by* when it is important to know who does the action.
>
> Pasta **was brought** to Italy from China **by Marco Polo**.
> BUT
> Pasta **was eaten** in China before it **was eaten** in Italy.
> (= It is clear that people ate pasta. *By* is not necessary.)

1. People cultivated corn in Mexico more than 2,000 years ago.

   <u>Corn was cultivated in Mexico more than 2,000 years ago.</u>

2. Native Americans used fish as fertilizer for corn.

   _____

3. Christopher Columbus brought corn to Europe.

   _____

4. The Spanish introduced turkeys to Europe in the 16th century.

   _____

5. In the 16th century, people confused turkeys with another bird from Turkey.

   _____

6. That's why people gave turkeys this name.

   _____

TIME to TALK

GROUPS.   **Step 1:** Study the food history that you have learned in the unit. Then prepare a list of five questions to ask students in other groups.

Step 2: Each group asks another group one question. The first group that answers correctly gets a point. Continue playing until there are no new questions.

Example:
Group A: *How were the workers who built the pyramids in Egypt paid?*
Group B: *Were they paid with bread?*
Group A: *That's right. You get one point.*

Food   **77**

Grammar to Communicate 3

i. In general, the active is much more common than the passive. We only use the passive when it is necessary.

We ~~bought pasta for dinner last night.~~
NOT Pasta was bought by us last night.

ii. We use the passive to focus on the result of the action, not the agent (the person or thing that does the action).

Pasta is **boiled**.
(= It is not important who boils it.)

Some food **was stolen** from the restaurant.
(= We do not know who stole it.)

I **was told** about the robbery last night.
(= I don't want to say who told me.)

A **Circle the correct verbs.**

> **Look**
>
> produce = grow or make something

1. Germans **consume / are consumed** the most potatoes in the world.

2. Cheese **first made / was first made** in Central Asia.

3. Salt **used / was used** for money a long time ago.

4. India **produced / was produced** the most bananas in 2003.

5. The Chinese **drank / was drunk** tea before the British.

B **Circle the sentences that use more natural English.**

1. **a.** In Japan, fish is often served raw.

   b. Japanese waiters often serve raw fish.

2. **a.** When were ice cream cones invented?

   b. When did someone invent ice cream cones?

3. **a.** In your family, who is dinner usually made by?

   b. In your family, who usually makes dinner?

4. **a.** Dinner is eaten late in the evening by Argentinians.

   b. Argentinians eat dinner late in the evening.

5. **a.** Over 350 kinds of cheese are produced in France.

   b. People in France produce over 350 kinds of cheese.

PAIRS. **Compare your answers.**

C   **Complete the paragraphs with the active or passive form of the verbs. Use the present or past.**

Nowadays, lobsters _____

1. (eat)

at expensive restaurants, and people

_____ a lot of money

2. (pay)

for them. But 100 years ago people

_____differently about lobsters.

3. (think)

In fact, lobsters _____ popular at all. They _____ only by poor

4. (be / not)   5. (eat)

people.

People _____ French fries all over the world. In England they

6. (eat)

_____"chips" and they _____ with vinegar. In the United States,

7. (call)   8. (eat)

people _____ fries with ketchup. When did fries become popular? Where

9. (prefer)

_____? Nobody knows for sure. But people from Belgium_____

10. (the dish / create)   11. (consider)

"frites" their national dish, and these delicious fried potatoes _____ in "friteries"

12. (sell)

in every village in the country.

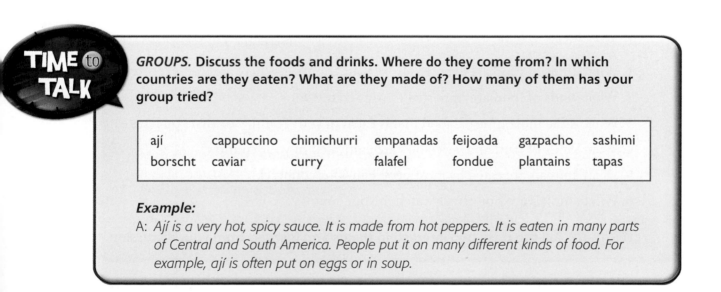

TIME to TALK

GROUPS. **Discuss the foods and drinks. Where do they come from? In which countries are they eaten? What are they made of? How many of them has your group tried?**

ají	cappuccino	chimichurri	empanadas	feijoada	gazpacho	sashimi
borscht	caviar	curry	falafel	fondue	plantains	tapas

Example:

A: *Ají is a very hot, spicy sauce. It is made from hot peppers. It is eaten in many parts of Central and South America. People put it on many different kinds of food. For example, ají is often put on eggs or in soup.*

Grammar

Correct the conversation. There are seven mistakes. The first mistake is corrected for you.

Customer: How is ~~cooked the fish~~? *the fish cooked*

Server: It grilled.

Customer: ~~Does it come with anything?~~

Server: It is serve with vegetables.

Customer: How is the vegetables prepared?

Server: They're sautéed by a cook.

Customer: Is the fish fresh?

Server: Of course. All of our fish is caught daily from local fishermen. They are deliver it every morning, fresh off the boat.

Dictation

 Listen. You will hear five sentences. Write them in your notebook.

Speaking

GROUPS. **Discuss the questions. Take notes while your group is talking. Write in your notebook.**

> ## Look
> **export** = sell merchandise (food, clothes, etc.) to another country
>
> **import** = bring merchandise into one country from another in order to sell it

1. What kinds of food are exported from your country? Where are they exported to?

2. What kinds of food are imported to your country?

3. What is the most unusual food that is eaten in your country or that you have eaten?

4. What kinds of fruit and vegetables are cultivated in your country?

5. What animals are eaten by most people in your country?

6. What animals are not usually eaten in your country?

WRAP-UP. **Tell the class two interesting things you learned from your discussion.**

Listening

A **35** Listen to the radio report. Check (✓) the main topic of the report.

ginger

garlic

honey bee

❏ 1. cooking with garlic, ginger, and honey

❏ 2. the history of garlic, ginger, and honey

❏ 3. your health and garlic, ginger, and honey

> **Look**
>
> dietary supplement =
> something, such as a vitamin,
> that you take to improve your
> health

B **35** Listen again. Check (✓) the correct type of food for each statement, according to the speaker.

	GARLIC	GINGER	HONEY
This is taken by pregnant women to stop nausea.			
This is often made into a drink.			
People with heart problems are often told to take this.			
This is usually taken in pill form.			
This is sometimes used to clean and soften the skin.			
This can be taken to help prevent plant allergies.			

TIME to TALK

GROUPS. Talk about how food is used as medicine in your country. Use the ideas in the box and your own ideas.

cold liquids	ginger	hot liquids	milk	mustard
garlic	honey	lemon	mint	salt

Example:

In Japan, a very hot mustard called wasabi *is served with raw fish. It tastes delicious, but it also kills any bacteria that might be in the fish.*

Reading

Getting Ready to Read

Read the first paragraph. Visualize a clambake on the beach.

Reading

**Reading Skill:
Visualizing**

Try to form pictures in your mind of what you read. **Visualizing** can help you understand ideas or steps in a process.

Read the article. Try to visualize the steps. What does a clambake look like? Tell a partner.

A traditional summer feast

During the summer months along the coast of Massachusetts and Rhode Island, you sometimes see large groups of people at the beach enjoying a traditional **feast** called a clambake. It looks like a large barbecue or a picnic, but it is actually a **unique** and delicious way of cooking **clams** and other shellfish. How did this tradition start?

This **region** of the Northeast was **inhabited** for thousands of years by Native Americans called the Wampanoags. [Wam puh NO ahgs]. When the colonists from England came to Plymouth, Massachusetts, in 1620, the Wampanoag people helped them by bringing them food such as corn and turkey. This was the famous first Thanksgiving. The Wampanoags understood how to use the natural tools around them to survive. They knew, for example, that lobsters could be used as fertilizer, and they also invented the clambake.

The Wampanoag clambake has several steps. First, some smooth round stones are collected from the beach. Next, a large round pit is made in the ground, and the stones are placed inside the pit. Dry wood is **gathered** from the forest. Then a fire is made on top of the stones. After that, seaweed is collected from the ocean. The wet seaweed is **piled** on top of the hot rocks. Then the clams and lobsters and corn are placed on top of the seaweed and covered with more seaweed. The food is steamed for several hours. As the food cooks, the people give thanks for all the gifts from the land and the ocean.

Massasoit, a Wampanoag Indian chief, visits with colonists in 1621

Look

colonist = a person who is sent to a place to live there and take control of the area

pit = a hole in the ground

After You Read

A Find the boldfaced words in the article. Guess their meaning from the context. Then circle the correct meaning.

1. feast
   a. large meal   **b.** beach

2. unique
   a. modern   **b.** special

3. clams
   a. vegetables   **b.** shellfish

4. region
   a. a particular area land   **b.** a large number of people

5. inhabited
   a. stopped something   **b.** lived in

6. gathered
   a. collected   **b.** burned

7. piled
   a. placed on top of other things   **b.** cooked a long time

B Read the article again. Circle the correct answers.

1. People usually have clambakes _____.
   a. in the mountains   **b.** near the ocean

2. The Wampanoags helped the early colonists by
   a. giving them food   **b.** having a clambake

3. The _____ invented this method of cooking clams.
   a. Wampanoags   **b.** English colonists

4. For a traditional clambake, a fire is made on top of the _____.
   a. seaweed   **b.** stones

5. The clams are cooked by steam coming out of the _____.
   a. ocean   **b.** firewood

6. While the clams are cooking, people give thanks for _____.
   a. food from the land and ocean   **b.** the Wampanoags

Writing

Writing Skill: Using Transition Words for Steps in a Process

To describe a process, you can show steps with transition words such as: *first, next, then,* and *after that.*

A   Complete the paragraph with the words in the box.

Next	Finally	then	First	After that

St. Nicholas Day is a festival day in Bulgaria. This is a great winter holiday that is celebrated in Bulgaria on December 6. On this festival day, people cook *Ribnik,* a fish called carp, wrapped in bread. _____ the fish is cleaned, and the scales are removed.
1.

_____ , the fish is seasoned with lemon juice
2.
or vinegar. It is_____ left to dry for four hours. While the fish is drying, the dough
3.
is prepared. The filling for the fish is made by mixing grated onions, parsley, celery, stewed tomatoes, and vegetable oil. _____ , the dough is rolled out and the fish is stuffed
4.
with the filling and wrapped in the dough. _____ , *Ribnik* is roasted in an oven and
5.
served with two loaves of bread.

B   Read the model paragraph. Circle the four transition words.

A Traditional Feast in Argentina

A traditional feast in Argentina is the *Asado*. It is a kind of meat barbecue. Family, friends, and neighbors are all invited. At an Asado, beef is cooked with some vegetable side dishes. First, the meat is cut up and prepared. Next, some salt is added, and sometimes pepper or spices. After that, the meat is placed on the grill. Usually the men prepare and cook the meat while the women prepare the drinks, vegetables, and salad. Finally, when the meat is cooked, everyone gathers around to try it. There is so much meat that it usually cannot be eaten in one day.

Prewriting: Listing Steps

A   You are going to write about a process. First, choose a topic from the box or your own idea.

Chinese New Year   Easter   Shivriti

Day of the Dead (Día de los Muertos)   Eid al-Adha

OR Other food festival: _____

OR Your favorite recipe: _____

B   Make a list of steps. Then describe the process.

A traditional feast: _____

OR

My favorite recipe: _____

Step 1:

_____

_____

Step 2:

_____

_____

Step 3:

_____

_____

Step 4:

_____

_____

Step 5:

_____

_____

Writing

Write a paragraph about the topic you chose. Make sure to show the steps. Use the model paragraph and your notes to help you. Write in your notebook.

Unit 7
Safety

Grammar
- Present Perfect Passive
- Passive with *Need(s) to*
- Present Progressive Passive

Vocabulary

CD 1 TRACK

36 Match the pictures with the words. Write the numbers. Then listen and check your answers.

_____ clear

_____ disappear

_____ evacuate

_____ inspect

_____ post

_____ rescue

_____ replace

_____ search

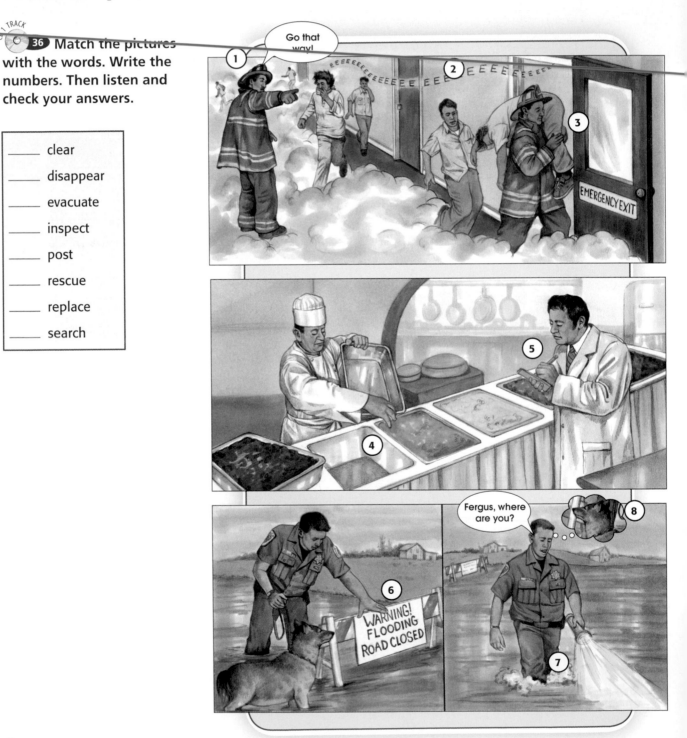

 Unit 7

Listening

 A **Listen. The owner of a building is talking to the building superintendent. Look at the owner's "To Do" list. Cross off the things that have been done.**

smoke detector

> **Look**
>
> **install** = connect equipment so that it may be used
> **sprinkler system** = equipment that puts out fires with water

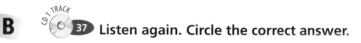

TO DO

1. change lock to laundry room door
2. replace batteries (3rd floor smoke detectors)
3. install sprinkler system
4. install safety locks
5. repair front stairs and post warning sign
6. do elevator inspection

B **37** **Listen again. Circle the correct answer.**

1. The batteries in the smoke detectors **need to be replaced / have been replaced**.

2. The superintendent **has been given / hasn't been given** an installation date for the sprinkler system.

3. The safety locks **have already been installed / are being installed tomorrow**.

4. The stairs **haven't been repaired yet / are being repaired right now**.

5. A sign **needs to be posted / has been posted**.

6. The elevators **need to be inspected / don't need to be inspected**.

C **37** **Listen again. Check (✓) the sentences that you can infer from the conversation.**

❏ **1.** The superintendent is lazy.
❏ **2.** The building owner isn't easy to work for.
❏ **3.** The superintendent has a difficult job.
❏ **4.** The building is an apartment building.
❏ **5.** The superintendent talks to the owner every day.

Grammar to Communicate 1

PRESENT PERFECT PASSIVE

i. The form of the present perfect passive is *has been* or *have been* + past participle.	ACTIVE: A dog **has bitten** a man. PASSIVE: A man **has been bitten** by a dog.
ii. Only a transitive verb (verb with an object) can be passive.	ACTIVE: A car **has hit** someone. *object* PASSIVE: Someone **has been hit** by a car.
iii. An intransitive verb (verb without an object) can never be passive.	ACTIVE: Two people **have died**. NOT: ~~Two people have been died.~~

A **38** Listen to the news headlines. Complete the sentences.

Escaped Bear Found

Cleveland, Ohio A missing black bear from Metroparks Cleveland Zoo was found yesterday. The search began two days ago and ended when

1. _____ has been found.

2. A _____ has been injured in a hunting accident.

3. Several _____ on the north side of town have disappeared.

4. A _____ has been rescued from Lake Erie.

5. A _____ has been reported at an old paint factory on 143rd Street.

B Complete the sentences with the passive. Use the present perfect.

1. Route 110 _____ (close).

2. Over 300 residents in the area _____ (evacuate).

3. Only a small part of the highway _____ (clear) so far.

4. One person _____ (take) to the hospital.

5. People _____ (tell) very little about what happened.

PAIRS. Read your sentences. What do you think happened?

C Rewrite the sentences in the passive. Write in your notebook. If the passive can't be used, write —.

1. Two hikers have disappeared in the Black Mountains.

2. People haven't seen the hikers in several days.

3. Someone has sent rescue dogs to the area.

4. Someone has called their families.

5. The search has continued for two days.

6. Over the past few years, someone has rescued several lost hikers in the same area.

D Complete the sentences. Use the present perfect passive or active.

> **Look**
>
> require = be necessary because of a rule or law

1. In the past twenty years, more people _____ in swimming pools than
   (die)
   in airplane crashes.

2. Since they were invented, seat belts _____ the lives of many thousands
   (save)
   of people.

3. Automobile accidents _____ the leading cause of accidental deaths in
   (become)
   many countries.

4. New cars without air bags _____ in the United States since the 1980s.
   (not / sell)

5. Small children _____ to ride in car seats for many years.
   (require)

6. Smoking _____ on airplanes for many years.
   (not / allow)

TIME to TALK

PAIRS. Imagine that you are television reporters. Prepare a list of headlines. Do not include any details. Use Exercise A as a model.

Example:
There has been a serious accident on Route 128 More than twenty people have been taken to the hospital. . . There has been a bank robbery...

WRAP-UP. Perform your report for the class.

Grammar to Communicate 2

PASSIVE WITH *NEED(S) TO*

We often use *need to* with the passive.
To form the passive with *need to*, add *be*
+ past participle.

ACTIVE: You **need to lock** the door.
PASSIVE: The door **needs to be locked**.

ACTIVE: You don't **need to close** the windows.
PASSIVE: The windows **don't need to be closed**.

 A **Match the parts of the sentences.**

Look

fire drill = when people practice
how to leave a building safely in
case of a fire

_____ 1. Sprinkler systems need to be

_____ 2. Fire drills need to be

_____ 3. Exit signs need to be

_____ 4. Zoo visitors need to be

_____ 5. Medicine needs to be

_____ 6. Meat in a supermarket needs to be

a. held every few months in public schools.

b. told not to feed the animals.

c. kept in locked areas in a hospital.

d. cut in a clean area.

e. posted in all public areas.

f. installed in all hotels.

B **Complete the sentences. Use the passive with**
need(s) to and the underlined verbs. Make the
sentences negative where necessary.

1. The broken window hasn't been **fixed** yet.
   It _____ immediately.

2. The smoke detector hasn't been **installed** yet.
   It _____ today.

3. The batteries in the smoke detector have been
   replaced. They _____ every six months.

4. The fire extinguishers have been **checked**.
   They _____ next week.

5. That electrical outlet still hasn't been **changed**.
   It _____ this week.

fire extinguisher

electrical outlet

Small children are coming to visit. What needs to be done? Write sentences in your notebook. Use the passive and the verbs in the box.

| clean up | close | lock up | put away | repair | tie up |

chemicals

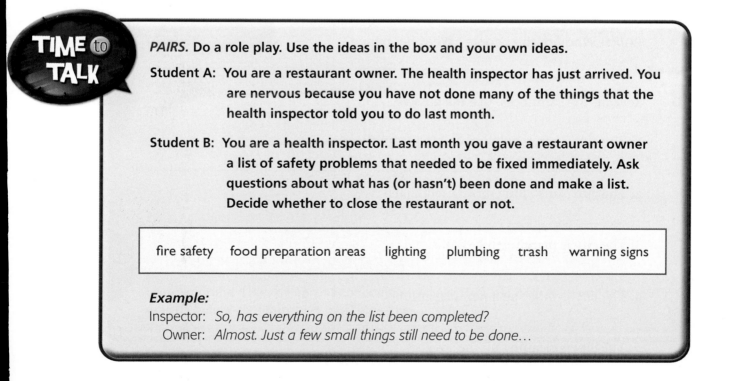

TIME to TALK

PAIRS. Do a role play. Use the ideas in the box and your own ideas.

Student A: You are a restaurant owner. The health inspector has just arrived. You are nervous because you have not done many of the things that the health inspector told you to do last month.

Student B: You are a health inspector. Last month you gave a restaurant owner a list of safety problems that needed to be fixed immediately. Ask questions about what has (or hasn't) been done and make a list. Decide whether to close the restaurant or not.

| fire safety | food preparation areas | lighting | plumbing | trash | warning signs |

Example:
Inspector: *So, has everything on the list been completed?*
Owner: *Almost. Just a few small things still need to be done...*

Grammar to Communicate 3

i. The form of the present progressive passive is *am/is/are* + *being* + past participle.

ACTIVE: The workers **are repairing** the road.
PASSIVE: The road **is being repaired**.

ACTIVE: The electric company **is changing** the lights.
PASSIVE: The lights **are being changed**.

A Read the conversation. Underline the passive verbs.

A: What is being done to take care of the problem?

B: Well, first of all, the streets are being cleared so that traffic can get through.

A: Is that being done by city workers?

B: Yes, they're doing a terrific job.

A: And what about the town's drinking water? Is it safe?

B: No, not yet. But it's being tested every day.

A: And when are people being allowed to go home?

B: Later today. They are being contacted right now.

A: Well, thank you for speaking to me today.

PAIRS. Who are the people? What happened?

B Rewrite the sentences. Use the passive.

1. The city is removing broken glass from the park.

   _____

2. The city is installing more streetlights.

   _____

3. The city is planning bike paths.

   _____

4. The city is building a new playground.

   _____

5. The city is cleaning up the streets.

   _____

C Read the newspaper articles. Complete the sentences with the present progressive. Use the passive or active.

NO MORE RESTAURANT FIRES

After last month's fire at the Seaside Grill, the city _____ every
 1. (inspect)
restaurant for fire safety. Fire extinguishers _____ and inspectors
 2. (check)
_____ for any possible dangers. If there is a problem, the owner
 3. (look)
_____ one week to fix it.
 4. (give)

Serious About Meat

After last month's problem at Cowtown Market, all meat _____ for
 5. (test)
possible disease. The city's health inspectors _____ to every
 6. (go)
restaurant and supermarket in the area. They _____ the places and
 7. (inspect)
products very carefully. Owners _____ the exact date of the
 8. (not / tell)
inspection.

Safe Pools

Before the tourist season begins, the city _____ hotel swimming
 9. (check)
pools in the area. The water in every hotel pool _____. The city
 10. (test)
_____ the owners one week to fix the problem.
 11. (give)

TIME to TALK

GROUPS. First, tell the group where you live. Talk about the things that are (or aren't) being done in your neighborhood and in the city to improve public safety. Make a list. If you need ideas, look at Exercises A and B.

Example:
A: *More streetlights are being installed.*
B: *Really? Not in my neighborhood!*

Review and Challenge

Grammar

Correct seven mistakes in this conversation. The first is corrected for you.

A: I think the batteries in the smoke detector need to ~~change~~. *be changed*

B: But we changed them last September.

A: They need to be changed every year. Do you remember the fire on Bartlett Street?

B: No. When was that? What was happened?

A: The batteries in the smoke detector were old, so the smoke detector didn't work.

B: Oh, yeah. But nobody was died in the fire, did they?

A: No, but there was a lot of damage. The house still hasn't repaired.

B: It's being repair now. I have been seen trucks in front of the house for the past week.

A: And so? We don't want that to happen to us, do we?

B: Right. So I need to be changed the batteries in the smoke detector.

Dictation

 39 **Listen. You will hear five sentences. Write them in your notebook.**

Speaking

PAIRS. **How safe is your home? What have you or your landlord or superintendent done to make it as safe as possible? What still needs to be done? Use the ideas in the box and your own ideas.**

carbon monoxide detector	fire alarm	heating system	smoke detectors
door locks	fire extinguishers	lights	stairs
exits	hallways	sprinkler system	window safety locks

Example:
A: *My landlord has done several things to make the building safe, but a lot more needs to be done.*
B: *What hasn't been done?*

Listening

CD 1 TRACK

A **40** Listen to the news. Check (✓) the topics that are mentioned.

❏ a lost child ❏ an injured child ❏ a car accident

❏ a plane crash ❏ a bridge repair ❏ a bank robbery

❏ a fire ❏ street repairs ❏ a park clean-up

❏ streetlights ❏ pool repairs ❏ summer safety problems

B **40** Listen. According to the news report, what has been done? What is being done? What needs to be done? Check (✓) the correct column. Then listen again and check your answers.

	THIS HAS BEEN DONE.	THIS IS BEING DONE.	THIS NEEDS TO BE DONE.
1. search for Matthew Perry			
2. clear an accident from Route 55			
3. repair the Charlestown Bridge			
4. close the roads to the office park			
5. evacuate the buildings			
6. install streetlights			
7. close the swimming pools			

TIME to TALK

PAIRS. Student A: Look at the list on page 295. You are the building inspector. You gave the landlord a list of things to do. Ask the landlord questions. What has he done or not done on the list. Student B: Look at the picture on page 297. You are the landlord. Answer the building inspector's questions.

Example:
A: *Has the elevator been fixed yet?*
B: *Not yet. But the repairman has been called.*

Now change roles. Student B: You are the building inspector. Student A: You are the landlord. Ask and answer questions.

Getting Ready to Read

GROUPS. **Do you think restaurants are generally clean or dirty places? Why? Have you ever seen any of these problems in a restaurant?**

cockroaches or rats	dirty kitchen
dirty bathrooms	workers not washing their hands

Reading

Read the article. Does the article change your feelings about restaurants?

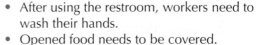

RESTAURANT HORROR STORIES

Whether people eat at a fancy restaurant or at the local deli, they almost all have a "restaurant horror story" to tell. They know someone who has gotten **food poisoning** from an **undercooked** burger or who found a cockroach in his taco or a hair in his pizza.

Most customers will be **concerned** and not want to eat at a restaurant if it isn't clean. Customers may see problems in the dining area. For example, they may see servers with dirty hands or fingernails; garbage that hasn't been cleared away; greasy **silverware** and dishes; and servers who touch both food and money.

In fact, the most serious problems are usually in the kitchen, which most customers never see. However, if you are able to see the cooking area, you may want to check if these rules are being followed:

- Workers' fingers need to be kept away from their face and hair.

- After using the restroom, workers need to wash their hands.
- Opened food needs to be covered.
- Spilled food needs to be cleaned up immediately.
- Cartons or boxes should not be placed on a **surface** used for food preparation.
- **Raw** food needs to be kept away from cooked and ready-to-eat foods.

Several cities and states in the United States have introduced new laws concerning restaurant cleanliness. They require all restaurants to post a report card showing their city health inspection **score**. Restaurants are rated A, B, or C according to how well they follow safety rules. The report is posted in the restaurant window and online. As a result of this law, restaurants are becoming cleaner, and are attracting more customers. Also, because restaurants are practicing higher standards of cleanliness, fewer people are getting food-related illnesses.

"I'm sorry, but your restaurant has failed on a number of health and safety issues."

www.cartoonstock.com

After You Read

A Find the boldfaced words in the article and guess their meaning from the context. Then match the words with their meanings.

_____ 1. food poisoning   **a.** the top of something, such as a countertop or tabletop

_____ 2. undercooked   **b.** uncooked

_____ 3. concerned   **c.** worried

_____ 4. silverware   **d.** how well you do on a test or an inspection

_____ 5. surface   **e.** knives, forks, and spoons

_____ 6. raw   **f.** an illness caused by eating bad food

_____ 7. score   **g.** not completely cooked

B Circle the correct inference for each statement.

> **Reading Skill:**
> **Making Inferences**
>
> An **inference** is a logical conclusion. Often, writers do not say all of their ideas directly. They expect the reader to make inferences based on the information in the text.

1. Whether people eat at a fancy restaurant or the local deli, they almost all have a restaurant horror story to tell.

   a. Even expensive restaurants can be dirty.

   b. Expensive restaurants are safer than a local deli.

2. People can get food poisoning from an undercooked burger.

   a. Food temperature and cooking time are important to food safety.

   b. Refrigerating food is important to food safety.

3. Workers need to wash their hands after they use the restroom.

   a. Washing hands is important to avoid spreading illness.

   b. Personal cleanliness makes people more attractive to others.

4. Cartons or boxes should not be placed on a surface used for food preparation.

   a. Surfaces may be dirty.

   b. Cartons may be too heavy.

5. Restaurants with a high health inspection score attract more customers.

   a. More people are eating out.

   b. People check the inspection report before they choose a restaurant.

Writing

Writing Skill: Writing a Letter of Complaint

When you write a **letter of complaint**, first state the reason you are writing. Describe the problem, then state an action that you will take or that needs to be taken.

Read the model letter. Then complete the tasks.

209 Washington Street
Phoenix, AZ 85007

August 9, 2007

Manager, Fiesta Restaurant
2376 Field Avenue
Phoenix, AZ 85004

Dear Sir:

I am writing to complain about the food I ate in your restaurant on August 1, 2007. I am very concerned about food safety in your restaurant.

I ordered the Beef Burger Deluxe with French fries. When the food arrived, my burger was cold in the middle. I think it had been frozen and had not been correctly defrosted. Afterward, I had a bad stomach ache, and I was sick most of the night.

I am including my restaurant bill for $15.50. I would like a full refund. Also, I am sending a copy of this letter to the local health department. I hope you will follow food safety rules more carefully. Thank you for your attention.

Sincerely,

Miguel Gonzalez

Miguel Gonzalez

1. Circle the sentence that tells the writer's reasons for writing the letter.
2. Underline the sentences that describe the problem.
3. Circle the sentences that tell the actions the writer wants the manager to take.

Prewriting: Using a Problem-Solution Diagram

 A Read the problems. Then state an action that someone could take to correct each problem.

PROBLEM	ACTION
Raw food is not being washed before it is served.	
Servers are touching money and food.	
Rats are getting into garbage cans outside the restaurant.	

B Think of a safety problem at your school, your child's school, at work, or in a restaurant or supermarket. Write the problem in the diagram. Then write the action that needs to be taken.

PROBLEM	ACTION

Writing

 Write a letter of complaint about the problem you chose. Use the model letter and your notes to help you. Write in your notebook.

Unit 8
Advertising

Grammar
- Adjectives ending in –*ing* and –*ed*
- Adjectives with *so* and *such*
- Adjective Word Order

Vocabulary

CD 1 TRACK **41** Match the pictures with the words. Write the numbers. Then listen and check your answers.

_____ advertisement

_____ amazed

_____ annoyed

_____ change the channel

_____ commercial

_____ embarrassed

_____ exhausted

_____ refreshing

_____ satisfying

Listening

A   CD 1 TRACK **42** Listen to the radio advertisement. Which car does the advertisement talk about first? Second? Third? Put the pictures in the correct order. Write the numbers.

_____ a.   _____ b.   _____ c.

B   CD 1 TRACK **42** Listen again. Complete the sentences with the words in the box. (Be careful! There are four extra answers.)

comfortable	embarrassing	great	safe	satisfying	tiring
embarrassed	expensive	high	satisfied	tired	worried

1. Are you _____ of high gasoline prices?

2. Listen to what some of our _____ customers have said.

3. I had such a _____ time!

4. It's a little _____ to say this.

5. It's a _____ efficient automobile.

6. I have three small children, so I need a large, _____ vehicle.

7. But gas prices are so _____ now that I had to sell my van.

8. They're so _____ that only rich people can afford them, right?

C   CD 1 TRACK **42** Listen again. Check (✓) the sentences that you can infer from the ad.

❑ 1. The people in the advertisement have not bought a Topline yet.

❑ 2. Up until now, most hybrids have been sports cars.

❑ 3. Up until now, most hybrids have been inexpensive.

❑ 4. Up until now, most hybrids have not been very attractive.

❑ 5. Topline hybrids are new on the market.

> **Look**
>
> hybrid car = a car that sometimes uses a battery to run instead of the gasoline engine

Grammar to Communicate 1

ADJECTIVES ENDING IN –ING AND –ED

i. Some adjectives are formed from verbs. They end in *–ing* or *–ed*.	Commercials **bore** me. (*bore* = verb) Commercials are **boring**. (*boring* = adjective) I feel **bored** when I watch commercials. (*bored* = adjective)
ii. Adjectives with *–ing* describe something or someone that causes a feeling.	The actors in the ad are **amazing**. (= The actors cause me to feel amazed.)
iii. Adjectives with *–ed* describe a person's feeling about something or someone.	I'm **amazed by** their acting. (= Amazed describes my feeling about them.)

A 🔊 **43** Listen to the commercials. Circle the words that you hear.

1. So why wait? Enjoy a **refreshing / refreshed** Tepsi today!

2. Hungry? Have some Snap, the **satisfying / satisfied** snack.

3. Play it now… Run for Your Life! The most **exciting / excited** game of the year.

4. You don't need to feel **depressing / depressed** anymore. Talk to your doctor today!

5. You'll be **amazing / amazed** at your savings at the gas pump.

6. Try Grow Back. We guarantee you won't be **disappointed / disappointing**.

PAIRS. Match the commercials with the products. Write the numbers.

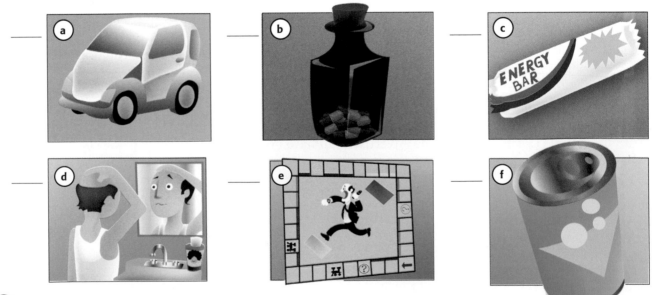

B Complete the sentences. Change the underlined verbs to adjectives with –ing and –ed.

1. Grow Back <u>doesn't interest</u> me.

   I'm not __interested__ in Grow Back.

   Grow Back isn't __interesting__.

2. The gas mileage of my car <u>surprises</u> me.

   The gas mileage is _____.

   I'm _____ at the gas mileage.

3. Playing Run for Your Life <u>excites</u> me.

   I'm _____ when I play it.

   Run for Your Life is an _____ game.

4. My problems <u>worry</u> me.

   I feel _____ all the time.

   My problems are _____.

5. The ad for Tepsi <u>annoys</u> me.

   I feel _____ when I see the Tepsi ad.

   The ad for Tepsi is _____.

6. Snap <u>satisfies</u> me.

   When I eat Snap, I feel _____.

   Snap is a _____ snack.

C Write the correct adjective. Add –ed or –ing.

1. "Do you feel exhaust_____ in the middle of the day? Do you need an energy boost?"

2. "Are you sick of housework? Have you had another tir_____ day?"

3. "You don't feel satisfi_____by eating grapefruits? Try Tastes Great! today, and lose weight without giving up good taste!"

4. "With Cat and Mouse Chase, your children will never be bor_____ again."

5. "Are you confus_____ by all the hair products out there? Well, now there's One-In-All."

6. "No more embarrass_____ moments. You can get as close as you want."

7. "All of your friends will be amaz_____. They won't believe it's you."

8. "Have the most relax_____ time of your life. Call now for reservations."

PAIRS. The sentences above come from advertisements. What kinds of products are the ads for? Tell your partner.

TIME to TALK

PAIRS. Choose one of the sentences from Exercise C, and use it in a radio ad. Use –ed and –ing adjectives. Then perform your ad for the class.

Example:
A: *Have you had another tiring day at the office?*
B: *Do you need a break? Something relaxing?*
A: *Capital Cruises has the answer. Just imagine…a relaxing afternoon by the pool…*
B: *…a refreshing afternoon swim…*
A: *And an exciting night of entertainment under the stars…*
B: *Capital Cruise Lines has it all. Call your travel agent today.*

Grammar to Communicate 2

ADJECTIVES WITH *SO* AND *SUCH*

i. *So* and *such* make an adjective stronger.	The product looks **so good**. (= The product looks really good.) That was **such a bad ad**. (= The ad was really bad.)
ii. We use *so* before an adjective. We use *such* before an adjective and noun. · Use *such a* and *such an* with singular nouns. · Use *such* with plural nouns and noncount nouns.	The woman in the ad is **so beautiful**. She's **such a pretty woman**. They're **such handsome men**. She has **such beautiful jewelry**.
iii. We use a *that* clause after *so* and *such* to give the result.	The product looks **so good that** I might buy it. It was **such a bad ad that** nobody will ever buy the product.

A   Match the parts of the sentences.

_____ 1. It is such a good product

_____ 2. The games are so exciting

_____ 3. The coffee looks so good

_____ 4. They are such good-looking men

_____ 5. The floor looks so clean

_____ 6. It is such a funny ad

a. that I can almost smell it.

b. that it will make everyone laugh.

c. that every kid will want them.

d. that it sells itself.

e. that women will love the ad.

f. that you could eat off it.

B   Complete the sentences. Write *so* or *such*.

1. People were _____ confused by the commercial that it was canceled.

2. Why are the actors in laundry soap commercials always having _____ a great time?

3. The magazine has _____ bad ads that I will never buy it again.

4. The ad was _____ confusing that the product didn't sell well.

5. The picture in the ad is _____ different from the real product.

6. The woman in the ad has _____ an annoying voice.

C **Rewrite the sentences with _so_.**

1. That was such a long commercial.   That commercial was _so long._
2. They make such boring products.   Their products are _____
3. It is such an embarassing ad.   The ad is _____
4. That was such an annoying phone call.   That phone call was _____

Now rewrite the sentences with _such_.

5. The idea is so great.   It is _such a great idea._
6. The actors are so good.   They are _____
7. The music is so amazing.   It is _____
8. The idea is so exciting.   It is _____

PAIRS. **Add clauses with _that_ to the sentences.**

Example:
The commercial was so long that she changed the channel.

D **Combine the sentences with _so...that_.**
Write in your notebook.

1. Most ads are boring. I leave the room when they come on.
   Most ads are so boring that I leave the room when they come on .

2. The animals in the ad are cute. I always enjoy watching it.

3. The ad was strange. I didn't understand it.

4. It was an interesting ad. I wanted to watch it again.

Combine the sentences with _such...that_. Write in your notebook.

5. It was a silly ad. Nobody will buy the product.

6. It looked like delicious candy. I went out and bought some.

7. It is a funny ad. It makes me laugh.

TIME to TALK

PAIRS. **Bring in some magazines and look at the ads. Find some ads that you think are effective and some ads that are not. Explain your opinions. Use _so_ and _such_.**

Example:
A: _I think this is a great ad. The food looks so real and delicious._
B: _I agree. It looks so real that it's making me hungry!_

Grammar to Communicate 3

ADJECTIVE WORD ORDER

i. We sometimes put two or three adjectives before a noun.	The ad shows a **tall young** woman. She is holding a **big black leather** bag.
ii. We usually put adjectives of opinion before adjectives of fact.	The ad is for a **nice Italian** bag. (= **Nice** is an opinion. **Italian** is a fact.)
iii. This is the usual order of fact adjectives.	size age color origin material purpose NOUN large new red Indian wool baby **blanket**

A Complete the sentences about the pictures. Write the nouns.

1. There are brown Italian leather _____.
2. There is a new plastic office _____.
3. There is a small red Japanese _____.
4. There is a tall young _____.
5. There is a lovely white wedding _____.
6. There is a wonderful wool _____.

B Underline the adjectives in Exercise A. Then write them in the correct columns.

OPINION	SIZE	AGE	COLOR	ORIGIN	MATERIAL	PURPOSE

C Rewrite the sentences. Add the adjectives in parentheses.

1. There is a young man. (handsome)
There is a handsome young man.

2. There is a large lake. (beautiful)

_____

_____

3. There is a fast Italian car. (sports)

_____

_____

4. Smiling young children are playing. (Chinese)

_____

_____

5. Look at the delicious vegetables. (green)

_____

6. They bought Italian business suits. (fashionable)

_____

TIME to TALK

GROUPS. Invent a product and write a one-minute television commercial for it. Remember, your job is to sell your product. Be creative. Use adjectives. Make or bring in props. Then perform your commercial for the class. The class will vote on which group's commercial is most effective.

Review and Challenge

Grammar

Find the mistake in each sentence. Circle the letter and correct the mistake.

1. I had <u>such a</u> <u>tired</u> <u>day</u> <u>that</u> I went to bed early.
        A   B   C   D

2. That was <u>such an</u> <u>interesting</u> ad for the <u>new small</u> <u>Korean car</u>.
             A   B   C   D

3. Those are <u>such black nice shoes</u> <u>that</u> I'm going to buy them.
            A   B   C   D

4. That's <u>so a nice</u> jacket <u>that</u> <u>I want to</u> get one, too.
         A   B   C   D

5. I am <u>such</u> <u>confused</u> <u>that</u> I <u>don't know</u> the answer.
       A   B   C   D

Dictation

 44 Listen. You will hear five sentences. Write them in your notebook.

Speaking

PAIRS. **Bring in some magazines and look through the advertisements. Find ads to match the sentences below.**

1. When I see this ad, I'm confused. I'm not sure what the product is.

2. This ad is annoying.

3. This is an ad for a small expensive product.

4. When you look at this ad, you feel embarrassed.

5. The people in this ad look depressed.

6. The food in this ad looks satisfying.

7. This ad is for an amazing new product.

Example:
A: *When I saw this ad, I was confused. It's not clear why the people are wearing the letter* W.
B: *Are they selling T-shirts?*
A: *No, it's an ad for a subway line.*

WRAP-UP. **Show one of your ads to the class. Can your classmates guess which sentence matches it?**

Listening

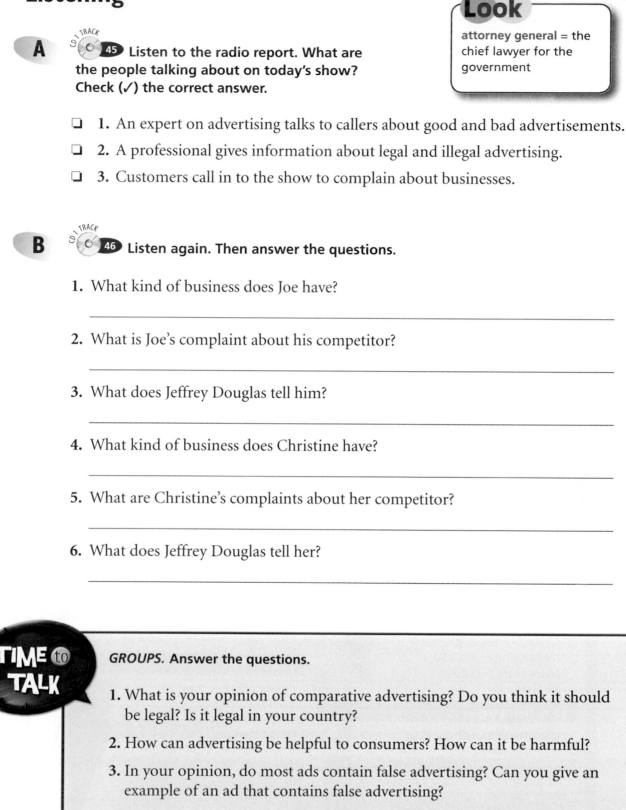

A CD 1 TRACK **45** **Listen to the radio report. What are the people talking about on today's show? Check (✓) the correct answer.**

> **Look**
>
> **attorney general** = the chief lawyer for the government

❏ 1. An expert on advertising talks to callers about good and bad advertisements.

❏ 2. A professional gives information about legal and illegal advertising.

❏ 3. Customers call in to the show to complain about businesses.

B CD 1 TRACK **46** **Listen again. Then answer the questions.**

1. What kind of business does Joe have?

_____

2. What is Joe's complaint about his competitor?

_____

3. What does Jeffrey Douglas tell him?

_____

4. What kind of business does Christine have?

_____

5. What are Christine's complaints about her competitor?

_____

6. What does Jeffrey Douglas tell her?

_____

TIME to TALK

GROUPS. Answer the questions.

1. What is your opinion of comparative advertising? Do you think it should be legal? Is it legal in your country?

2. How can advertising be helpful to consumers? How can it be harmful?

3. In your opinion, do most ads contain false advertising? Can you give an example of an ad that contains false advertising?

4. In what ways does advertising influence you? For example, have you ever bought a product because you liked the ad?

Reading

Getting Ready to Read

PAIRS. What makes an advertisement successful? Think of one advertisement you have seen recently. What made you remember it?

Reading

Read the first paragraph of the article. Underline the sentence that gives the main idea of the reading.

> **Reading Skill:**
> **Identifying the Main Idea from the Introduction**
>
> When you read, pay attention to the first paragraph, or introduction. It usually gives the main idea of the text.

THE LANGUAGE OF ADVERTISING

Advertising is a multi-million dollar industry. Advertisers spend a lot of money and time to make effective ads that will sell their products. Sometimes advertisers use dishonest language in their ads. Here are some dishonest techniques they use:

Misleading Language

"Orange Tree Shampoo helps control dandruff with regular use." This sounds like a convincing argument, but in fact it does not **claim** very much. It doesn't say that this shampoo controls dandruff. It says that it *helps* control it.

Incomplete Comparisons

"Koolau coffee gives you more taste and more flavor." This ad does not tell us what product Koolau coffee is being compared to. More taste and more flavor than what?

It's Unique

"Ultrasoft Body Lotion—Only Ultrasoft is so kind to your skin." This ad suggests that this lotion is so amazing that no other product is like it. But most lotions are good for your skin, so what is so special about this one?

False Science

"Crunch breakfast cereal–lose ten pounds a week as part of a calorie-controlled diet. You won't be disappointed." This sounds like such a good diet cereal that it will help you lose weight right away. But you can lose ten pounds a week without the cereal, if you are on a calorie-controlled diet.

Flattery

"Lemon Shine, the furniture polish for people who care about furniture." This ad **flatters** the consumer. It says that if you buy this product, you are an excellent homemaker.

Advertisements surround us. They influence what we buy and how we spend our money. Taking a close look at the language they use can make us aware of how they influence us.

After You Read

A Find the boldfaced words in the article and guess their meaning from the context. Then circle the correct meaning.

1. consumers   **a.** sellers   **b.** customers

2. techniques   **a.** special advertisements   **b.** ways of doing something

3. misleading   **a.** making someone think   **b.** telling lies to make someone do
                   something is true when it is not   something stupid

4. claim   **a.** to ask for money   **b.** say that something is true,

5. flatters   **a.** gives a lot of compliments   **b.** says lies about

6. surround   **a.** be all around us   **b.** be far away

7. influence   **a.** decide   **b.** have an effect

B Read the article again. Write *T* (true) or *F* (false) for each statement. Write *?* if you cannot infer the information.

_____ **1.** The ad for shampoo says that it controls dandruff.

_____ **2.** Koolau coffee has more taste than all other coffees.

_____ **3.** The ad for body lotion explains why it is unique.

_____ **4.** The ad for cereal claims that it will help you lose weight.

_____ **5.** The ad for furniture polish says that if you buy it, you care about your furniture.

_____ **6.** If we pay attention to the language of ads, they will not influence us.

C Write the name of the product. Which ad says that . . .

1. it is better than other products?   _____

2. people who buy it are good homemakers?   _____

3. you should use the product regularly?   _____

4. you will be completely satisfied?   _____

5. there is no other product like it?   _____

Writing

A Read the paragraph. There are three off-topic sentences. Cross them out.

Advertising is not new. Today it is all around us: on television and the radio, in movies, magazines, and newspapers, on the Internet, and on the street. Some people think that there was less advertising in the past, but advertising started with very early civilizations. Rock paintings in caves were used for advertising thousands of years ago in South America. I have visited some caves in Southern Brazil. Advertisements were also used on walls and buildings in ancient Egypt, Greece, and Rome. Much later, technology improved and advertisements were printed on paper. The first time advertisements were printed on paper was in the 17th century, in English newspapers. Advertising can cause problems. Many people complain about how much advertising we see in modern times, but in fact, advertisements have been around for thousands of years. All kinds of advertising are interesting to me.

B Read the model paragraph. Cross out the sentence that is off-topic.

Chanel® Perfume—a Lifestyle

My favorite advertisement is an ad for Chanel® perfume. Nicole Kidman stars in this ad as a romantic movie star with a handsome boyfriend, beautiful clothes, and diamonds. Of course, she is wearing Chanel® perfume. The ad looks like a film from the 1940s. It has an elegant, sophisticated atmosphere. You feel that if you buy this perfume, you will be elegant and sophisticated, too. My problem with Chanel perfume is that it's very expensive. The best thing about the ad is that there are almost no words. This ad works by selling an idea, a feeling, a lifestyle.

Prewriting: Using a Cluster

A   Look at the brainstorming cluster the writer used for the model paragraph.

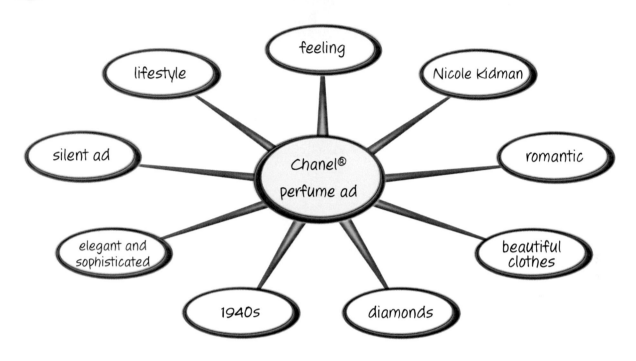

feeling

lifestyle

Nicole Kidman

silent ad

Chanel® perfume ad

romantic

elegant and sophisticated

beautiful clothes

1940s

diamonds

B   Choose an ad that you like or dislike. Write words in the cluster to describe the ad.

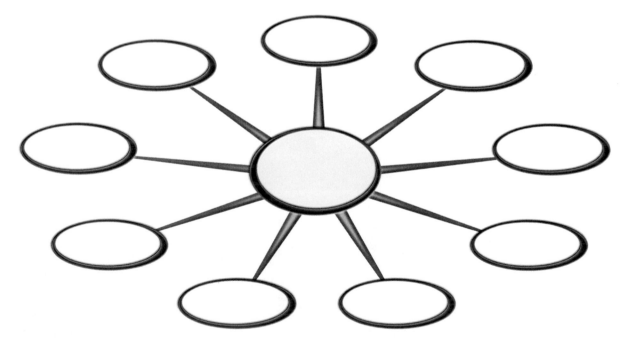

Writing

Write a paragraph about the ad you chose. Make sure your topic sentence gives your opinion. Use the model paragraph and your cluster to help you. Write in your notebook. Describe the ad in your supporting sentences.

Vocabulary

CD2 TRACK

2 Match the pictures with the words. Write the numbers. Then listen and check your answers.

_____ appliance

_____ assemble

_____ electricity

_____ engine

_____ gadget

_____ instruction manual

_____ tool

_____ toolbox

_____ useless

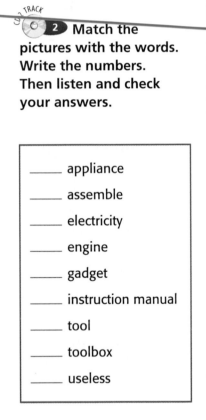

Listening

A 🔘 **3** Listen. The man helps several customers. How many of the customers buy things? Circle the correct number.

0   1   2   3   4

B 🔘 **4** Listen again. For each pair of sentences, circle the sentence that you hear.

1. **a.** People who have newborn babies put one in the baby's room.

    b. People with newborn babies put one in the baby's room.

2. **a.** I'm looking for a gift for a neighbor who just had a baby.

    b. I'm looking for a gift for a neighbor. She just had a baby.

3. **a.** I'm looking for a gadget that I saw on TV.

    b. I'm looking for a gadget I saw on TV.

4. **a.** It's an appliance that you can use to cut all kinds of food.

    b. It's an appliance that is used to cut all kinds of food.

5. **a.** It's one of those gadgets sold only on TV.

    b. It's one of those gadgets which is sold only on TV.

6. **a.** Is there anything else that I can help you with today?

    b. Is there anything else with which I can help you today?

7. **a.** But I called this morning and the man that I spoke to said there were plenty.

    b. But I called this morning and the man who I spoke to said there were plenty.

C 🔘 **5** Listen again. Check (✓) the statements that you can infer from the conversations.

❏ **1.** The first customer and her husband have a newborn baby.

❏ **2.** The salesman works in the department where things are sold.

❏ **3.** We use the word *thingamajig* when we can't think of the name of an object.

❏ **4.** The third customer comes into the store sometime in the afternoon.

❏ **5.** The salesman hopes that the third customer has a nice day.

Grammar to Communicate 1

ADJECTIVE CLAUSES

i. An adjective clause describes a noun. The adjective clause comes after the noun it describes.	I have a new cell phone that takes pictures. adjective clause People who like gadgets love cell phones. adjective clause
ii. We can combine two sentences by using an adjective clause. The adjective clause must be connected to main clause.	I have a lot of gadgets. They are easy to use. I have a lot of gadgets that are easy to use. main clause adjective clause
iii. An adjective clause usually begins with a relative pronoun (*that, who,* or *which*). Use *that* or *who* for people. Use *that* or *which* for places, events, ideas, and things.	I know people **that** love gadgets. I know people **who** love gadgets. I bought a clock **which** changes colors.

A Underline the adjective clause. Draw an arrow from the adjective clause to the noun that the clause describes.

1. A piece of equipment is a special machine that is used to do something.

2. A tool is a hand-held object that is used to fix or make things.

3. A gadget is a small tool that makes a particular job easier and fun.

4. A device is an object which was invented for a specific job.

5. An appliance is an electrical device that is used in people's homes.

PAIRS. Think of an example of a tool, a gadget, a device, and an appliance.

B Complete each sentence with an adjective clause.

1. An appliance ____that makes coffee____ is called a coffee maker.

2. A device _____ is called a can opener.

3. A device _____ is called a vegetable peeler.

4. An appliance _____ is called a dishwasher.

5. A small machine _____ is called a hair dryer.

C Combine the sentences. Change the second sentence to an adjective clause.

1. People use canes. People can't walk very well.

<u>People who can't walk very well use canes.</u>

2. People have hearing aids. People can't hear well.

_____

3. People have talking clocks. People can't see well.

_____

4. People use baby monitors. People have infants.

_____

5. People have alarm systems. People want to be safe.

_____

6. People need good tools. People repair a lot of things in their home.

_____

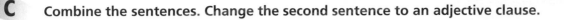

cane

D Write definitions of the words. Use adjective clauses and the information in the box.

He is good at repairing and making things.	It is used in the ear to help people hear.
It allows you to hear sounds in another room.	It makes a noise if someone breaks into your home.
It keeps food cold.	It removes dust and dirt from floors and carpets.

1. a refrigerator (appliance) <u>It's an appliance that keeps food cold.</u>

2. a baby monitor (device) _____

3. a vacuum cleaner (appliance) _____

4. an alarm system (device) _____

5. a hearing aid (device) _____

6. a handyman (person) _____

TIME to TALK

GROUPS. Write definitions for five objects that are often found in a classroom. Use adjective clauses. Then read your definitions to the class. Can they guess the objects?

Example:
Group A: *This is something that is white and is used by the teacher every day.*
Group B: *Is it chalk?*

Grammar to Communicate 2

SUBJECT AND OBJECT RELATIVE PRONOUNS

i. The relative pronouns *that*, *who*, and *which* can be the subject or the object of an adjective clause.

> AS SUBJECTS:
> I bought a clock. **The clock** tells me the weather.
> I bought a clock **which** tells me the weather.
>
> AS OBJECTS:
> The clock tells me the weather. I bought **the clock**.
> The clock **that** I bought tells me the weather.

ii. You do not need to include *that*, *who*, or *which* when it is the object of the adjective clause. However, you <u>must</u> include the relative pronoun when it is the subject of an adjective clause.

> The clock I **bought** tells me the weather.
>
> Do you know anyone **who** can help me?
> NOT Do you know anyone can help me?

A Add *that*, *which*, or *who* to the sentences.

1. I own at least one gadget I don't know how to use. (which)
    <u>I own at least one gadget which I don't know how to use.</u>

2. A handyman I know has over 100 tools. (that)
    _____

3. He is the guy we call when we can't fix something. (who)
    _____

4. I hate to buy things I need to assemble. (that)
    _____

5. I have many instruction manuals. I never have time to read. (which)
    _____

6. I use every tool I have quite often. (that)
    _____

B Underline the adjective clauses. Then complete the sentences.

1. One of the gadgets which I use in the kitchen is _____.

2. The person that I know with the most gadgets is _____.

3. A device I have learned how to use recently is _____.

4. A tool that I use all the time is _____.

5. A friend who I can always ask about the latest gadgets is _____.

C **Rewrite the sentences. Describe the underlined nouns with adjective clauses. Use the words in the box. Rewrite each sentence three ways.**

I bought a can opener years ago.	You installed a smoke detector.
I have gadgets.	You met a guy at the party.
She had used it with her kids.	You saw a technician last week.

1. <u>The guy</u> loves gadgets.

   The guy **who** you met at the party loves gadgets. The guy **that** you met at the party
   loves gadgets. The guy you met at the party loves gadgets.

2. I use the same <u>can opener</u>.

   _____

   _____

3. A friend gave me the <u>baby monitor</u>.

   _____

   _____

4. The <u>smoke detector</u> isn't working.

   _____

   _____

5. All the <u>gadgets</u> are hard to use.

   _____

   _____

6. The <u>technician</u> doesn't work here anymore.

   _____

   _____

ON YOUR OWN. Look at the pictures on page 291. Write sentences that describe each group of things in the pictures. Use adjective clauses.

PAIRS. Now read each other your sentences. Do you have the same description?

Example:
A: *Picture A shows equipment that a doctor uses.*
B: *My answer was different. Picture A shows equipment that a nurse's aide uses.*
A: *I think both answers are right.*

RELATIVE PRONOUNS AS OBJECTS OF PREPOSITIONS

i. *That*, *who*, or *which* can be the object of a preposition. *That*, *who* or *which* comes before the preposition. (*Whom* can also be an object. See page 283.)

> The woman loved the watch. I talked **to the woman**.
>
> The woman **who** I talked **to** loved the watch.

ii. You do not need to include *that*, *who*, or *which* when it is the object of a preposition.

> The woman I talked **to** loved the watch.

 A Read the advertisements. Underline the adjective clauses.

King Shaver

The King Shaver will give you the best shave that you have ever had. It's perfect for the man who never has enough time in the morning. The King Shaver has a high-performance motor for a fast shave. It also has three separate moving heads that give a close shave. It's a great gift for that special man you've been thinking of.

Only $29.95

Hot Clothes Steamer

Are there people in your family who hate to iron? Do you want to buy them something that you know they will like? The Hot Clothes Steamer does the job of an iron in much less time. It has a powerful motor that heats up in less than two minutes. It's the steamer that you've been dreaming about.

Only $29.99

Shake-It Flash

Do you want a flashlight that doesn't need new batteries every few months? Are you tired of flashlights that never work when you need them? Then the Shake-It Flash is just for you. Just shake the flashlight when you need it, and the batteries that you bought three years ago will still work. This is a flashlight that you'll never be disappointed with.

Only $34.95

PAIRS. Take turns reading the sentences you have underlined. Include *that*, *which*, or *who* only if necessary.

B   **Complete the sentences with adjective clauses. Put the words in the correct order. Add *who*, *that*, or *which* only where necessary.**

1. I need something   (can / things / see / me / better / help)

    I need something (that OR which) can help me see things better.

2. I'm looking for a gadget   (with / see / I / better / can / things)

_____

3. Did you see the talking clock   (about / I / talking / was)

_____

4. I couldn't find any appliances at the store   (I / to / went)

_____

5. Are you going to buy those gadgets   (looking / you / at / are)

_____

6. I want to speak to the woman   (this device / me / sold)

_____

C   **Complete the sentences.**

1. I would like a gadget that _____.

2. I don't understand people who _____.

3. People who know how to fix things _____.

4. I've never seen a gadget which _____.

5. I don't like gadgets that _____.

TIME to TALK

Student A: Look at the pictures on page 292.
Student B: Look at the pictures on page 298.
What were the inventions made for? When and where were they used? Write a description of each invention in your notebook.

PAIRS. Student A: Read your descriptions. Student B: Look at Student A's pictures. Then tell Student A the answers. Now change roles. Student B: Read your descriptions. Student A: Look at Student B's pictures. Then tell Student B the answers.

Example:
A: *This is a phone that lets you see the people that are calling.*
B: *You're right. When do you think it was made?*

Grammar

Correct the seven mistakes in this advertisement. The first is corrected for you.

> *person who has*
> Do you need something special for the ~~person has~~ everything? Do you have all the appliances ~~you~~ need them at home? Do you want a gadget who will make your life easier? Then come to Feldman's, the store that it has everything. We have every gadget you are looking for them, and our prices are the best in town. There isn't a store has lower prices than Feldman's. And next Monday morning we will have a special gift for customers which visit our store between 10:00 o'clock and noon. So come on in. We are always happy to answer any questions you have.

Dictation

6 Listen. You will hear five sentences. Write them in your notebook.

Speaking

GROUPS. Imagine an invention that would be useful to have. Use the topics from the box or your own ideas. If you wish, draw a picture of your invention. Then write an advertisement for it. Use adjective clauses.

entertainment	food preparation	sports	travel

Example:
This baseball bat has a computer that tells you how fast and where to swing the bat.

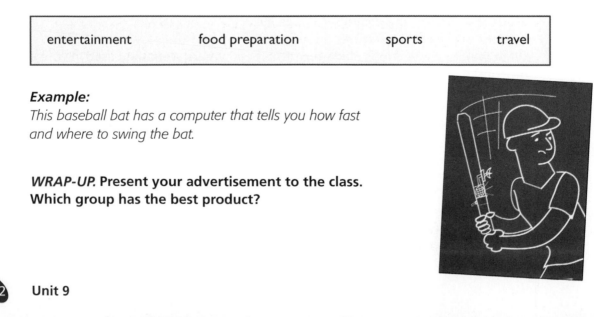

WRAP-UP. Present your advertisement to the class. Which group has the best product?

Listening

A **7** **Listen. Check (✓) the sentence that expresses the opinion of John Parker, the person who wrote the e-mail.**

❏ **1.** Most of the gadgets that are sold today are only for young people.

❏ **2.** There are a lot of gadgets that make our lives easier.

❏ **3.** Too many gadgets these days make our lives harder, not easier.

B **7** **Listen again. Check (✓) the statements that are true, according to the listening.**

❏ **1.** John Parker knows a lot about new technology.

❏ **2.** John Parker likes gadgets that are simple and make his life easier.

❏ **3.** John Parker is probably younger than 30.

❏ **4.** John Parker would like someone to invent a gadget that could make his bed in the morning.

❏ **5.** John Parker would like to buy a cell phone that only makes and receives calls.

GROUPS. Answer the questions.

1. Do you agree with John Parker? Why or why not?

2. Have you ever had trouble using a gadget that was supposed to make your life easier? What happened?

3. Are you the kind of person who likes to have the latest electronic equipment or gadgets? If not, do you know anyone who does?

4. What was the last piece of electronic equipment or gadget that you bought? Does it work well? Has it made your life better or worse? In what way?

5. In general, do you think that technology is improving most people's lives? Why or why not?

Reading

Getting Ready to Read

Scan the article. Find two advantages
and two disadvantages of microwave ovens.

Reading

Read the article. Why are microwave ovens useful?
What problems could they have?

Gadgets that make our lives easier:
The microwave oven

There are millions of them everywhere—
in restaurants, supermarkets, and in our
homes. Microwave ovens are popular
because they cook food fast and are easy
to use. They save time and energy because
they heat only the food, not all of the air
in the oven. Microwaves are also smaller
than conventional ovens, so they're perfect
for people who have small kitchens.

How do microwave ovens work?
Microwave ovens use microwaves, which
are short waves of electromagnetic energy,
like radio waves. Microwaves heat food
by moving the water molecules around in
the food. Microwaves must be used only
with glass, ceramic, or plastic containers
that are labeled "microwave safe." These
are safe containers because microwaves
pass through them without heating them.
Plastic wrap should not be used because
it **melts** from the heat. Also, metal and
aluminum foil should never be used. They
reflect microwaves and sharp thin metal
can start a fire in a microwave.

Can I get sick from eating microwaved food?
Some people worry that microwaves

contaminate food with poisons. There
is no scientific **evidence** for this. On
the other hand, microwave ovens can
sometimes leave cold spots in large pieces
of food. These could contain **bacteria** that
can make you sick. You can avoid this
problem if you turn or **stir** the food once or
twice during cooking.

Can microwave ovens be dangerous?
Sometimes. You should be careful if you
heat water in a microwave. If you **overheat**
water, it can become extremely hot. It
may not appear to be boiling, but when
you pick up the container, the hot water
can make the cup suddenly **explode**. You
can avoid this problem by warming water
and liquids for the correct amount of
time. There is also a very small risk that
microwave ovens can **leak** microwaves.
However, this is not a great concern.
Microwaves are not very **intense**. They
contain very low amounts of radiation,
so they do not cause cancer. However,
you should always keep the door to the
microwave closed. The metal door keeps
the radiation from escaping from the oven.

Look

molecule = the smallest part into which a substance (water,
etc.) can be divided without changing its form

radiation = a form of energy that can be dangerous

After You Read

A Find the boldfaced words in the article and guess their meaning. Then complete the sentences with the words.

1. When ice cream gets very hot, it _____.

2. You should _____ food so that it cooks evenly and does not get cold spots.

3. You should not _____ water because it could burn you.

4. Microwave ovens can _____ microwaves, but the radiation is not dangerous.

5. _____ are micro-organisms that sometimes can make people sick.

6. Microwaves do not _____ food with poisons. However, some plastic containers may have chemicals that are bad for you.

7. If you overheat a bottle in the microwave, the bottle can _____.

8. There are many types of electromagnetic energy. Some are powerful. Others are not. Microwave energy is not very _____.

9. There is no scientific _____ that microwave ovens cause cancer.

B Read the article again. Write *T* (true) or *F* (false) for each statement.

_____ 1. Microwave ovens save more energy than gas and electric ovens do.

_____ 2. Microwaves are waves of light.

_____ 3. Microwaves heat food by heating the air.

_____ 4. It is possible to get sick from microwaved food.

_____ 5. You can avoid cold spots by stirring food while it cooks.

_____ 6. You can use any kind of plastic dish in a microwave oven.

_____ 7. You can't use glass containers in the microwave.

C Complete the sentences.

1. A microwave oven is an oven that ___*uses microwave energy*___.

2. Microwaves are waves of energy _____.

3. You should only use plastic containers that _____.

4. Cold spots are parts of food which _____.

5. Microwave ovens are perfect for people who _____.

Writing

Writing Skill: Using Signpost Words

Signpost words let your reader know what kind of idea your sentence will contain. They can:
- contrast ideas (*however, on the other hand*)
- list ideas (*first, second, next*)
- give examples (*for example*)

A Read the model paragraph. Underline the signpost words.

Vending Machines: Popular but Controversial

Vending machines have been around since the 19th century. These days, vending machines are very popular but also controversial. They are popular for several reasons. First, they are very convenient. You can buy a snack or a drink at work anytime you feel like it, even if you work late at night. Second, vending machines can sell the snacks that employees like most, for example, peanuts. On the other hand, vending machines also have disadvantages. Sometimes they break, and you can lose your money. Often you have to hit the machine to make the candy or snack come out. The most obvious disadvantage of vending machines is that they sell mostly junk food. For this reason, they are controversial. Many people think that if vending machines don't carry healthy food, they should not be allowed in schools.

B Complete the paragraph with good and bad points about cable TV. You may want to talk about cost, convenience, or programs.

There are both advantages and disadvantages to cable TV. One advantage is that

_____.

For example, _____.

Another advantage of cable TV is that _____.

On the other hand, there are sometimes problems with cable service. One disadvantage

is _____. Another disadvantage is _____

_____.

In conclusion, _____

_____.

Prewriting: Using a T-Chart

A   Choose a gadget from the box or your own idea.

cell phone	DVD player	_____
digital camera	iPod	invention / gadget

B   Read the T-chart that the writer used for the model paragraph. Then complete your own.

VENDING MACHINES	
Advantages	**Disadvantages**
• convenient • sell snacks that employees like	• sometimes they break • you can lose money • sell mostly junk food

GADGET: _____	
Advantages	**Disadvantages**

Writing

 Write a paragraph about the gadget or invention you chose. Make sure that your topic sentence gives an idea or opinion. Describe its advantages and disadvantages. Use the model paragraph and the T-chart to help you.

Shopping

Grammar
- Noun Clauses: Question Words and *That*
- Noun Clauses: Indirect Questions
- Noun Clauses: *If / Whether*

Vocabulary

CD 2 TRACK 8 **Match the pictures with the words. Write the numbers. Then listen and check your answers.**

_____ be in business

_____ be sold out

_____ exchange

_____ find out

_____ fitting room

_____ rain check

_____ refund

_____ restroom

_____ try on

_____ wonder

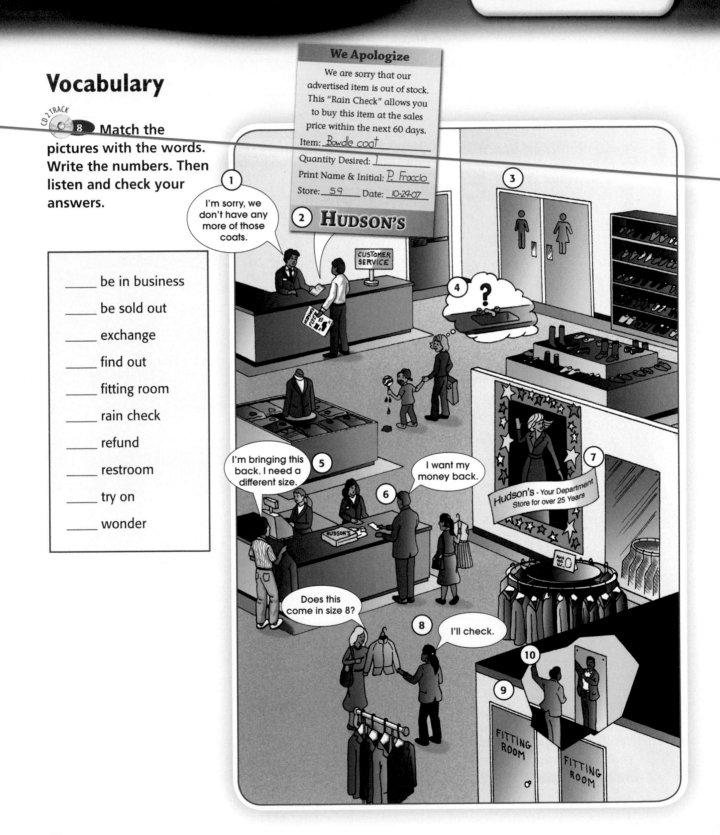

Listening

A **9** **Listen. Who are the people? Where are they? Check (✓) the correct answer.**

- ❏ 1. The man is a cashier in a supermarket. Shoppers are asking him about prices.
- ❏ 2. The man works at the information booth at a mall. Shoppers are asking different questions.
- ❏ 3. The man is a sales associate at a department store. Shoppers are asking him about new products.

B **10** **Read the sentences. Listen again and put the sentences in the correct order. Write *1* (first sentence), *2* (second sentence), and so on. Then listen again and check your answers.**

- _____ **a.** "Oh no! I loved that bookstore. Do you know whether they've opened another store?"
- _____ **b.** "Excuse me, could you tell me where the bookstore is?"
- _____ **c.** "I heard that they were having trouble."
- _____ **d.** "I'm not even sure if they're still in business."
- _____ **e.** "Better Books? I'm afraid they closed last month."
- _____ **f.** "Sorry, but I have no idea where they went."

C **11** **Listen again to the conversations. Check (✓) the statements that you can infer.**

Conversation 1

- ❏ 1. The bookstore has moved to another location.
- ❏ 2. The bookstore's owner is in trouble with the police.

Conversation 2

- ❏ 3. The ATM machine on the first floor has not been working lately.

Conversation 3

- ❏ 4. The woman is not a good mother.

Grammar to Communicate 1

NOUN CLAUSES: QUESTION WORDS AND *THAT*

i. A noun clause is a part of a sentence. A noun clause begins with a connector, such as *that*, or a question word such as *where*. The connector is followed by a subject and verb.

> I don't think <u>that the store is open</u>.
> main clause   noun clause
>
> I don't know <u>where the store is</u>.
> main clause   noun clause

ii. In noun clauses that begin with a question word, do <u>not</u> use question word order.

> I don't know <u>what time it is</u>. = (What time is it?)
> noun clause

iii. Use a noun clause after certain verbs—for example, *think, know, believe*. You can use *that* after the verb, but it is not necessary.

> I think <u>that the shoes are expensive</u>. OR
> noun clause
>
> I think <u>the shoes are expensive</u>.
> noun clause

iv. Use a noun clause after the verb *be* and certain adjectives (for example, *afraid, glad, sorry*, and *sure*).

> I'm afraid <u>that we're all sold out</u>. OR
> noun clause
>
> I'm afraid <u>we're all sold out</u>.
> noun clause

A Underline the noun clauses. Then match each picture with the correct sentences.

> **Look**
>
> come in = be available in a particular size or color (clothes, shoes)
> fit = be the right size for someone.

_____ 1. I wonder what other colors these come in.

_____ 2. I'm not sure that this is going to fit.

_____ 3. I don't understand why you want to wear things like that.

_____ 4. I have no idea how long they're going to be on sale.

_____ 5. I'm sorry that I bought you the wrong size.

B What are the people probably going to say to each other?
Write sentences. Add *not* in the noun clause where necessary.

Look

afford = be able to pay for something

1. a mother to her teenage child   (I / afraid / we / can / afford / $100 / for a pair of shoes)

   "I'm afraid (that) we can't afford $100 for a pair of shoes."

2. a salesperson to a customer   (I / hope / the shirt / fit / your boyfriend)

   _____

3. two friends   (I / glad / you / try it on / before you bought it)

   _____

4. a wife to her husband   (I / happy / you / buy / that bag for me / yesterday)

   _____

5. a salesperson to a customer   (I / sorry / we / could / help / you)

   _____

C Write true sentences about yourself and people you know. Use one word or phrase in each box. Write in your notebook.

I my father my mother my friends my brother _____ **(your idea)**	have no idea know should find out want to know	how much what what color(s) what kind what size where	go shopping like to wear spend on clothes wear would like as a gift

Example: My father has no idea what size I wear.

PAIRS. **Tell your sentences to a partner.**

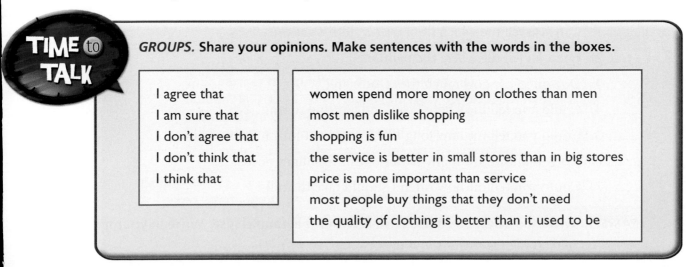

TIME to TALK

GROUPS. **Share your opinions. Make sentences with the words in the boxes.**

I agree that I am sure that I don't agree that I don't think that I think that	women spend more money on clothes than men most men dislike shopping shopping is fun the service is better in small stores than in big stores price is more important than service most people buy things that they don't need the quality of clothing is better than it used to be

Grammar to Communicate 2

NOUN CLAUSES: INDIRECT QUESTIONS

i. We use questions with noun clauses to ask for information in a polite way.	Do you know **where the hardware store is?** 　　main clause　　　　　　noun clause
ii. Use question word order in the main clause. Do <u>not</u> use question word order in the noun clause.	Do you know **what time it is?** = (What time is it?) 　　main clause　　noun clause
iii. Do not use *do, does,* or *did* after question words in noun clauses.	Do you know **what time the store opens?** = (What time does the store open?) Do you know **how much you paid?** = (How much did you pay?)

A Where are the people? Write *D* (department store), *H* (hardware store), or *P* (pharmacy).

_____ 1. "Can you tell me which floor men's clothing is on?"

_____ 2. "Can you tell me where the paint is?"

_____ 3. "Do you know how much these tools are?"

_____ 4. "Could you tell me where I can find a fitting room?"

_____ 5. "Could you tell me how long I'll have to wait for my prescription?"

_____ 6. "Do you know how many batteries this flashlight needs?"

_____ 7. "Could you tell me how often I should take the pills?"

PAIRS. Rewrite the questions in Exercise A without a noun clause. Write in your notebook.

1. Which floor is men's clothing on?

B Write questions. Put the words in the correct order.

1. nearest / is / you / do / pharmacy / where / the / know

   _____

2. remember / shoes / cost / you / your / do / how much

   _____

3. can / can / buy / I / you / me / where / some batteries / tell

   _____

4. when / cell phone / remember / you / you / can / bought / your

   _____

5. which store / know / sells / you / inexpensive / do / shoes

   _____

PAIRS. Ask and answer the questions above.

C Read the answers. Then complete the questions.

1. **A:** Can you tell me _____

   B: The fitting rooms? They're on the third floor.

2. **A:** Could you tell me _____

   B: We close at 8:00 P.M.

3. **A:** Do you know where _____

   B: I'm sorry, but the restrooms are for employees only.

4. **A:** Do you happen to know _____

   B: I think the batteries last for four years.

5. **A:** Do you know _____

   B: Nobody took your bag. It's over there.

TIME to TALK

PAIRS. Look at the questions in Exercise A. Make a short conversation for each one. Take turns asking and answering the questions.

Example:
A: *Can you tell me which floor men's clothing is on?*
B: *I'm sorry. I'm afraid that I don't work here. But I think there's a store directory near the escalator.*

Grammar to Communicate 3

NOUN CLAUSES: *IF / WHETHER*

i. We can use a noun clause to ask a *yes / no* question. Use *if* or *whether* at the start of the noun clause.	*if* subject verb Do you know **if** **the store** **has** an elevator? *whether* subject verb Can you ask **whether** **we** **can** use it?
ii. Do not use *do, does,* or *did* after *if* or *whether* in noun clauses.	Do you know **if the store sells batteries?** = (Does the store sell batteries?) Do you remember **whether you got a receipt?** = (Did you get a receipt?)
iii. You can also use *if* or *whether* in statements with noun clauses.	I don't know **if Sue will like this jacket.** I can't remember **whether the jackets were on sale.**

A Look at the sentences from a conversation between a customer and a sales associate. Put the sentences in the correct order.

Look

return = take something back (to the store)

_____ **a.** "Yes?"

_____ **b.** "Do you know if she's coming back soon?"

_____ **c.** "Can you tell me whether anyone else can help me?"

_____ **d.** "You'll have to ask the manager, and she's not here right now."

__1__ **e.** "Excuse me. I wonder whether you can help me."

_____ **f.** "I want to find out if I can return these jeans without the receipt."

_____ **g.** "In about a half an hour. She's on her lunch break."

_____ **h.** "I'm sorry, but if you don't have your receipt, she's the only one who can help you."

Now underline the noun clauses in the conversation.

B Rewrite the questions in your notebook. Begin the questions with *Do you know...?*

1. Do they give refunds?

2. Can all products be returned?

3. Does the store take credit cards?

4. Are there often things on sale?

5. Do they give rain checks?

6. Is a manager always in the store?

7. Are their prices low?

8. Do they have a restroom?

PAIRS. Think of a store you both know. Then ask and answer the questions you wrote.

C Complete the conversations.

1. **A:** Are they sold out?

   B: I don't know if ___they're sold out.___

2. **A:** Did you buy the shirt on sale?

   B: I can't remember if _____

3. **A:** Do you want a rain check?

   B: I'm not sure whether _____

4. **A:** Does your wife want a refund?

   B: I don't know whether _____

5. **A:** Did other customers have a problem with the machine?

   B: I have no idea whether _____

6. **A:** Can I exchange this?

   B: I'm not sure if _____

7. **A:** Is the supermarket open yet?

   B: I don't know if _____

D Imagine you are in the stores. Complete the questions.

1. (shoe store) Could you find out if ___you have these in a size 8?___

2. (hardware store) Can you tell me whether _____

3. (supermarket) Do you know if _____

4. (clothing store) I'd like to know whether _____

5. (electronics store) I wonder if _____

6. (pharmacy) I need to know whether _____

PAIRS. **Are any of your questions the same?**

TIME to TALK

PAIRS. **Choose one of the questions from Exercise D and role-play the conversation.**

Example:
A: *Excuse me. Could you find out if you have these in a size 8?*
B: *I'm afraid that we're sold out of that size. But we have some very similar styles in an 8. Would you like to see them?...*

WRAP-UP. **Now choose another question and change roles. Student A will be the sales associate, and Student B will be the customer.**

Grammar

**Find the mistake in each sentence. Circle the letter
and correct the mistake.**

1. Could you tell me how much does this rug costs?
   A   B   C   D
2. I don't know that if they are in business anymore.
                  A   B   C   D
3. Do you know whether the store does give rain checks?
   A   B   C   D
4. I'm afraid whether we don't have those in black.
   A   B   C   D
5. I wonder that there is more than one department
   A   B   C   D
   store at the mall.

Dictation

12 Listen. You will hear five sentences. Write them in your notebook.

Speaking

PAIRS. **Combine the information in the two boxes. Make questions about shopping
in the place where you live now. Then ask and answer the questions.**

Can you tell me
Do you happen to know
Do you have any idea
Do you know
I'd like to know

of a good butcher shop
how much will a reliable used car cost me
when is the best time of year to buy a new car
where can I find a good bakery
where can I get a good deal on a used car
which mall has the best stores
which pharmacy has the best prices on prescription drugs
which store has the freshest fruits and vegetables
which stores have public restrooms

Example:
A: *Do you know when the best time of year to buy a new car is?*
B: *I have no idea. You should ask Angel. I think he works for a car dealership.*

WRAP-UP. **Share what you learned with the class.**

Listening

Look

chain stores = a group of stores owned by the same company
competition = when businesses sell the same products or services
economy = the way that money, businesses, and products are organized in a country or area

A CD 2 TRACK 13 **Listen to the radio report. Check (✓) the sentence that best expresses Ms. Caldwell's opinion.**

❏ **1.** It will be good when there are no more small stores.

❏ **2.** People like superstores.

❏ **3.** Small stores and superstores are good for the economy.

❏ **4.** It would be bad for the economy if small stores disappeared.

❏ **5.** Superstores are dangerous places and should be closed.

❏ **6.** Superstores should not be allowed to offer discounts to their customers.

B CD 2 TRACK 13 **Check (✓) the statements that you think Ms. Caldwell would agree with. Then listen again and check your answers.**

❏ **1.** Small-business owners make important contributions to their communities.

❏ **2.** Family-owned businesses are a thing of the past, whether we like it or not.

❏ **3.** Small businesses can offer their customers products or services that superstores cannot.

❏ **4.** Superstores should not lower their prices so that they hurt small stores.

❏ **5.** Small-business owners should lower their prices to compete with superstores.

❏ **6.** No large supermarket chain should be allowed in a town that already has a family-owned supermarket.

TIME to TALK

GROUPS. **Discuss the questions.**

1. What kinds of superstores are there in your country?

2. Why might someone prefer to pay more to shop at a small store rather than a superstore? Where do you prefer to shop? Why?

3. Do you believe that small family-owned businesses are "a thing of the past"? Explain your answer.

4. Do you know anyone who owns a small business? If so, do you know what he or she thinks of superstores?

Reading

Getting Ready to Read

PAIRS. Have you ever shopped online? If you have, what did you like or dislike about it? If you haven't, would you like to? Talk with a partner.

Reading Skill:
Recognizing Purpose

Understanding the writer's **purpose** (reason for writing) can help us to understand the main idea of a text.

Reading

Read the article. Circle the letter of the writer's purpose.

a. to convince us to shop online

b. to help people avoid the dangers of online shopping

c. to discuss the advantages and disadvantages of online shopping

Online Shopping

Millions of people use the Internet for shopping every day. It's fast, convenient, and it can save you money. But there are risks. Do you know what the dangers of online shopping are?

One danger is that the company may not be **legitimate**. It's a good idea to use companies that you know or that someone has recommended. If you choose an **unfamiliar** company, check that they have a real address rather than a P.O. Box. Do you know what their phone number is? Call the company and ask if it is correct. Check the web address carefully to see if the company is legitimate or a fake.

Another problem is making sure your payment is safe. Look for web sites that have a **secure** payment method. The web page is secure if the web address begins with https://. (The extra *s* means secure). You will also see a closed padlock. 🔒 If there is no padlock,

you should **think twice** about buying. If you do make a purchase, it is safer to pay by credit card than by debit card. A credit card offers some protection against theft. If someone steals your credit card number, you are usually only **liable for** a fixed amount, for example $50.

Remember to save and print out all the information about your **transaction**, including the payment details, the company information, and any e-mail correspondence. You may need this information if you want a refund or have a complaint.

Finally, never give out unnecessary personal information to a web site. Your bank account number and social security number can be stolen online and used to buy products or borrow money in your name. Don't become a victim of **identity theft**!

Shopping online can be safe, but you need to protect yourself whenever you make an online transaction.

After You Read

A Find the boldfaced words in the article and guess their meaning from the context. Then circle the best definition.

1. I called the number on the web site, but no one answered. I hope the site is **legitimate**.

   a. very busy   **b.** real

2. I am **unfamiliar** with that company. I'd better check before I buy something from them.

   a. know a lot about   **b.** don't know a lot about

3. When you see the padlock symbol, you know that the web site is **secure**.

   a. safe to buy from   **b.** will give fast service

4. If I were you, I'd **think twice** before I bought something from that company.

   a. consider it carefully   **b.** look in other stores

5. Someone stole my credit card and spent $500! Am I **liable for** the whole amount?

   a. have to report   **b.** responsible for paying

6. The **transaction** with QuickBuy.com was great—fast and secure.

   a. buying or selling   **b.** protection

7. I was a victim of **identity theft**, so I changed my credit cards and bank accounts.

   a. paying too much money for something   **b.** stealing and using of personal information.

B Read the article again. Write *T* (true) or *F* (false) for each statement.

_____ **1.** It is better to use companies that you already know.

_____ **2.** A post office box number is safer than a street address.

_____ **3.** It's better to use a debit card than a credit card.

_____ **4.** You usually cannot get a refund if you buy online.

_____ **5.** Identity theft means that someone steals and uses your personal information.

Writing

A Choose the best concluding sentence for the paragraph. Circle the letter.

   Paypal® is a business that offers a popular service. It allows people to pay and transfer money through the Internet. Customers can register their credit card with Paypal®. Then if they want to buy something online, they can pay for it with Paypal® as long as the seller is also a Paypal® member. This means people can do quick business transactions. It also means they do not have to give their credit card information to the person or company they are buying from _____.

   a. Today, Paypal® does business transactions in 55 countries.

   b. Paypal® is almost as popular as my favorite service, YouTube.

   c. Paypal® is popular with consumers because it makes them feel safe.

B Read the model paragraph. Then circle the topic sentence. Underline the concluding sentence.

Problems with Warehouse Discount Stores

   Many people love large warehouse discount stores because they sell inexpensive food. However, there can be unexpected problems with shopping at these stores. First, you must buy food in large quantities, and it might spoil before you can eat it. Also, it's easy to spend more than you can afford. The prices are so low that customers fill their shopping cart with extra things. When they get to the checkout counter, they are surprised at how much they have spent. However, you don't have to waste food or money when you shop at a warehouse discount store. Before you go, make a list of things you need and a list of things that can spoil. When you go to the store, check the "sell by" dates of food items. Take a calculator with you and add up prices. Then you will not be surprised by the cost at the checkout. By planning ahead, you can shop wisely at warehouse stores and save money.

Prewriting: Freewriting

A   *PAIRS.* **Discuss the freewriting for the model paragraph. Why are some sentences crossed out?**

- groceries at large warehouse discount stores. . . ~~free parking.~~
- convenient because you can buy a lot of stuff low prices. You don't buy one jar of coffee—you buy ten. Open 24 hours. . . Buying ~~a lot of food is not always good~~ . . . spoil—waste money, buy too much. . . shopping cart full! ~~Buy other things too, not just food.~~
- . . . Better to make a list first then you don't buy too much—Also check the dates make sure the food won't go bad . . . ~~close to my house~~ . . . bring calculator—Add it up Can U afford it?

B   **Choose one of the topics in the box. What are the dangers of this type of shopping? Freewrite for seven minutes. Write in your notebook if you need more room.**

| shopping from a catalog | shopping on eBay | shopping on TV | using a credit card |

_____

_____

_____

_____

_____

_____

Writing

Write a paragraph on the topic you chose. Write in your notebook. Make sure to include a topic sentence, supporting sentences, and a concluding sentence.

Grammar
- Reported Speech: Statements
- Reported Speech: Information Questions
- Reported Speech: Yes / No Questions

Vocabulary

CD 2 TRACK

🎧 Match the pictures with the words. Write the numbers. Then listen and check your answers.

_____ accept someone to a university

_____ dormitory

_____ financial aid

_____ give your notice

_____ live on-campus

_____ move in

_____ salary requirements

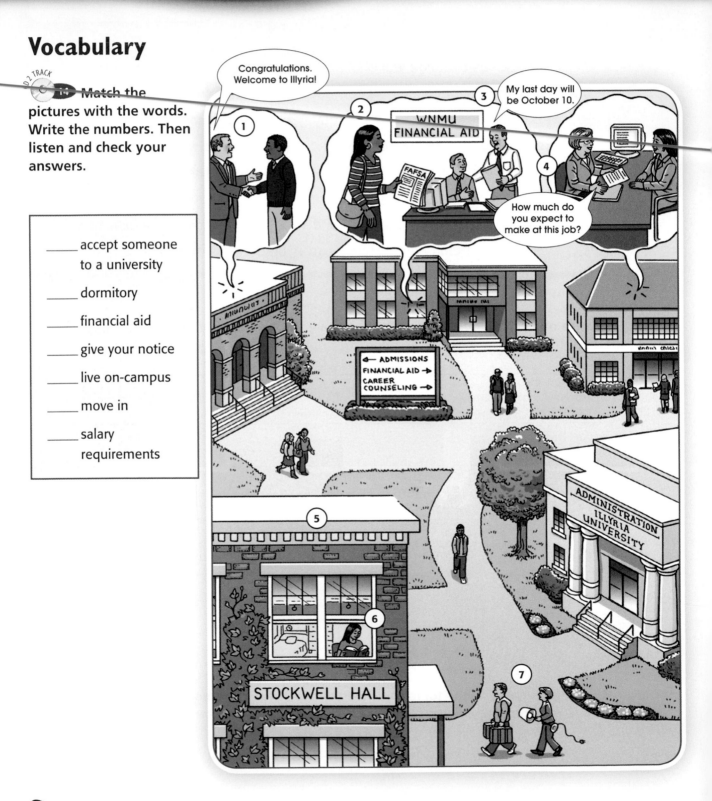

Listening

A   🔊 **15** **Listen. Tony Wells is telling his friend Myrna about his job interview. Check (✓) the statement that best describes what happened.**

❑ **1.** The interview started off badly but got better.

❑ **2.** The interview started off badly and never got better.

❑ **3.** The interview started off well but then there were problems.

B 🔊 **15** **Read the sentences. Write *T* (true) or *F* (false). Then listen again and check your answers.**

_____ **1.** Myrna asked Tony where he had gone.

_____ **2.** The doorman said to Tony, "The elevator is out of order."

_____ **3.** The receptionist asked Tony why he was late.

_____ **4.** Ms. Doe wanted to know if Tony was working.

_____ **5.** Ms. Doe said that she couldn't discuss salary at the first interview.

_____ **6.** Ms. Doe said that she would call Tony for a second interview.

C 🔊 **15** **Listen again. Then check (✓) the sentences that you can infer from the conversation.**

❑ **1.** Tony is not really interested in the job.

❑ **2.** Myrna helped Tony prepare for the interview.

❑ **3.** The interview was on the eighth floor.

❑ **4.** Ms. Doe is the manager of the department.

❑ **5.** Tony is going to have a second interview.

❑ **6.** Tony is probably not going to get the job.

Grammar to Communicate 1

REPORTED SPEECH: STATEMENTS

i. When we write someone's exact words, we use a reporting verb—for example, *said* or *told*. We put the person's words in quotation marks.

When we report what someone says, we do not use quotation marks. We use a reporting verb and a noun clause.

Henry said, "I'm busy."

Henry **said that he was busy**.
noun clause

ii. When we report what someone says, we change the pronoun in the noun clause. We can use *that* at the beginning of the noun clause, but it is not necessary.

Amy said, "I don't have any money."

Amy **said (that) she didn't have any money**.

iii. When the reporting verb is in a past form, we change the form of the verb in the noun clause.

These are some of the verb form changes in the noun clause.

Lee said, "I am sick."

Lee **said** that she **was** sick.

am / is → was   do / does → did
are → were   did → had done
can → could   will → would
has done / have done → had done

 A   Underline the examples of reported speech in the e-mail.

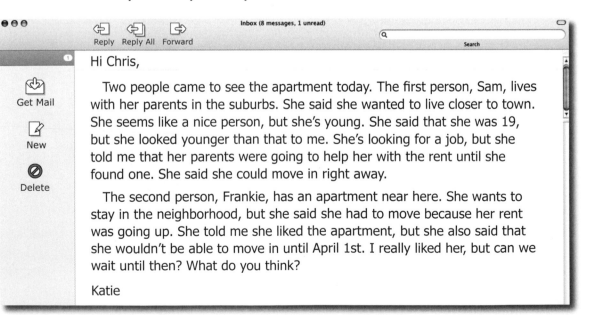

Hi Chris,

Two people came to see the apartment today. The first person, Sam, lives with her parents in the suburbs. She said she wanted to live closer to town. She seems like a nice person, but she's young. She said that she was 19, but she looked younger than that to me. She's looking for a job, but she told me that her parents were going to help her with the rent until she found one. She said she could move in right away.

The second person, Frankie, has an apartment near here. She wants to stay in the neighborhood, but she said she had to move because her rent was going up. She told me she liked the apartment, but she also said that she wouldn't be able to move in until April 1st. I really liked her, but can we wait until then? What do you think?

Katie

PAIRS. **Who do you think Katie and Chris are going to choose?**

B Write the exact words of Katie's conversations with Sam and Frankie. Use quotation marks (" ") Write in your notebook.

1. Sam said, "I want to live closer to town."

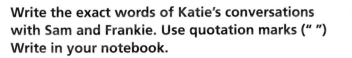

Look

Tell has an object before the noun clause. *Say* does not.

          object   noun clause
He told **me**   **that he had a job**.
               noun clause
He said **that he had a job**.

C Complete the sentences with *said* or *told*.

1. You _____ me you didn't like loud music, but your stereo is loud all the time.

2. You _____ you would use your cell phone to make calls, but you use our phone a lot.

3. I _____ you that you couldn't have any pets, so the cat can't stay.

4. I _____ that you had to give me the rent by the end of the month. It's now June 1st.

5. You _____ us you were neat, but your room is always a mess.

D Make sentences that are true about you. Circle the words.

1. **I'm / I'm not** a quiet person.

2. **I've had / I've never had** a roommate before.

3. **I will / I won't** have a lot of visitors.

4. **I need / I don't need** a parking space.

5. **I can / I can't** cook.

6. **I'm / I'm not** living with my family now.

7. **I have / I don't have** a pet.

8. **I'm / I'm not** going to be at home a lot.

ON YOUR OWN. **Imagine you want to share an apartment. Katie in Exercise A interviewed you yesterday. Report what you said. Write in your notebook.**

1. I said I was a quiet person. OR I said I wasn't a quiet person.

TIME to TALK

PAIRS. **Role play a conversation between two roommates. They have been living together for one month, but they are not getting along and are upset with each other.**
Student A: You think that Student B was not honest about his or her habits and personality during the interview.
Student B: You think that Student A was not honest when he or she told you about the apartment.

Example:

A: *You told me you weren't messy, but you always leave dirty dishes in the sink!*
B: *I only did that once. And anyway, you didn't tell me that the dishwasher wasn't working.*

Grammar to Communicate 2

REPORTED SPEECH: INFORMATION QUESTIONS

i. When we report information questions, we do <u>not</u> use question word order in the noun clause. We also do <u>not</u> use the auxiliaries *do*, *does*, or *did*.	How much **is the salary?** I asked how much **the salary was.** What days do you work? He asked what days **I worked.**
ii. When the reporting verb is in a past form, we change the form of the verb in the noun clause. We also change the pronoun.	She asked, "Why do you want the job?" → She asked why I wanted the job.
iii. We can use the reporting verb *ask* with or without an object.	They asked, "Where do you work?" → They **asked** where I worked. OR They **asked me** where I worked.

A **16** **Listen to the job interview. Then put the questions in the order they were asked.**

____1____ **a.** She asked me why I had left my other job.

_____ **b.** She asked me who they could call for a reference.

_____ **c.** She asked me what my salary requirements were.

_____ **d.** She asked me how long I had been working at my present job.

_____ **e.** She asked me what kind of experience I had.

_____ **f.** She asked me when I would be able to start.

B **Write the exact words of the questions from Exercise A. Use quotation marks (" ").**

1. *She asked, "Why did you leave your other job?"* _____

2. _____

3. _____

4. _____

5. _____

6. _____

C Read the questions these people were asked at job interviews. Match each question with the correct picture. Then rewrite the questions in your notebook. Use indirect speech.

Example:
The interviewer asked Caleb how many kinds of soup he could make.

___d___ **1.** "How many kinds of soup can you make, Caleb?"

_____ **2.** "Where did you learn how to cut hair, Koko?"

_____ **3.** "How many kinds of cars do you know how to fix, Jin?"

_____ **4.** "When did you get your trucker's license, Dan?"

_____ **5.** "Which grades have you taught, John?"

_____ **6.** "What hospital are you working at, Lynn?"

TIME to TALK

PAIRS. **Student A: Look at page 293. You asked questions at a job interview. Tell your partner the questions that you asked.**
Student B: Discuss which questions were appropriate. Now change roles. Look at page 296. An interviewer asked you questions at a job interview. Tell Student A the questions the interviewer asked you.
Student A: Discuss which questions were appropriate.

Example:
A: *I asked when I would get my first paycheck.*
B: *Hmmm. . . I don't think that's an appropriate question since he hadn't offered you the job yet!*

REPORTED SPEECH: YES / NO QUESTIONS

i. When we report *yes / no* questions, we do <u>not</u> use question word order in the noun clause. We also do <u>not</u> use the auxiliaries *do*, *does*, or *did*.	**Are you** interested in sports? → She asked <u>if **I was** interested in sports</u>. noun clause **Does** the school **have** many students? → I asked <u>if the school **had** many students</u>. noun clause
ii. When the reporting verb is in a past form, we change the verb form in the noun clause. We also change the pronoun.	He asked, "Do you want to start in June?" → He asked <u>if I wanted to start in June</u>. noun clause
iii. When we report *yes / no* questions, we use *if* or *whether* after *asked*.	I asked, "Are professors friendly?" I asked **if** professors were friendly. OR I asked **whether** professors were friendly.

A Carol had a college interview. Which questions did Carol ask, and which questions did the interviewer ask? Write *C* (Carol) or *I* (Interviewer).

_C_ **1.** I asked whether she could give me information about the dorms.

_____ **2.** I asked if she had taken a campus tour.

_____ **3.** I asked if she had chosen a major.

_____ **4.** I asked if I would be able to live off-campus.

_____ **5.** I asked whether the food on campus was good.

_____ **6.** I asked whether there were small classes.

_____ **7.** I asked whether she had applied to many colleges.

_____ **8.** I asked if she was applying for financial aid.

17 **Listen to the conversation between a father and his son. Complete the sentences with reported speech.**

A: Well, first of all, are they going to give you any financial aid?

B: I was too embarrassed to ask ___*if they were going to give me*___ financial aid.
        1. (give)

A: Too embarrassed? Well, how about the dorms? Do you have to live on-campus?

B: I forgot to ask _____ on-campus.
        2. (have to live)

A: Can you take classes in the evening?

B: I never asked _____ evening classes. I forgot.
        3. (can take)

A: What about the number of students? Are the classes big?

B: I didn't ask _____ big, and he didn't mention it.
        4. (be)

A: Do they accept many international students?

B: I asked _____ a lot of international students, but he
        5. (accept)
never answered.

A: Well, do you think he liked you?

B: I don't know! I didn't ask _____.
        6. (like)

TIME to TALK

PAIRS. **Student A: Turn to page 293.**
          Student B: Turn to page 296. Imagine that you went to a college interview yesterday. Share information about the two colleges. Start your sentences with the phrases in the boxes.

The interviewer	asked me if… didn't mention… wanted to know…	I	asked… forgot to ask… wanted to know…

Example:
A: *I asked if Hillside had a soccer team, but the interviewer said no.*
B: *Really? The interviewer at Midway told me that there was a great soccer team. Did you ask if they had a sports center?*
A: *No, I forgot to ask.*

WRAP-UP. **Which college would you prefer to attend?**

Grammar

Correct the note. There are seven mistakes. The first is corrected for you.

> I think my interview with Mr. Rogers went pretty well. He told me ~~you~~ **I** had a very good résumé. I said that it is very nice of him to say that. He then asked me why I did want to work for the company. I said that many people have told me it was a great place to work. Mr. Rogers asked me that I could give him three references. I gave him your name and told him that we work together for five years. At the end of the inverview, Mr. Rogers told me that he wanted to make another appointment to see me. I asked when would he call me, but he said he wasn't sure.

Dictation

18 Listen. You will hear five sentences. Write them in your notebook.

Speaking

PAIRS. **Tell your partner about an interview that you have had—for example, an interview for a job, an apartment, a loan, or an interview at a school or a government agency. What questions did they ask you? How did you answer?**

Example:

A: *When I applied for a visa to come here, I had to go to the embassy in Venezuela for an interview.*

B: *What kinds of questions did they ask you?*

A: *A lot…They asked me if I had any relatives here. I told them that I had a sister in L.A.*

Listening

A 🔊 **19** **Listen to two interviews. Circle the correct answers.**

1. The first interview was for **a college / a job / a roommate**.

2. The second interview was for **a college / a job / a roommate**.

3. The interviewer did something wrong in the **first / second / first and second** interviews.

B 🔊 **19** **Listen again. Which questions were the people asked during their interviews? Write *1* (Conversation 1), or *2* (Conversation 2).**

_____ 1. How long have you been married?   _____ 4. Why should we accept you?

_____ 2. Do you have any questions for me?   _____ 5. What do you do in your free time?

_____ 3. What was your best subject in school?   _____ 6. Do you plan to have children?

> **Look**
>
> **discrimination** = treating a person unfairly because of his or her race, sex, age, marital status, etc.

TIME to TALK

***ON YOUR OWN.* Read what happened at two job interviews.**

Jack Miller: "First, the interviewer asked me about my experience and how long I'd been an accountant. Then she asked me how old I was, and I said 59. She didn't say anything, but the interview ended quickly after that. She said she'd call me in a few days, but it's been two weeks and she still hasn't called."

Beth Yee: "The interview was terrible. The interviewer didn't even look at my application. He just asked me what I was doing there. When I told him that I was applying for a construction job, he smiled. I told him I'd been working in construction for five years, but he didn't ask me any questions at all. He said he would call me if there were any openings. But that was a lie. I know two guys with no experience who were hired that same day."

***GROUPS.* Talk about Jack's and Beth's experiences. Were they victims of discrimination? If so, how? Should Jack or Beth do anything? If so, what?**

Reading

Getting Ready to Read

PAIRS. Talk with a partner. What are some reasons a job interview may go badly?

Reading

Read the article. Did you find your answer to the question?

JOB INTERVIEW Tips

Have you ever left a job interview and wondered if you said the wrong thing? Daniel Richmond, a career expert, answers questions from people who made common mistakes at job interviews. He explains what interviewers want to hear and how to answer difficult job interview questions.

Q I recently interviewed for a job at a hotel front desk. The interviewer asked me to tell her about myself. I said that I was very creative and that I enjoyed cooking. The interviewer looked confused. She asked me if I was applying for a position in the kitchen.

A Remember, during a job interview, always talk about your **relevant** skills and experience for the job. It is appropriate to mention cooking if you are applying for a job as a chef, but those interests are not important for a position at the front desk.

Q The interviewer asked me why I had given notice at my **previous** job. I told him that my boss made the employees work too much overtime and that he was rude. The interview didn't go well after that.

A Interviewers do not like to hear you say bad things about a past employer, even if the information is true. You want to **make a good impression** on the interviewer, so try not to talk about **negative** things, especially about your previous employer.

Q The interviewer asked me to tell him about myself, so I did. After about ten minutes, he started to look annoyed and said, "May I say something?"

A The interviewer may have thought that you were not a good listener. At an interview, you should answer the questions, but also show that you can listen and not **take over** the conversation.

Q The interviewer asked why I wanted to work for them. I didn't know what to say.

A The interviewer was probably wondering how much you know about the company. It is important at a job interview to show that you are serious, that you are **genuinely** interested in the position and in the company. You can often get information about a company before the interview, on the company's web site. Then if you are asked this type of question, you can say something positive about the company's new products or services.

Remember, at a job interview, you want to show your best qualities: your skills, a good attitude, polite manners, and a strong interest in the job.

After You Read

A Find the boldfaced words in the article and guess their meaning from the context. Then circle the best definition.

1. I wanted to talk about how much I love my dog, but I knew it wasn't **relevant**.

   a. important   **b.** necessary

2. The interviewer wanted to know why I left my **previous** job.

   a. last   **b.** next

3. In a job interview, it's very important to **make a good impression** in a short time.

   a. show your strongest skill   **b.** show your best qualities

4. It's never a good idea to say a lot of **negative** things when you are on a date.

   a. unhappy or angry   **b.** impolite

5. A good listener never **takes over** a conversation.

   a. interrupts   **b.** does all of the talking in

6. I told the interviewer I had been researching his company for a very long time. I wanted to show him that I was **genuinely** interested in working for him.

   a. really   **b.** not at all

B Read the article again. Check (✓) the statements you can infer from the article.

❑ **1.** It's important to wear nice clothes for a job interview.

❑ **2.** To make a good impression, listen to the interviewer; don't just talk.

❑ **3.** It's a good idea to look at a company's web site before a job interview.

❑ **4.** You shouldn't ask questions at the first interview.

❑ **5.** You should be completely honest about your previous employer.

Writing

Writing Skill: Writing a Cover Letter

To apply for a job, use the standard letter format below. Make sure to say your purpose for writing in the first paragraph. Mention the job position you are interested in.

Read the model letter. Label the parts of the letter.

a. margins (space)

b. inside address (address of recipient)

c. heading (your address and the date)

d. salutation (greeting)

e. purpose (reason for writing)

f. body (details about yourself)

g. signature (sign your name)

h. closing (e.g. *Yours sincerely*)

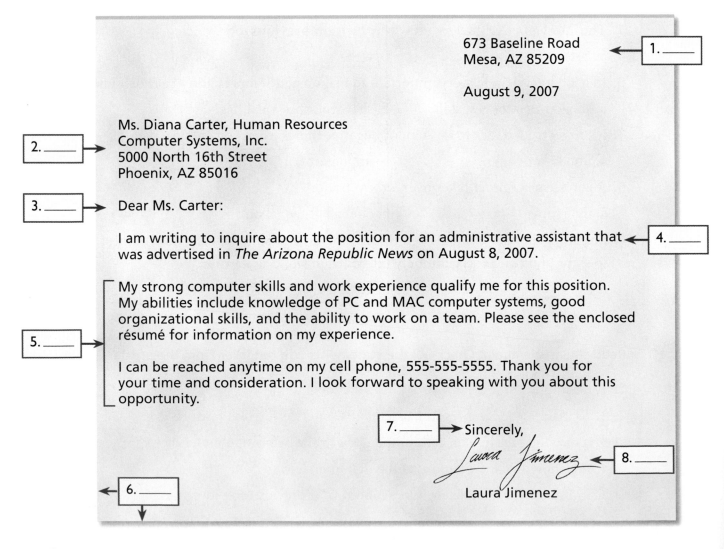

673 Baseline Road
Mesa, AZ 85209

1. _____

August 9, 2007

2. _____

Ms. Diana Carter, Human Resources
Computer Systems, Inc.
5000 North 16th Street
Phoenix, AZ 85016

3. _____

Dear Ms. Carter:

4. _____

I am writing to inquire about the position for an administrative assistant that was advertised in *The Arizona Republic News* on August 8, 2007.

5. _____

My strong computer skills and work experience qualify me for this position. My abilities include knowledge of PC and MAC computer systems, good organizational skills, and the ability to work on a team. Please see the enclosed résumé for information on my experience.

I can be reached anytime on my cell phone, 555-555-5555. Thank you for your time and consideration. I look forward to speaking with you about this opportunity.

7. _____

Sincerely,

8. _____

Laura Jimenez

6. _____

Prewriting: Completing a Y-Chart

Read the advertisement. Complete the Y-chart with the qualifications necessary for this job.

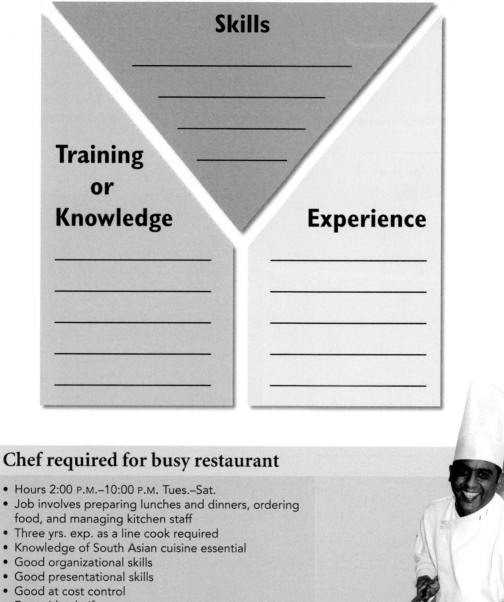

Skills

_____

_____

_____

_____

Training or Knowledge

_____

_____

_____

_____

Experience

_____

_____

_____

_____

Chef required for busy restaurant

- Hours 2:00 P.M.–10:00 P.M. Tues.–Sat.
- Job involves preparing lunches and dinners, ordering food, and managing kitchen staff
- Three yrs. exp. as a line cook required
- Knowledge of South Asian cuisine essential
- Good organizational skills
- Good presentational skills
- Good at cost control
- Fast with a knife

Fax cover letter and résumé to Mr. Weston
619-555-1700
The Green Parrot
8 Figueroa Street
Los Angeles, CA 90017

Writing

Write a cover letter for the job advertisement above or one from your local newspaper.

Grammar
- Gerunds as Subjects
- Gerunds as Objects of Prepositions
- Gerunds as Objects of Verbs

Vocabulary

20 **Complete the sentences with the words in the box. Then listen and check your answers.**

| has trouble | takes pride in |
| socialize | waste time |

Dan loves to study and learn new things. He _____ his grades. He does well
1.
in school, but he _____ making
2.
friends. He never wants to _____
3.
with his classmates after school. He doesn't like to _____ sitting
4.
around talking and drinking coffee.

can't help	curious about
postpones	is capable of
succeeds in	

Olga is very smart and _____ doing
5.
many different things. She is good at sports, and she is a talented musician. She
_____ everything she does. She is also
6.
_____ many things, so she always
7.
asks many questions. Olga always likes doing things on time. She never
_____ anything. Olga is a very special
8.
person. People _____ loving her.
9.

Listening

 A   **Look at part of this personality quiz.**

> ① **How do you feel about being alone?**
> **a.** I avoid being alone.
> **b.** I can spend hours alone without getting bored.
> **c.** Being alone doesn't bother me, but spending time with people is more interesting.

CD 2 TRACK 21   **Now listen to the conversation between Jackie and Alex. Why is Jackie taking the personality quiz? Check (✓) the correct answer.**

❏ **1.** just for fun

❏ **2.** to help her choose a career

❏ **3.** to learn how to be a better student

❏ **4.** to understand why she doesn't like being alone

B   **CD 2 TRACK 22**   **Who said it? Write _J_ (Jackie) or _A_ (Alex). Then listen again and check your answers.**

_____ **1.** "I don't think you're capable of spending more than a few minutes alone."

_____ **2.** "I just enjoy spending time with other people."

_____ **3.** "I'm not good at socializing."

_____ **4.** "So you avoid socializing."

_____ **5.** "Being messy is not the worst thing in the world."

_____ **6.** "I never have any trouble studying."

C   **CD 2 TRACK 23**   **Check (✓) the sentences that you can infer from the conversation.**

❏ **1.** Jackie and Alex know each other pretty well.

❏ **2.** Jackie really likes her job.

❏ **3.** Jackie has a lot of friends.

❏ **4.** Alex doesn't have very many friends.

❏ **5.** Alex is probably neater than Jackie.

Grammar to Communicate 1

GERUNDS AS SUBJECTS

i. Gerunds are nouns that are formed from verbs. The form of a gerund is verb + *–ing*. To make a gerund negative, add *not* before the gerund.	gerund **Being** alone can be enjoyable. **Not having** any friends can be lonely.
ii. Like nouns, gerunds can be the subject of a sentence.	subject **Having friends** is important. OR subject **Friends** are fun.
iii. Use the singular form of the verb after a gerund.	**Having** friends is important.

A Circle the gerunds. Are the statements true for you? Check (✓) the correct column.

	YES	NO	IT DEPENDS
1. Meeting new people is exciting.			
2. Doing things alone is boring.			
3. Listening to people's problems is interesting.			
4. Not having a lot of friends is depressing.			
5. Not knowing what to talk about is embarrassing.			
6. Being with people all day long is tiring.			

B Complete the sentences. Use the correct form of the verbs in the box. Are the statements true for you? Check (✓) the correct column.

get   go   meet   spend   talk

	YES	NO	IT DEPENDS
1. _____ new people is easy for me.			
2. _____ to strangers makes me uncomfortable.			
3. _____ along with people is something I'm good at.			
4. _____ to parties is a great way to meet people.			
5. _____ time with family is important to me.			

PAIRS. Compare your answers in Excercises A and B. Are you and your partner similar?

C **Rewrite the sentences. Begin with a gerund.**

1. It takes a long time to get to know people well.

Getting to know people well takes a long time.

2. It is relaxing to take walks alone.

_____

3. It doesn't bother me at all to live alone.

_____

4. It's very important to me to be popular.

_____

5. It's hard to get along with other people.

_____

PAIRS. **Which statements do you agree with?**

D **Write sentences in your notebook. Say which quality you think is more important.**

1. be popular / be respected

Being respected is more important than being popular.

2. have a few good friends / socialize with a lot of people

3. make people laugh / be a good listener

4. make people feel good / tell people what you really think

5. be very intelligent / be kind to other people

TIME to TALK

ON YOUR OWN. **Check (✓) the qualities important to succeed in life.**

BEING...	NOT IMPORTANT	SOMEWHAT IMPORTANT	IMPORTANT	VERY IMPORTANT
attractive				
curious				
friendly				
honest				
intelligent				
neat				
responsible				

GROUPS. **Compare your answers and explain your opinions.**

Example:
A: *I think that being attractive is very important. It makes life easier.*
B: *Really? How does being attractive make life easier?*

Grammar to Communicate 2

Use a gerund after a preposition. The preposition can come after a verb, an adjective, or a noun.

I believe **in working** hard.
I'm bored **with studying** all the time.
They always make excuses **for not being on time**.

A **Listen to the definitions of different types of learners. Complete the sentences. What kind of learner are you?**

> ## Look
>
> We often use the preposition *by* to explain how we do something.
> **Some people learn by touching.**

1. Visual learners learn best by _____ at pictures, diagrams, and charts.

2. Verbal learners learn best by _____ and discussing things.

3. Physical learners learn best by _____ things with their hands and bodies.

4. Aural learners learn best by _____.

5. Logical learners learn best by _____ about things.

B **Circle the correct prepositions. Then listen and check your answers.**

1. Lynn is interested **at / for / in** reading books about many subjects. She's very curious **about / to / with** a lot of different things.

2. Robert is very good **at / for / in** doing things with his hands. He can look **at / in / with** a picture and understand exactly what he has to do.

3. Sammi takes great pride **about / for / in** doing things on time. She is capable **at / of / to** staying up all night if she has to finish something.

4. Claudia believes **at / in / to** learning by doing. She is not interested **at / in / on** reading instruction manuals.

C **Write true sentences about yourself. Make the sentences negative where necessary. Remember to use the correct prepositions.**

1. I / be / good / memorize

_____

Look

memorize = learn and remember words, music, and other information

2. I / be / good / read fast

_____

3. I / worry / make mistakes

_____

4. I / take pride / be / neat and organized

_____

5. I / be capable / do / two different things at the same time

_____

6. I / often / succeed / solve problems

_____

7. I / get tired / learn new things

_____

PAIRS. **Compare your sentences. How are you and your partner similar?**

TIME to TALK

PAIRS. **Look at the types of learners in Exercise A. Then discuss which type of learner each sentence below describes. Write** *Vis* **(visual),** *Ver* **(verbal),** *A* **(aural),** *P* **(physical); or** *L* **(logical).**

_____ **1.** You are not good at sitting in one place for a long time.

_____ **2.** Closing your eyes helps you remember things.

_____ **3.** You often succeed in solving a problem when you are walking or exercising.

_____ **4.** You are better at pronouncing new words than spelling them.

_____ **5.** You are good at solving puzzles.

_____ **6.** You succeed in solving problems faster if you discuss them with someone else.

_____ **7.** You remember new words by putting them into categories.

_____ **8.** You remember new words by drawing pictures of them.

Example:
A: *I don't think that physical learners are good at sitting in one place for a long time.*
B: *I agree. So the answer to Number 1 is P.*

Grammar to Communicate 3

GERUNDS AS OBJECTS OF VERBS

i. Use a gerund after some verbs—for example, *enjoy*, *can't help*, and *can't stand*.	I **enjoy being** with friends. I **can't help laughing**. I **can't stand eating** alone.
ii. Use a gerund after some verb + object combinations.	I **have trouble remembering** new words. I **have a hard time meeting** new people. I don't like to **spend time writing** e-mails. I try not to **waste time talking** on the phone.

A **Make sentences that are true about you. Circle the verbs.**

1. I **practice / don't practice** doing the same thing again and again until I can do it perfectly.

2. I **can stand / can't stand** having to do things that I don't think are important.

3. I **avoid / don't avoid** doing things that are difficult for me.

4. I **keep / don't keep** working on a problem until I find a solution.

5. I **stop / don't stop** doing things that I know are bad for me.

Look

can't stand = strongly dislike

B **Complete the sentences about the pictures.**

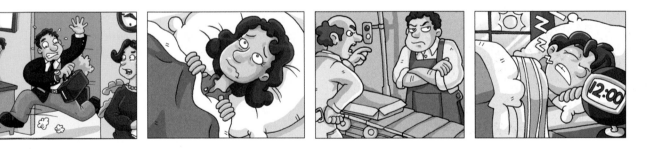

1. My brother _____ . If he _____
   (have trouble / be on time)   (keep / arrive)

   late to work, he's going to lose his job.

2. My mom _____ . When I go out at night,
   (can't stop / worry about me)

   she _____ .
   (have a hard time / sleep)

3. My boss _____ . If he _____
   (keep / lose his temper)   (not stop / yell)

   at me, I'm going to quit.

4. My son _____ .
   (waste too much time / sleep)

C **Read the situations and give advice. Use the words in parentheses.**

1. My nephew moved in with me last year. He is having trouble making friends, so he spends all of his free time with me. I think he needs friends his own age. (keep)

   Tell him he can't keep spending his free time with you. He needs to keep

   trying to make friends.

2. When my cousin talks about her ex-boyfriend, she usually cries. I can't stand listening to her talk about him all the time! (avoid)

   _____

   _____

3. I want to get my own apartment, but my mother gets depressed when I say that. I feel sorry for her, but I resent not being able to live my own life. (postpone)

   _____

   _____

4. My niece avoids being with the family. We invite her to everything, but she hardly ever comes. We have a hard time understanding her behavior. (stop)

   _____

   _____

5. I'm very afraid of speaking in public. I've been asked to give a speech at my graduation. I'm thinking about saying no, but I don't want my teachers to be disappointed in me. (practice)

   _____

   _____

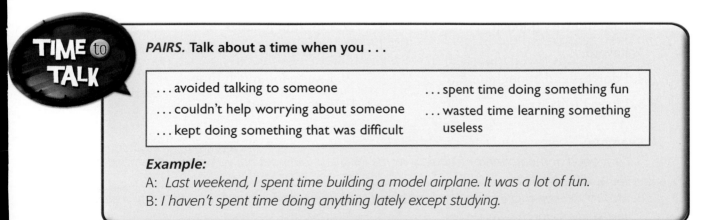

TIME to TALK

PAIRS. **Talk about a time when you . . .**

. . . avoided talking to someone

. . . couldn't help worrying about someone

. . . kept doing something that was difficult

. . . spent time doing something fun

. . . wasted time learning something useless

Example:

A: *Last weekend, I spent time building a model airplane. It was a lot of fun.*

B: *I haven't spent time doing anything lately except studying.*

Review and Challenge

Grammar

Correct the advertisement. There are six mistakes. The first mistake is corrected for you.

Strangers Today, Friends Tomorrow

Do you know people who spend all their free time ~~to sit~~ *sitting* in front of a computer? Are they bad at socializing? If you are interested in help them, tell them about the new book *Strangers Today, Friends Tomorrow*. They won't have trouble to find it in their local bookstore or library, and read it will not take long. The writer succeeds in give a lot of useful advice in just 100 pages. But the most important information is the last sentence of the book: "Being with other people are important, and everyone is capable of changing."

Dictation

CD 2 TRACK **26** **Listen. You will hear five sentences. Write them in your notebook.**

Speaking

PAIRS. **Talk about your experience as a language learner. Complete the sentences. Then give each other advice.**

1. I am good at…

2. I am not very good at…

3. I avoid…

4. I don't spend enough time…

5. I have difficulty…

6. I have fun…

7. I need to practice…

8. I take pride in…

9. I waste too much time…

10. I worry about…

Example:

A: *I am good at memorizing vocabulary words for a test, but I am not very good at remembering them after the test.*

B: *Maybe you can make vocabulary cards and study them a couple of times every day, instead of just studying them before a test.*

 Unit 12

Listening

A 🔘 **27** **Listen to a college lecture. Who is the lecture for? Check (✓) the correct answer.**

❏ **a.** students who are studying to be teachers

❏ **b.** students who are having trouble at school

❏ **c.** visual, verbal, and logical learners

B 🔘 **27** **Check (✓) the sentences that are true according to the lecture. Then listen again and check your answers.**

❏ **1.** This is the first class on learning styles.

❏ **2.** Most teachers are good at teaching aural and physical learners.

❏ **3.** Aural learners are good at remembering people's names.

❏ **4.** Reading out loud is a good way for many aural learners to study.

❏ **5.** Listening to music and studying at the same time is never a good idea.

❏ **6.** Sitting and listening to the teacher is not easy for physical learners.

❏ **7.** Physical learners are better at remembering things if they move around when they study.

TIME to TALK

GROUP. **Discuss the questions.**

1. Are you or is anyone you know an aural or a physical learner? How do you know?

2. Do you agree with the lecturer that teachers are better at teaching visual, verbal, and logical learners than they are at teaching aural and physical learners? Use specific examples from your own experience to explain your answer.

3. When you are having trouble learning something, what do you do? Give a specific example.

4. Are you good at remembering things? If so, what kinds of things are you good at remembering? Is there anything that you are not good at remembering? What do you do when you want to remember something?

Reading

Getting Ready to Read

Read the article as fast as you can. Use one of the techniques in the box.

Reading

Read the article. What makes someone a good entrepreneur?

> **Reading Skill: Improving Reading Speed**
>
> When you read too slowly, it may be difficult to understand the text. To read faster, try these techniques:
> 1. Try not to focus on every word.
> 2. Increase your vocabulary to recognize more words.
> 3. Don't move your lips when you read. This slows down your reading.
> 4. Use your hand or an index card to guide your eyes down the page.

WHAT MAKES A SUCCESSFUL ENTREPRENEUR?

Many people dream of starting their own business. However, few of them actually try it, and even fewer succeed. So what makes the lucky few successful? Is it their good ideas? Is it luck? Is it personality?

Entrepreneurs are people who start their own company and take financial risks to do so. Their company sometimes offers a completely new product or service. It is not always certain if the company will succeed, but entrepreneurs are very hardworking. Even when their company has problems, entrepreneurs refuse to **give up**. They believe anything is possible and they can persuade others, too, that their company will succeed. What makes entrepreneurs work so hard? It is not only money. Entrepreneurs want to make a profit, but **achievement** is also important to them.

Two examples of successful entrepreneurs are Debbie Fields, who started Mrs. Fields Cookies, and Jeff Bezos, who started the Internet company amazon.com.

Debbie Fields had always loved making cookies. She got married when she was 19 years old and quickly became bored with being a housewife. So in 1977, she persuaded her bank manager to **back** her business idea for a cookie store. Halfway through her first day of business, she had not sold a single cookie, so she went outside and started handing out her cookies for free. Soon people were waiting outside to buy more cookies. Now there are hundreds of Mrs. Fields cookie stores all over the country.

Jeff Bezos started in business by **analyzing** the top twenty mail order businesses. These companies sell products by mailing catalogs to customers at home. Jeff tried to think of a product that could be sold more effectively online. He **came up with** the idea of selling books, because a book catalog is too big to mail but is perfect for the Internet. He left his job and started his business in his home garage. His parents **invested** $300,000. It was most of their life savings. "We weren't **betting on** the Internet," his mother said, "We were betting on Jeff." Now they are billionaires.

After You Read

 A   **Find the boldfaced words in the article and guess their meaning from the context. Then complete the sentences with the words.**

1. You should be proud of yourself. The work you did is a real _____.

2. She's so creative and she writes music so fast! She _____ a new song last night.

3. They were willing to _____ my idea for a business.

4. _____ will accept financial risks in order to start a business.

5. Sometimes life is difficult, but it is important not to _____.

6. I _____ my money in a new company.

7. Of course, I don't know who the winner will be, but I'm _____ Joe. He's great!

8. Before you start a company, you should spend time _____ the risks.

B   **Read the article again. Then circle the statements that you can infer.**

1. So in 1977, she (Debbie Fields) persuaded her bank manager to back her business idea for a cookie store.

   a. Debbie Fields needed to borrow money to open her business.
   b. Debbie had enough money to open her business on her own.

2. Halfway through her first day of business, she had not sold a single cookie, so she went outside and started handing out her cookies for free.

   a. Debbie was a person who gave up easily.
   b. Debbie found ways to overcome problems.

3. He (Jeff Bezos) left his job and started his business in his garage.

   a. Jeff Bezos was a person who took risks.
   b. Jeff didn't like his boss.

4. His parents invested $300,000. It was most of their life savings.

   a. Jeff's parents were careless with their money.
   b. Jeff's parents were confident that their son would succeed.

Writing

Read the model essay. Then answer the questions.

Factors for a Pilot's Success

(1) When people think about a career, they often think about the education or training that it requires. However, the right skills and personality are also important for success. To become a successful pilot, a person must have specific skills and the right personality to fly a plane.

(2) First of all, pilots have to have strong logical and mathematical skills in order to control heavy aircraft in all kinds of weather. These skills help them make fast, correct decisions about distances. About half of all airplane crashes happen during approach and landing, so pilots need to make the best decision about how to fly or land the plane in bad weather.

Personality is also an important factor for a pilot. Pilots need to be watchful and careful. An airplane can be worth over a hundred million dollars, and pilots need to check many details, such as aircraft condition, departure, destination, weather, and fuel. A pilot cannot be careless with these details or the plane could crash. Pilots also need to be calm. For example, if one of the plane's engines fails, the pilot must make a safe emergency landing. He must not panic.

(3) Of course, education and training are often important for career success. Pilots need to find a good flight instructor. But education by itself does not mean success. For many careers, natural skills and personality may be equally important.

1. Look at the introduction. What is the main idea of the essay? Circle the letter.

a. Education and training are less important than skills for a job.

b. Pilots must have math skills and a calm personality.

c. The right skills and personality are important for a pilot's success.

2. Underline the topic sentence in each body paragraph.

Prewriting: Using Guided Writing

Choose one of the jobs in the box or your own idea. Then answer the questions. Write in complete sentences or notes.

| sales person | police officer | childcare worker | (your idea): _____ |

Introduction

What is the job you have chosen to write about? Describe it. _____

_____

What two skills or personality traits are important for the job? Write your main idea:

_____

_____

Body Paragraph 1

What is the first important skill or personality trait? Write your topic sentence:

_____

_____

Why is this skill or trait important? List two reasons:

A: _____

B: _____

Body Paragraph 2

What is the second important skill or personality trait? Write your topic sentence:

_____

_____

Why is this skill or trait important? List two reasons:

A: _____

B: _____

Conclusion

What is your final idea? What qualities are needed for this job? _____

_____

_____

Writing

Write an essay about the topic you chose. Use your ideas from your guided writing. Add or change sentences as necessary. Make sure to include a main idea and topic sentences. Write in your notebook.

Unit 13
Looking Back

Vocabulary

CD 2 TRACK **28** Complete the sentences with the words in the box. Then listen and check your answers.

convinced	promised	warned

My parents didn't want me to go so far away, but
I _____ them to let me go. When the day
1.
came to leave, I _____ to write often. When
2.
my father _____ me to be careful, I told
3.
him not to worry.

didn't mind	pretended	refused

I _____ being alone on the plane because
4.
I didn't want to talk to anyone. I felt very sad
about leaving my family. The flight was long,
but I _____ to eat or drink anything. I was
5.
hungry, but I _____ not to be. The only
6.
food I wanted was my mother's.

encouraged	expected	managed

When I arrived, I _____ my cousin to meet
7.
me, but he wasn't there. I looked at some maps
and _____ to get to his place by bus.
8.
I've been here four months now. My cousin
_____ me to register for Spanish classes. Now
9.
I know some Spanish, and I feel more comfortable.

Listening

A **29** **Listen to the conversation. What are the man and woman talking about? Check (✓) the correct answer.**

❏ **1.** They are comparing life on a farm to life in the city.

❏ **2.** The woman is telling the man about her past.

❏ **3.** They are talking about taking horseback riding lessons.

> **Look**
>
> **freedom** = when you are able to do and live as you wish without being afraid
>
> **look back** = think about the past

cowboy

B **29** **Listen again. Complete the sentences with the words in the box. (Be careful! There are four extra words.)**

alone	cowboy	freedom	horse	live
back	difficult	fun	inside	work

1. The woman used to _____ on a farm.

2. It was _____ for her to get used to living in the city.

3. She still isn't used to being _____ all day.

4. She was used to having a lot of _____.

5. She often pretended to be a _____.

6. Her mother taught her not to look _____.

C **29** **Listen again. Check (✓) the sentences you can infer from the conversation.**

❏ **1.** This is the first time that the man has asked the woman about her childhood.

❏ **2.** The woman was a lonely child.

❏ **3.** The man has lived on a farm.

❏ **4.** The woman wanted to move to the city.

❏ **5.** The woman misses living in the country.

❏ **6.** The woman has good memories of her childhood.

USED TO DO AND BE USED TO DOING

i. We use *used to* + verb for past habits or states (something that happened again and again in the past). Notice the spelling of the negative form.	I **used to get up** early every day, but now I get up late. College **used to be** cheap. Now it costs a lot. We **didn't use to** pay so much.
ii. We can also use the simple past for past habits and states, but *used to* + verb emphasizes that the situation is no longer true.	There **was** a school on Pine Street. (= Maybe it is still there, and maybe it isn't.) There **used to be** a school on Pine Street. (= There isn't a school there anymore.)
iii. We use *be used to* + gerund for something that is not difficult because it has happened many times before.	I **am used to waking up** early. (= It isn't difficult for me to wake up early because I do it all the time.)
iv. We use *get used to* + gerund for something that becomes easier because it has happened many times before.	I'm **getting used to waking** up early. (= It's still a little difficult for me to wake up early, but it's not as difficult as it was before.)

A Read Nguyen's story. Then complete the chart with verbs from the story.

> I used to live in a small village in Vietnam. I used to walk everywhere. I never went anywhere in a car, and I had never seen a subway. When we moved here to Canada, it was so different. I wasn't used to living in a big city and I couldn't get used to hearing cars and trucks all night long. I also had to take the subway to school, and that was frightening. Now I'm used to taking the subway everywhere. The other big change for me was English. I didn't speak any English when I came here, so I didn't use to play with the other kids during recess. Now I've gotten used to speaking English at school, but I still speak Vietnamese at home.

USED TO + VERB	BE OR GET USED TO + GERUND (OR NOUN)
used to live	wasn't used to living

B Maritsa talks about changes in her life since she moved from Brazil. Write sentences with *used to*.

1. Now I live in a house. _I used to live in an apartment._

2. I hardly ever cook now. _____

3. Now I drive all the time. _____

4. I don't see my family now. _____

5. I'm busy all the time now. _____

C Lydia moved to a new country two months ago. Write sentences with *be used to*.

Before	Now
1. She lived in a small town.	_She isn't used to living_ in a big city.
2. She ate a big meal at lunchtime.	_____ a sandwich for lunch.
3. She always walked to work.	_____ public transportation.
4. She shopped at street markets.	_____ supermarkets.
5. She wore summer clothes all the time.	_____ winter clothes.

PAIRS. Imagine that it is one year later. What has Lydia gotten used to? What is she still getting used to? Talk to your partner.

Example: I think she's still getting used to living in a city. That's hard to get used to.

D Make true sentences about how your life has changed since you were a child.

1. I used to _____ when I was a kid.

2. I didn't use to _____, but now I do.

3. Now I'm used to _____.

4. I didn't think I'd ever get used to _____, but I did.

5. I don't think I'll ever get used to _____.

PAIRS. Talk about an important change in your life. Choose a topic from the box, or your own idea. Use *used to*, *be used to*, and *get used to*.

graduating from school	moving out of your parents' house	starting a new job
losing a job	moving to a new city or country	

Example:
A: *I used to live in Los Angeles. I moved to San Francisco last year. It's very different here. I had to get used to walking a lot. I never used to walk in L.A.*

Grammar to Communicate 2

VERB + INFINITIVE OR GERUND

i. Use an infinitive after some verbs such as *decide* and *hope*.	He **decided not to go** to college. He **hopes to find** a job when he graduates.
ii. Use a gerund after some verbs such as *dislike* and *can't stand*.	I **dislike doing** homework, and I **can't stand taking** tests.
iii. Use an infinitive or gerund after some verbs such as *like*, *begin*, and *hate*. The meaning doesn't change.	I **don't like to speak** English. OR I **don't like speaking** English. I **began to learn** a few years ago. OR I **began learning** English a few years ago.
iv. Put *not* before a gerund or infinitive to make it negative.	I hated **not being** outside. OR I hated **not to be** outside.

A   **30** **Three people talk about their memories. Listen and complete the sentences.**

1. Gary

2. Miriam

3. Ryan

1. I wasn't the greatest student at first. I _____ to do homework, so I never knew the answers when teachers called on me. I _____ reading too. I hardly ever went to the library. I didn't study, but I _____ to pass the tests. I _____ to do better in ninth grade. That's when we moved, and I _____ going to a new school.

2. I was scared a lot in school. I used to _____ raising my hand because I didn't want people to laugh at me. I _____ to be sick when we had a test because I was afraid of doing badly. I _____ being so afraid when I _____ to relax.

3. I wasn't a very nice student. I never _____ to clean the board, and I _____ to work in a group with the other students. I _____ getting into trouble because I didn't want to listen to the teacher. I don't know how the teachers and other students _____ being around me.

B Look at the verbs in the box. Write them in the correct columns of the chart. For help, look at page 287.

avoid	hate	learn	offer	refuse	stop
can't stand	keep	manage	pretend	start	

VERB + INFINITIVE	VERB + GERUND	VERB + INFINITIVE OR GERUND
pretend		hate

C Complete the sentences about Andy when he was little. Write the gerund or infinitive.

1. I could only manage _____ still for a few minutes.
   (sit)

2. Every day I had to promise _____ out of my seat.
   (not / get)

3. I enjoyed _____ school in the summer.
   (not / have)

4. I kept _____ my classmates.
   (bother)

5. I disliked _____ inside all day.
   (be)

6. I pretended _____ my teachers.
   (not / understand)

D Complete the sentences about your childhood. Use a gerund or an infinitive.

1. By the time I was 10, I had learned _____

2. When I was a kid, I used to avoid _____

3. When I was little, I couldn't stand _____

4. I never minded _____

5. When I was young, I planned _____

TIME to TALK

PAIRS. Talk about what you were like as a child. Use the sentences in Exercises C and D and your own ideas.

Example:
A: *I sometimes pretended not to understand my teachers.*
B: *I didn't, but I used to pretend to be sick a lot.*

Grammar to Communicate 3

VERB + OBJECT + INFINITIVE

i. Some verbs can have an infinitive or an object + infinitive after them—for example, *ask, expect, need, want, would like*. The meanings of the two sentences are different.

verb	infinitive
I want	to go.

verb	object	infinitive
I want	you	to go.

ii. Some verbs must have an object before the infinitive—for example, *advise, allow, convince, encourage, teach, tell, warn*.

	verb	object	infinitive
My mother	taught	me	to work hard.

NOT My mother taught to work hard.

 A **31** **Listen to Dan talk about his relationship with his parents when he was a teenager. Complete the sentences. Then listen again and check your answers.**

allowed	expected	will teach
didn't allow	taught	would like
encouraged	wanted	

When I was a teenager, my parents were very strict.

They _____ me to come home right after
1.

school and do my homework. They _____ me
2.

to go out with my friends during the week. Saturday

was the only night that they _____ me to go
3.

out. My parents also _____ me to get a good education, and they _____
4. 5.

me to work hard. They really _____ me to succeed. When I have kids, I
6.

_____ them to work hard too, but I'm not going to be as strict as my parents were.
7.

I _____ my kids to have more freedom than I did. It's important for children to
8.

obey their parents, but I think it's also important for children to have fun.

 Unit 13

B Rewrite the underlined sentences. Use the words in parentheses.

1. George said to Rita, "Will you marry me? I love you."

   George asked Rita to marry him.
   (ask)

2. Rita's mother said, "Finish college first. You can always get married later."

   _____
   (advise)

3. Rita's grandmother said, "Don't rush into marriage. You don't want to make a mistake."

   _____
   (warn)

4. Rita's father said, "Marry George. He'll be a good husband."

   _____
   (encourage)

5. Rita's best friend said, "Don't get married now. You're too young."

   _____
   (tell)

6. Rita's sister said, "Don't make a decision right away. Think about it for a while." Rita agreed.

   _____
   (convince)

C Write sentences with the words in the boxes. Make the sentences negative where necessary. Write in your notebook.

Most parents My parents	advise encourage expect want would like	me their children their daughters their sons	be independent get a good education get married get married at a young age give them grandchildren live with them forever make a lot of money move far away

Example:
Most parents want their children to get a good education.
My parents wanted me to get a good education.

GROUPS. **Talk about what kind of parent you would like to be.** OR
If you have children, talk about what kind of parent you are.

Example:
When I have children, I will expect them to listen to me all the time. OR
I have two children. I don't allow them to play outside after dark.

Review and Challenge

Grammar

Find the mistake in each sentence. Circle the letter and correct the mistake.

1. I used to refuse helping around the house, but now I do the housework all the time.
   A   B   C   D

2. Young people are used to offer to help elderly people a lot more than they do now.
   A   B   C   D

3. Our kids are used to speaking English in school, but we expect them speaking Chinese at home.
   A   B   C   D

4. I am used to live far away from my family and friends, but I don't like it.
   A   B   C   D

5. I used to make all the meals, but now I want that my wife to cook.
   A   B   C   D

Dictation

CD 2 TRACK **32** **Listen. You will hear five sentences. Write them in your notebook.**

Speaking

ON YOUR OWN. **Check (✓) the sentences that were true when you were growing up.**

❏ 1. Boys used to have more freedom than girls.

❏ 2. Many mothers warned their daughters not to get married at a young age.

❏ 3. Most girls expected to get married and have children.

❏ 4. Most men did not want their wives to work.

❏ 5. Most women didn't mind staying at home and taking care of the house and kids.

❏ 6. Most men were not used to helping with the housework.

❏ 7. Most parents encouraged their daughters to go to university.

❏ 8. Women's lives used to be a lot easier than they are today.

GROUPS. **Tell your classmates where you grew up. Then compare your answers and talk about your experiences growing up there. Talk about whether things have changed or not.**

Example:
I grew up in Shanghai, China. Boys definitely used to have more freedom than girls, but things are different today. Nowadays girls in Shanghai expect to have the same opportunities as boys. And parents encourage their daughters to go to university.

Listening

A  **33** Listen. Why did Isabel Muñoz call her new book *Half and Half*? Check (✓) the correct answer.

❏ **1.** because she used to spend six months of the year in Ecuador and six months in the United States

❏ **2.** because she is an American married to an Ecuadorian, just like her mother and father

❏ **3.** because she grew up in two very different cultures

B **33** Write *T* (true) or *F* (false). Then listen and check your answers.

_____ **1.** Isabel's father convinced his best friend to have a party and invite Isabel's mother.

_____ **2.** Before she was married, Isabel's mother was used to having a lot of freedom.

_____ **3.** Isabel's mother finally got used to living with her husband's family.

_____ **4.** Isabel's mother used to pretend to be happy living with her husband's family.

_____ **5.** Isabel's mother moved back to the United States when she and her husband stopped loving each other.

GROUPS. **Discuss the questions.**

1. What is the hardest thing for you to get used to about English?

2. What are you used to doing in English: speaking? listening? writing? reading? If you haven't gotten used to doing these things in English, do you think you will ever be completely comfortable using English? Why or why not?

3. Do you consider yourself to be bicultural, like Isabel? Why or why not?

4. What are some of the advantages of being bicultural? What are some of the disadvantages?

Reading

Getting Ready to Read

What do you think schools in the United States were like 100 years ago? Write two ideas in your notebook.

Reading

Read the article. Look up the meaning of the words *slave* and *slavery*. Write definitions in your notebook. Then try to write a sentence with each word.

> **Reading Skill:**
> **Using a Dictionary**
>
> When you see new words in a text, it is best to first try to guess the meaning from the context. Sometimes, however, there may not be enough context to guess. Then you should look in a dictionary.

Schools in the 19th century

Nowadays we are used to the idea of **public** education that is open and free to all children, but 200 years ago in the United States, there was no public education system. Education was a family or local responsibility. In much of the United States, families lived on **isolated** farms that were far away from towns. These people had few books, newspapers, or opportunities for education. Many children never went to school. Parents expected boys to learn farming and girls to learn homemaking. Only **wealthy** families were able to hire **tutors** for their young children. Sometimes boys from wealthy families went to college, but girls **rarely** did.

During this period, citizens of a local community sometimes got together and managed to hire a teacher. The teacher, usually a man, was not paid much, and sometimes received food and housing from members of the community instead of money. Children used to go to school in the mornings. In the afternoons, they worked on the farm or at home.

The schoolhouse was often just one room. Students from ages six to twenty-one were sometimes in the same class. They studied basic reading, writing, and math. During the lessons, students used to read aloud and memorize texts. They learned from reading books with a strong moral message.

Discipline in these schools was **harsh** and children were used to being **punished**. If they were late for class or didn't listen, the teacher often hit them.

In the 19th century, most African-American children could not go to school. In northern states such as Pennsylvania, New York, and Massachussetts, some African-American children attended schools as early as 1760. There were also separate schools in some southern cities such as Charleston, Alexandria, and the District of Columbia. However, many southern states passed laws after 1830 that discouraged or did not allow education for African-Americans. Most African-Americans were slaves in the south. They could not attend schools until the end of the Civil War—and the end of slavery.

By the start of the 20th century, more children were receiving an education. By 1910, 72 percent of American children attended school. In 1918, every state required students to complete at least elementary school. By the early 20th century, most states had passed laws that made school **compulsory** for children until age 16. Also, in 1954, separate schools for African-American and white children were made illegal. By the mid-1960s, all states were following this law. At last, there was greater equality for all students.

After You Read

A Find the boldfaced words in the article. Guess their meaning from the context. Then complete the sentences with the correct words.

1. Their farm is _____ because it is far away from town and there is no road.

2. Education in the United States is _____ for children from the age of 6 to 16.

3. My cousin does not go to school. Two _____ teach him at home.

4. In the past, teachers in the United States _____ children for being late by hitting them.

5. His father owns several stores and he is very _____.

6. _____ schools are free to all children in the United States.

7. Nowadays in the United States, it is illegal for teachers to use any sort of violent _____.

8. My children are _____ sick, so they don't miss much school.

9. The teacher used _____ words with the class because everyone failed the test.

B Read the article again. Write *T* (true) or *F* (false) for each statement.

_____ 1. In the early 1800s, most children in the United States attended school.

_____ 2. In the early 1800s, rich people employed private teachers for their children.

_____ 3. Schools in the early 19th century usually had several teachers.

_____ 4. In 1840, every child under 16 had to go to school.

_____ 5. Most African-American children went to school by 1840.

Writing

The first paragraph of an essay is the **introduction**. The introduction tells the reader the **topic** (what the essay is about). The introduction should also be interesting to the reader. The introduction usually ends with a main idea sentence called a **thesis**.

Read the model essay. Then answer the questions.

My Summers in Poland

My best childhood memory is of the summers I spent with my grandmother. When I was a child, I lived in Krakow, Poland. City life was sometimes fast and confusing for a small child. But I was lucky—every summer I left Krakow behind and went to my grandmother's house in the little village of Bledzew. Those summers were my escape from the fast life of the city. When I was with my grandmother, time moved slowly. Those summers were a special time.

My grandmother had a farm with many animals. I used to help her take care of them. My favorite thing was to feed the sheep, pigs, and ducks. I also liked to milk the cows and collect eggs from the chickens. My grandmother baked her own bread and I helped her make butter for it from the cows' milk.

My grandmother loved to fish, so we used to go fishing almost every day. She had her favorite place at the river nearby. She was so skilled that we always came back with a bucket full of fish. At night we used to go back to the river and catch little crabs with our hands. We would shine a light into the water to attract them. They would come out from their hiding place under the rocks. Then we would catch them. While we were fishing, my grandmother taught me old folk songs. One of them was called "Little Bird from Krakow." When she sang this song, I imagined that I was that little bird and that I had left Krakow to spend the summer in Bledzew.

Now I live in Baltimore, Maryland. When I go to the market downtown and smell salty crabs, I think of my grandmother Helena. I will never forget the long summer days we spent in Bledzew, when time seemed to stand still.

1. What is the topic of the essay? Circle the best answer.

   a. the writer's childhood in Krakow, Poland

   b. the writer's summers in Bledzew

2. What is the thesis? Circle the best answer.

   a. The writer's childhood summers in Bledzew were special to her.

   b. The writer had a lot of fun with her grandmother and misses her.

Prewriting: Freewriting

A Choose a topic from the box or think of your own idea. Freewrite for ten minutes in your notebook.

a powerful memory from my childhood	my first day in school / at a new job
a difficult decision	my first month in this country

B Look at the ideas in your freewriting. What was important or powerful about the experience? Circle the sentences. Copy them below. Then write your thesis (main idea).

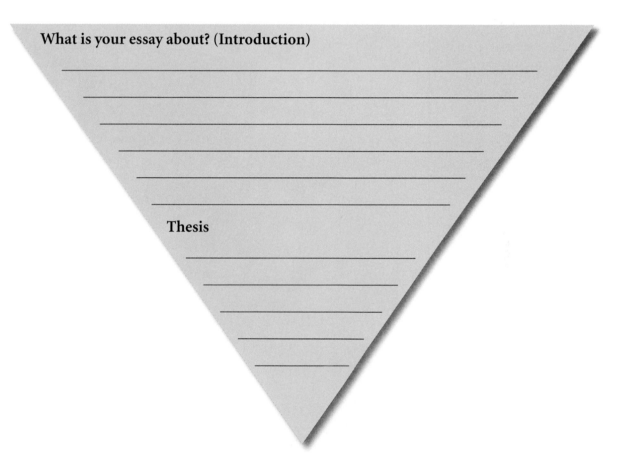

What is your essay about? (Introduction)

_____

_____

_____

_____

_____

_____

Thesis

_____

_____

_____

_____

_____

Writing

Write an essay about your powerful memory. Include your introduction above. Then write one or more body paragraphs that explain what happened. In the conclusion, say what you learned.

Unit 14
Socializing

Grammar

- Suggestions and Offers: *Let's / Let me / Why don't we / Why don't I*
- Preferences: *Would rather / Would prefer*
- Polite Requests: *Would you mind*

Vocabulary

CD 2 TRACK 34 Match the numbers with the words. Write the numbers. Then listen and check your answers.

_____ brunch

_____ get the door

_____ get-together

_____ go for a drive

_____ go out to a restaurant

_____ potluck

_____ take-out

_____ take your coat

BENNY'S

SPECIAL
10 AM – 1PM

Eggs Benedict
French Toast
Coffee Juice

$ 10.00

Tim! Welcome to the party!

Listening

A  **35** Listen to the conversations. Match the items to make correct sentences about the people.

_____ **1.** Gilda   **a.** is the new neighbor.

_____ **2.** Paul   **b.** lives in apartment 4C.

_____ **3.** Rita   **c.** is having a potluck.

_____ **4.** Tom   **d.** thinks the complex is noisy.

B **36** Listen again to the second conversation. Who said it? Write _T_ (Tom), _G_ (Gilda), _P_ (Paul), or _R_ (Rita).

_____ **1.** "Here, let me take your coat."

_____ **2.** "OK, let's go meet the neighbors."

_____ **3.** "Which would you prefer?"

_____ **4.** "Honey, would you mind getting Tom some coffee?"

_____ **5.** "Why don't we go and sit down?"

_____ **6.** "I'd prefer to live in a house."

_____ **7.** "I'd rather not live in an apartment either."

C **37** Listen again. Check (✓) the sentences that you can infer from the conversations.

❏ **1.** Gilda enjoys meeting new people.

❏ **2.** The people live in a big apartment complex.

❏ **3.** The guests bring food to a potluck.

❏ **4.** Gilda's apartment is small.

❏ **5.** It's cold outside.

❏ **6.** Paul has a busy life.

SUGGESTIONS AND OFFERS: *LET'S / LET ME / WHY DON'T WE / WHY DON'T I*

i. Use *Let's* and *Why don't we* to make suggestions. Use the base form of the verb (infinitive without *to*) after *Let's* and *Why don't we*.	**Let's stay** home tonight. OR **Why don't we stay** home tonight?
ii. Use *not* after *Let's* for something you don't want to do.	**Let's not go** to that restaurant. It's too expensive.
iii. Use *Let me* and *Why don't I* to make offers. Use the base form of the verb after *Let me* and *Why don't I*.	Your suitcase looks heavy. **Let me carry** it for you. = **Why don't I carry** it for you?

A CD 2 TRACK **38** **Are the people in the pictures making suggestions or offers? Listen and complete the sentences.**

1. **A:** Let _____ your coat.
   B: Thanks.

2. **A:** Let _____ some Chinese take-out.
   B: Mmmm. That sounds good.

3. **A:** Why _____ a break?
   B: Great idea.

4. **A:** Why _____ get the door?
   B: I'd really appreciate that.

PAIRS. **Practice the conversations.**

 186   Unit 14

B   **Complete the conversations. Make offers. Use the words in the box.**

check	make a reservation	show you
get you some water	pick you up	

1. **A:** I can't turn the air conditioner on.

   B: Let _____

2. **A:** Do you have any more of these shirts in a medium?

   B: Let _____

3. **A:** I'm thirsty.

   B: Let _____

4. **A:** It's going to be difficult for me to get to Pedro's place by bus.

   B: Why don't _____

5. **A:** The restaurant's probably going to be crowded. It always is on Saturdays.

   B: Why don't _____

C   **Read the situations. Make suggestions. Use the words in parentheses. Write sentences in your notebook. Make the sentences negative where necessary.**

1. You and a friend are going to get together on Sunday. Suggest a cookout. (Let's)

2. You are planning a party with your roommate. Suggest a potluck. (Why don't)

3. Your friend wants to invite a lot of people. Suggest that's not a good idea. (Let's)

4. You don't have enough plates. Suggest paper plates. (Why don't)

5. You don't want to forget to invite your neighbors to your party. (Let's)

6. Your friend wants to eat Italian food. You want to get Chinese take-out. (Why don't)

TIME to TALK

Role-play the situations in Exercise C. Take turns making suggestions.
Student A: Make a suggestion.
Student B: Respond to Student A.

Example:
A: *Let's have a cookout.*
B: *It's going to rain on Sunday. Why don't we have people over for brunch instead?*

Grammar to Communicate 2

PREFERENCES: *WOULD RATHER / WOULD PREFER*

i. Use *would rather* (*'d rather*) or *would prefer* (*'d prefer*) to talk about preferences.	I don't want to walk. **I'd prefer to take** the bus. We don't want to go to the movies. We**'d rather stay** home.
ii. Use the base form of the verb after *would rather*. Use the infinitive after *would prefer*.	I**'d rather stay** home. He**'d prefer to go** out.
iii. The negative forms are *would rather not* and *would prefer not*.	I**'d rather not do** anything this weekend. OR I**'d prefer not to do** anything this weekend.
iv. In questions, use *or* + the base form of the verb.	A: **Would** you **prefer** to walk **or take** the bus? B: I'd prefer to take the bus.

A Match the offers and suggestions with the responses.

_____ 1. Do you want to get take-out tonight?   **a.** I'd rather not have them over tonight.

_____ 2. Let's go for a drive.   **b.** I'd prefer to keep it. I'm cold.

_____ 3. Why don't we go for a walk?   **c.** I'd prefer not to spend the money.

_____ 4. How about a table in the shade?   **d.** I'd rather go for a drive.

_____ 5. Let me take your coat.   **e.** I'd prefer not to spend all day in the car.

_____ 6. Why don't we invite Tom and Sue?   **f.** I'd rather sit in the sun.

B Imagine you are planning a trip to New York. (Your home is 480 miles away, and you have plenty of money.) Write true sentences.

1. <u>I would prefer to drive. OR I would prefer to fly.</u>
   (would prefer / drive / fly)
2. _____
   (would rather / stay for 3 days / go for a week)
3. _____
   (would rather / stay at a hotel / stay with friends)
4. _____
   (would prefer / see the city on foot / go on a bus tour)
5. _____
   (would prefer / visit museums / go shopping)
6. _____
   (would rather / eat in nice restaurants / eat take-out food)

PAIRS. **Read your sentences to your partner. Explain your preferences.**

C **Write questions. Use *Would you rather . . . or . . .?***

1. _____
(have a cookout / have brunch)

2. _____
(lie in the sun / sit in the shade)

Now write questions in your notebook. Use *Would you prefer to . . . or . . .?*

3. take a walk / go for a drive

4. have a potluck / get take-out

5. go to a big party / stay at home with friends

6. run five miles / relax at home

7. cook a nice dinner / go out to eat

8. watch a sports game / read a book

TIME to TALK

PAIRS. **Ask and answer five questions about what your partner prefers to do over the weekend.**

Example:
A: *Would you rather go to the movies or go to the beach?*
B: *I'd rather go to the movies. I don't like to lie in the sun. How about you? Would you prefer to go to the movies or the beach?*

Grammar to Communicate 3

POLITE REQUESTS: *WOULD YOU MIND*

i. Use *Would you mind* + verb + *-ing* when you ask people to do things for you.

Would you mind handing me that paper?
(= Please hand me that paper.)

ii. When someone uses *Would you mind* to ask you to do something and you agree, do not say *yes*. Use the responses on the right.

A: Would you mind taking this to the post office?
B: **No, I'd be glad to.** OR B: **No problem.**
B: **Not at all. I'd be happy to.** OR B: **Sure.**

 A CD 2 TRACK **39** The people in the apartment building are making requests. Complete the requests. Then listen and check your answers.

1. (2C) **A:** Would you mind _____ the suitcases? **B:** No problem.

2. (3A) **A:** Would you mind _____ me a favor? **B:** Sure. What is it?

3. (3C) **A:** Would you mind _____ at the stove? **B:** Not at all.

4. (2A) **A:** Would you mind _____ the door? **B:** Of course not.

5. (3B) **A:** Would you mind _____ to the store? **B:** Sure. What do you need?

6. (2B) **A:** Would you mind _____ take-out? **B:** Not at all.

B Rewrite the requests. Use *Would you mind*.

1. Please help me with this. _Would you mind helping me with this?_
2. Could you close the door, please? _____
3. Would you lend me your pen, please? _____
4. Can you repeat what you said? _____
5. Could you please check my homework? _____
6. Please get me a coffee during the break. _____

Which requests might you ask a classmate? Which requests might you ask your teacher?

C You're preparing for a party. Ask different friends to help you. Use *would you mind*.

1. You don't have time to make the salad. Ask Kenny.
   Kenny, would you mind making the salad?

2. You need to get some extra chairs from the bedroom. Ask Tony.

   _____

3. You forgot to go to the store and get ice for drinks. Ask Sheila.

   _____

4. Two friends brought some extra glasses, but you need more. Ask Sandy.

   _____

5. You want to put the food in the living room. Ask Mike.

   _____

6. You wanted to take the dog for a walk, but now you don't have time. Ask Lynn.

   _____

PAIRS. Practice making the requests above and giving appropriate answers.

TIME to TALK

PAIRS. Think of at least five things that you need help with. Make requests with *Would you mind*. Then listen to your partner's requests and respond. If you can't do what your partner is asking, explain why not.

Example:
A: *Would you mind giving me a ride home after class?*
B: *I'd love to, but I didn't drive to school today.* OR *Sure. Where do you live?*

Review and Challenge

Grammar

Complete the conversation with the words in the box. Be careful. There are several extra words.

don't	I	Let's	not	rather	to go
don't we	Let me	mind	prefer to	rather not	you

A: Why _____ we go to the beach today?
   1.

B: That's a good idea. Would you prefer _____ to North Beach or South Beach?
   2.

A: Why _____ go to South Beach? It's prettier than North Beach.
   3.

B: OK, but I'd _____ take the train. Would you _____driving?
   4. **5.**

A: No, not at all. Would you _____ take the highway or drive along the coast?
   6.

B: _____ take the coast road. It's a beautiful day for a drive.
   7.

A: OK. Why don't _____ go and get gas while you make some sandwiches?
   8.

Dictation

CD 2 TRACK

40 Listen. You will hear five sentences. Write them in your notebook.

Speaking

PAIRS. Do the role-plays below.

Student A: Make suggestions or offers.
Student B: Say *no* to the suggestions or offers. Continue until Student A makes five suggestions. Then change roles.

1. Your friend's birthday is tomorrow. Suggest ways to celebrate it.

2. Your child is bored. It's raining. Suggest ways to have fun.

3. Your father is very old and needs help around the house. Offer help.

4. Your girlfriend or boyfriend is moving to a new apartment. Offer help.

Example:
A: *Why don't I treat you to lunch? Or would you rather go out to dinner?*
B: *Oh, I don't know. I don't really feel like going out.*

Listening

A **41** **Listen to the lecture. What is Professor Bryant's main point? Check (✓) the correct answer.**

❏ **1.** *Would you mind* is not polite.

❏ **2.** Students should not believe everything that is in their textbooks.

❏ **3.** To learn a language, you need to do more than just study it.

B **41** **Check (✓) the statements that are true according to Professor Bryant's lecture. Then listen again and check your answers.**

❏ **1.** *Would you mind* is not always polite.

❏ **2.** Using the correct grammar is not very important when you speak.

❏ **3.** Books and teachers cannot teach you everything about a language.

❏ **4.** Native speakers always use English the way it is taught in books.

❏ **5.** Studying and learning are not the same thing.

❏ **6.** If you go to language classes and study hard, you will learn a language quickly.

TIME to TALK

GROUPS. **Discuss the questions.**

1. How do you make polite requests in your native language? Do you use special words and grammar? Is your tone of voice important? Is your body language important?

2. When you study grammar in class, do you listen for it outside of class? If so, do you ever hear native speakers using the language in a way that is different from what you have learned?

3. What are the advantages and disadvantages of learning a language in the following ways?

getting a job that requires speaking the language	taking a class
living with native speakers	taking private lessons
making friends with native speakers	talking to native speakers
reading and studying on your own	watching television

Reading

Getting Ready to Read

Look at the picture. What do you think the article will be about?

Reading

Read the article. Did you correctly guess the topic?

Minding Our Manners

Many people think that the rules for polite behavior are the same everywhere. They may not realize that how you define **politeness** depends upon the culture that you grow up in.

For example, countries have different **customs** for offering and receiving food and drinks. In Latin America, offering food or drink to all visitors is very important. If a visitor refuses to accept the food, it is considered rude, unless there is a health reason. In the United States, on the other hand, it can be appropriate for a guest to say "no" if he or she doesn't want anything. Many hosts accept this **refusal** and are not **offended** by it.

Politeness is also expressed by the way people speak to each other. Some cultures are more open and friendly; others are more **reserved**. For example, in the United States, it is common for strangers to **strike up** a conversation. They may start talking on the bus, at a subway station, or in a

supermarket. In the United Kingdom, on the other hand, it is less common for strangers to talk. Many British people are more reserved than Americans, so talking to strangers is not always considered polite.

Different customs can also be seen in behavior at restaurants. In the United States, for example, people say "Excuse me" to call to a waiter or waitress. They do not snap their fingers, because they think it is rude. In some cultures, people **gesture** with their hands or snap their fingers. It is **appropriate** in those countries and the server will not be offended.

Politeness is based on a desire to **treat** other people well, but countries show politeness in different ways. Each culture has its own customs and expectations. If we understand this, we are less likely to be offended by customs that are different from our own.

After You Read

A   Find the boldfaced words in the article. Guess their meanings from the context. Then complete the sentences with the words.

1. Why was she _____ ? I only said, "That color looks terrible on you!"

2. When they want the waiter's attention, they _____ with their hands.

3. It's difficult to understand the _____ of a foreign country when you don't speak the language well.

4. She does not talk to people she doesn't know because she is a little bit _____.

5. I sometimes _____ a conversation with strangers when I am at the laundromat.

6. She always serves her guests first. She knows how important _____ is.

7. My parents are never unfair. They always _____ my brothers and me the same way.

8. He didn't accept her _____ of marriage. Finally she agreed to marry him.

9. My boss is a little too friendly with the women in the office. I don't think his behavior is

_____.

B   Read the article again. Circle the best response.

1. The writer of the article states that ____.

   a. polite behavior is the same everywhere

   b. countries show polite behavior in different ways

   c. some cultures are more polite than others

2. In Latin America people often think it is rude ____.

   a. for a visitor to say "no" to an offer of food or drink

   b. to offer food or drink to a visitor

   c. to accept food or drink from your host

3. According to the writer, people in the United States____.

   a. are more reserved than the British

   b. do not have good manners

   c. sometimes speak to strangers

4. According to the writer, in the United States _____.

   a. customers say "excuse me" to a waiter or waitress

   b. waiters are treated better than waitresses

   c. waiters and waitresses are expected to be polite

Writing

Writing Skill: Writing Body Paragraphs

The **body paragraphs** develop the **thesis** (the main idea of the essay). Each body paragraph has a topic sentence and supporting sentences. The supporting sentences may give examples, descriptions, reasons, or facts.

Read the model essay. Then complete the tasks.

From Guyana to New York

I come from Guyana, a small country in South America. My family is East Indian, and we lived in a small quiet village with only 200 people. Our neighbors were from different backgrounds—African, European, and East Indian—but everyone got along. Then when I was 18, my life changed completely. My parents decided to move to New York City. It was a huge change for me. In New York, there were more than 8 million people, and for the first time, I saw streetlights, elevators, and skyscrapers. But the most surprising thing for me was the way New Yorkers acted.

First of all, the relationships between men and women were different. When I rode on the subway, I saw high school boys and girls holding hands and kissing. I couldn't believe they were allowed to do that. In Guyana, my parents expected me to be home at 6 P.M. I was not allowed to go out at night or have a boyfriend.

I was also surprised by how impolite young people were. In Guyana, you said "Good morning" or "Good afternoon" to older people, and you called them by a title, like "Sir." It was especially important to respect your teacher. If you didn't, you were punished first by your teacher and again by your father when you got home. In New York, it was the opposite. The high school students often spoke impolitely to adults and used rude gestures.

Moving to New York from Guyana was an incredible change for me. The crowds, buildings, and traffic were so different, but the biggest difference was the attitude. I have become a little like a New Yorker, yet I am still traditional in certain East Indian ways. I consider myself about 30% New Yorker and 70% Guyanese.

---

1. **Circle the topic sentence in the body paragraphs.**
2. **Underline the supporting sentences.**

Prewriting: Using Guided Writing

Choose one of the topics in the box. Then answer the questions. Write in complete sentences or notes.

> differences between my native country and the United States
>
> differences between my parents' generation and my generation

Introduction

1. What are you contrasting? Differences between _____ and
_____ .

2. What can you say about this topic to make your reader interested?
_____
_____
_____

3. What is your most important idea about these differences? Write your thesis:
_____
_____

Body Paragraph 1

1. What is the first important difference? Write your topic sentence:
_____

2. List examples:
   A. _____
   B. _____

Body Paragraph 2

1. What is the second important difference? Write your topic sentence:
_____

2. List examples:
   A. _____
   B. _____

Conclusion

Remind the reader what the main differences are. How do you feel about the differences?
_____
_____

Writing

Write an essay on the topic you chose. Use your ideas from your guided writing. Add or change sentences as necessary. Make sure to include a thesis and topic sentences. Write in your notebook.

Unit 15
On the Road

Grammar
- *Should / Ought to / Had better*
- *Have to / Be supposed to / Can*
- *Had to / Was / Were supposed to*

Vocabulary

CD 3 TRACK

2 Match the pictures with the words. Write the numbers. Then listen and check your answers.

_____ crosswalk

_____ intersection

_____ left lane

_____ parallel park

_____ pass

_____ pedestrian

_____ pull over

_____ right lane

_____ speed

_____ walk signal

Listening

A **3** Listen. Tim tells Susan about taking the road test for his driver's license. Circle the things in the box that he had to do during the test.

Look

back up = move (a car) backward
turn signal = one of the lights on a car that shows if the car is going to turn right or left

back up	drive on the highway	park on a hill
drive in traffic	parallel park	turn left at an intersection

B **3** Read the sentences. Then listen again. Who said each sentence? Write *S* (Susan), *T* (Tim), or *D* (driving examiner).

_____ 1. "I had to go home to change my shoes."

_____ 2. "I was supposed to be there at 9:00, but I got there at 9:05."

_____ 3. "Then I had to parallel park."

_____ 4. "What do you have to do whenever you make a turn?"

_____ 5. "When can you take it again?"

_____ 6. "I have to wait at least two months."

_____ 7. "You really ought to go to driving school."

_____ 8. "Yeah, maybe I ought to do that."

C **3** Listen again. Check (✓) the sentences that you can infer.

❏ 1. The man and the woman do not know each other very well.

❏ 2. The man knew that he wasn't supposed to wear flip-flops.

❏ 3. The driving examiner did not notice that the man forgot to look over his right shoulder.

❏ 4. The man is not very good at parallel parking.

❏ 5. The man likes to drive in traffic.

❏ 6. When you fail the road test, you can't take it again for two months.

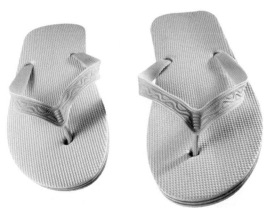

flip-flops

Grammar to Communicate 1

SHOULD / OUGHT TO / HAD BETTER

i. For advice or warnings, use *should* + base form of the verb or *ought to* + verb. They have the same meaning.	You **should drive** carefully. OR You **ought to drive** carefully.
ii. Do not use *ought to* with questions or negative statements. Use *should* and *should not*.	When **should I take** my driving test? You **shouldn't take** it until you are ready.
iii. For advice or warnings about very serious situations, use *had better* or *had better not* + base form of the verb.	You **had better obey** the traffic laws. (= If you don't, you will get into trouble.) We **had better not park** there. (= If we park there, you'll get a ticket.)
iv. The contracted form of *had better* is *'d better*.	He**'d better drive** safely during the road test.

 A **4** **Listen to the situations and write the missing words. Then listen again and check your answers.**

1. _____ slow down. There's a police car behind you.

Look
slow down = go more slowly

2. You_____ to the driver.

3. That boy _____ the old woman his seat.

4. _____ and look at a map?

5. You'd _____ there. You're too close to the fire hydrant.

B **Write affirmative and negative statements or questions. Use *ought to*. If *ought to* is not possible, use *should*.**

1. There's a lot of traffic. <u>You ought to leave early.</u>_____
   (you / leave early)

2. I think we're lost. _____
   (we / ask for directions)

3. It's difficult to find parking in town. _____
   (you / take the subway)

4. All the people aren't on the bus yet. _____
   (the driver / close the door)

5. The car is making a strange noise. _____
   (I / pull over)

6. There are two buses that go to the museum. _____
   (which bus / we / take)

C Write advice for each driver in your notebook. Use *had better* or *had better not.*

1. (get any more tickets)

2. (turn on the headlights)

3. (pull over)

4. (park there)

5. (slow down)

6. (back up)

TIME to TALK

GROUPS. Talk about good advice to give to a new driver. Use *should (not), ought to,* or *had better (not)* with the ideas in the box and your own ideas.

Example:
A: *You might be alone in a strange place when you get a flat tire.*
B: *You'd better learn how to change a flat tire.*

beep your horn	eat or drink while driving
buy a used car	flash your lights at slow drivers
buy cheap gasoline	learn how to change a flat tire
change the oil every _____ miles	talk on your cell phone while you drive

Grammar to Communicate 2

HAVE TO / BE SUPPOSED TO / CAN

i. Use *have to / has to* when you talk about something that is necessary. Use *have to / has to* + base form of the verb.

Use *don't / doesn't have to* when you talk about something that is not necessary.

> I have to stop at the light.
> He has to take his road test.
>
> I don't have to get gas. I have enough.
> She doesn't have to take the road test this week. She can take it next week.

ii. *Be + (not) supposed to* means that something is necesary (according to a law or rule), but people may or may not do it.

> I'm not supposed to turn here.
> She's supposed to stop.

iii. *Can* means that a law or rule allows you to do something. *Can't* means that a law or rule does not allow you to do something.

> I can turn here. (= It's allowed.)
> I can't turn right. (= It's not allowed.)

A **Ann Yu works at the Department of Motor Vehicles. Listen to the conversations and complete the sentences. Then listen again and check your answers.**

1. **Max Lee:** How old do I _____ to take the test?

   Ann Yu: You _____ at least 16.

2. **Sue Pike:** _____ the test today?

   Ann Yu: No. You're _____ three months. Then _____ it.

3. **Mr. Kay:** _____ today?

   Ann Yu: No. You _____ until the day of the test.

4. **Ms. West:** Does my daughter _____ to a driving school?

   Ann Yu: No, she doesn't. She _____ from you.

B **Complete the sentences with the correct form of *be + (not) supposed to* + verb.**

1. That man's going 70 miles an hour in town. He 's not supposed to go so fast.

2. The woman isn't waiting for the walk signal. She _____.

3. Look at those cars. They're all passing. They _____.

4. Why are you stopping? You _____ at a green light.

5. I'm in the right lane. I need to make a left turn, but I _____ left from this lane.

C **Complete the sentences with *can't, has to, have to, doesn't have to,* or *don't have to*.**

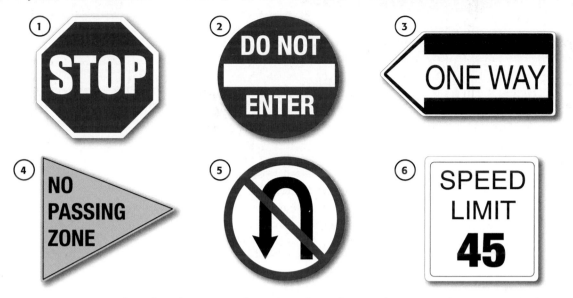

1. Lisa sees sign 1. She ___has to___ stop, but she ___doesn't have to___ wait for a green light.

2. Ms. Hassan is going down First Street. She sees sign 2 in front of her. She _____ go straight. She _____ turn left or right.

3. Mr. Gold wants to turn right. He sees sign 3. He _____ turn left.

4. A truck is going slowly. Other drivers want to pass, but they see sign 4. They _____ pass. They _____ stay behind the truck.

5. George wants to make a U-turn, but he sees sign 5. He _____ make a U-turn. He _____ go straight.

6. Mr. and Mrs. Bok are on the highway. They see sign 6. They _____ go faster than 40 miles per hour, but they _____ go 65 miles per hour.

TIME to TALK

PAIRS. **Read the sentences about driving rules. Discuss if they are true or false in your country. (If you are not sure, guess.) Then think of a few more rules to add to the list.**

1. People under the age of 18 can't drive.

2. You are supposed to wear seat belts, but many people don't.

3. Passengers in the back seat of a car do not have to wear a seat belt.

4. People older than 75 have to take a driving test every year.

5. You can't use a cell phone while driving.

6. Drivers do not have to have insurance.

Example:

Number 1 is false in my country. Teenagers can get a license when they are 16, but they aren't supposed to drive alone until they are 17. How about in your country?

Grammar to Communicate 3

HAD TO / WAS / WERE SUPPOSED TO

i. *Had to* means that something was necessary in the past. *Didn't have* to means that something was not necessary. Use *had to / didn't have to* + base form of the verb.

> I **had to have** my license with me.
> (= It was necessary.)
>
> I **didn't have to get** gas.
> (= It wasn't necessary.)

ii. *Was / Were* (*not*) *supposed to* means that there was a rule or law that someone did not obey. Use *was / were + supposed to* + base form of the verb.

> You **were supposed to stop**, but you didn't.
>
> She **wasn't supposed to turn**, but she did.

A CD 3 TRACK 6 **Listen to the sentences about Mae's bus rides last week. How did she probably feel? Check (✓) the correct column. Then listen again and check your answers.**

	MAE WAS HAPPY	MAE WAS UNHAPPY
1.		
2.		
3.		
4.		
5.		

B **Yi-Lan, George, and Paul had to do different things to get their driver's licenses. Write one sentence with *had to* and one sentence with *didn't have to* for each person.**

	TAIWAN Yi-Lan	GREECE George	GREAT BRITAIN Paul
a. take lessons at a driving school	No	Yes	No
b. drive in city traffic	No	Yes	Yes
c. stop and start the car on a hill	Yes	Yes	No
d. drive on a highway	No	No	No

1. _Yi-Lan didn't have to take lessons at a driving school._

2. _____

3. _____

4. _____

5. _____

6. _____

C

Write questions about the past with *have to*.

1. you / go / to a driving school   _Did you have to go to a driving school?_

2. you / practice / a lot before the road test   _____

3. where / you / drive / for your road test   _____

4. what / you / do / during your road test   _____

5. how many times / you / take / the road test   _____

PAIRS. **Now ask a classmate who has a driver's license (or your teacher) the questions.**

D

What did these people do wrong? Write sentences. Use a form of *be supposed to*. Use *not* when necessary.

1. Julia didn't change her oil every 3,000 miles.

   Now her car has broken down.

   Julia was supposed to change her oil every 3,000 miles.

2. Anna had an accident and drove away.

   _____

3. Peter got a parking ticket because he parked in front of a fire hydrant.

   _____

4. Two drivers got tickets because they didn't stop at the stop sign.

   _____

5. Dr. Berks got a ticket because he turned on a red arrow.

   _____

red arrow

6. I got a ticket because I didn't have my seat belt on.

   _____

7. The children didn't wait to cross the street, and a car almost hit them.

   _____

TIME to TALK

PAIRS. **Look at the pictures on page 294 and tell the story. What was the driver supposed to do? What wasn't he supposed to do? What did he have to do at the end?**

Example:
The man was supposed to stop at the red light, but he didn't.

Review and Challenge

Grammar

Correct the paragraph. There are nine mistakes. The first one is corrected for you.

My husband is a good driver, but he ~~ought be~~ *ought to be* more careful. For example, he knows he supposed to pass cars on the left, but he often passes them on the right. ~~He also shouldn't to drive too close to the car in front of him, but he does.~~ And he drives fast. I always have tell him, "You'd better to slow down." But he doesn't listen. In fact, last week he has to pay two speeding tickets. He hadn't better get another ticket soon. I'm glad I have my own car, and I haven't to drive with him all the time. And he can't to use my car either—not the way he drives!

Dictation

7 Listen. You will hear five sentences. Write them in your notebook.

Speaking

PAIRS. **Write a dialogue based on one of the situations. Act it out for the class.**

1. Student A: You are a teenager. You want to borrow the family car.

Student B: You are a parent. Your teenager wants to borrow your car. However, you're upset because he has not done the housework that he was supposed to do.

Begin like this:

Teenager: Mom, can I borrow the car tonight?

Mother: I don't think so. No, you know the rules. You were supposed to take out the garbage, but I had to do it.

2. Student A: You just took your road test, and everything went wrong. You are upset.

Student B: Your friend is very upset about failing the road test. Find out what went wrong, and give some advice.

Begin like this:

Student A: You had to take your road test today, right?

Student B: Yeah, and it was a disaster!

Listening

A **8** **Listen to the radio report. Check (✓) the sentence that best expresses Captain Thompson's opinion about teenage drivers.**

❏ **1.** Parents ought to teach their teenagers how to drive, but they shouldn't allow them to drive alone until they are 18.

❏ **2.** Parents ought to wait until their teenagers are 18 years old before they teach them how to drive.

❏ **3.** When teenagers know the rules of the road, they are ready to get their driver's licenses.

B **8** **Listen again. Answer the questions. Then listen again and check your answers.**

1. Why does Captain Thompson believe that teenagers cannot handle the responsibility of driving?

_____

_____

2. Why does Captain Thompson say that more than two teenagers in a car is usually trouble?

_____

_____

3. What four pieces of advice does Captain Thompson give to parents?

_____

_____

GROUPS. Discuss the questions.

1. Do you agree with Captain Thompson's opinion about teenage drivers? Why or why not?

2. How old should someone have to be to get a driver's license?

3. Insurance companies in the United States charge higher rates for teen drivers than for other drivers. Do you think this is fair? Why or why not?

4. Is there any other group of drivers who should pay higher insurance rates? Who? Why?

5. In your opinion, which of the following age groups has the safest drivers: 17 to 19 year-olds; 20 to 35 year-olds; 36 to 55 year-olds; or people 56 years-old and older? Explain your answer.

6. In your opinion, who are safer drivers, men or women? Explain your answer.

Reading

Getting Ready to Read

PAIRS. **Have you or has anyone you know ever been in a car accident? Was it serious? What do you think can be done to make driving safer?**

Reading

**Reading Skill:
Evaluating Arguments**

When a writer tries to persuade you to agree with a certain opinion, think about the arguments carefully. Are they good arguments?

Read the article. Circle the writer's three arguments. Do you agree with any of them?

Safer Roads

Early on a Sunday morning in April, 2006, Devon Knight, 17, died in a head-on car crash. It was 7:00 A.M., just hours after Devon's high school prom night. The passenger in Devon's car and the driver of the other car did not have serious injuries. But Devon, who was thrown from the car, died in the **collision**. He had been popular in school and successful on the high school football team. Now he is only a memory.

Car accidents are the leading cause of death among young people. In 2004, 3,620 drivers between the ages of 15 and 20 died in **fatal** car crashes in the United States. These numbers are not acceptable. Driving will always be dangerous, but we can reduce the number of deadly accidents.

First, the practical road test in the United States should be more difficult. In some states, you may only have to drive for ten minutes in a quiet neighborhood and turn left and right, back up, and parallel park. This road test is not good enough. Instead, driving tests ought to test drivers on major highways and in fast-moving traffic.

Second, we need to test drivers more often. Most drivers take their road test when they are 17 or 18 and never take the test again. But after many years of driving, things change. Highways get busier. Also, people may not drive as well when they become older. For these reasons, drivers should be required to take the test every ten years. Then they would be more likely to **maintain** their driving skills.

Finally, we need to make the consequences for **breaking the law** more serious after the first **violation**. In California, a drunk driver's license is **suspended** for at least four months the first time he is arrested. On his second arrest, his license is suspended for one year, and on the third arrest, for two years. I think that on their third arrest, **intoxicated** drivers in all states should lose their licenses **permanently**. Driving under the influence of alcohol (DUI) is a serious crime, and drivers should face the consequences of their actions.

Driving always involves risk, but we can make our roads safer. We ought to make road tests more difficult, retest drivers, and increase **penalties** for breaking the law. Then all drivers would be safer. In particular, young adults like Devon Knight would be less likely to die in **tragic** accidents.

After You Read

A Find the boldfaced words in the article. Guess their meaning from the context. Then circle the best definition.

1. collision
   - **a.** injury   **b.** accident

2. fatal
   - **a.** careful   **b.** deadly

3. maintain
   - **a.** keep the same   **b.** make something worse

4. breaking the law
   - **a.** doing something illegal   **b.** driving too fast

5. violation
   - **a.** crime   **b.** punishment

6. suspended
   - **a.** stolen for a time   **b.** taken away for a time

7. intoxicated
   - **a.** drunk   **b.** angry

8. permanently
   - **a.** for a good reason   **b.** forever

9. penalties
   - **a.** taxes   **b.** punishments

10. tragic
    - **a.** terrible   **b.** busy

B Scan the article again. Write *T* (true) or *F* (false) for each statement.

_____ **1.** Car accidents are the second cause of death among young people.

_____ **2.** The practical road test in all states makes people drive on major highways and in fast-moving traffic.

_____ **3.** People sometimes do not drive as well when they become older.

_____ **4.** The writer thinks that the penalty for drunk driving should be more serious.

_____ **5.** In 2003, almost 5,000 people died in car accidents.

On the Road **209**

Writing

Read the model essay. Then complete the tasks.

Traffic: The Road Ahead

Everyone agrees that bad traffic in our city is a problem today. Some people say the best solution to bad traffic is to have better public transportation. I think this is a good idea, but I also think that we need to build better roads and repair them at reasonable times.

First, we can prevent some traffic problems by good highway planning. For example, when cars enter a highway, sometimes they are going too slowly. They can't go fast because the on-ramp is too short, so they don't have time to build up to highway speed. The cars behind them have to slow down and this leads to bad traffic. If engineers make on-ramps longer, cars can enter the highway at the right speed and traffic will move better.

We can also prevent traffic jams by repairing roads at night. Often during the day, you have to change lanes on a highway or city street because of construction work. There are fewer lanes to drive in, so cars have to slow down and the traffic backs up. Repairs should be done at night. Then there will be less traffic in the day when more people are on the road.

Traffic in our city is a complex problem that needs several solutions. Better public transportation will help. However, many people will still continue to drive, so we need to find additional solutions. Good highway planning and night road repair are two ways that can help prevent bad traffic.

1. **What is the problem?** _____
2. **Underline the thesis.**
3. **Circle the topic sentence in each body paragraph.**

Prewriting: Using Guided Writing

Choose one of the problems in the box. Then answer the questions. Write in complete sentences or notes.

dangerous driving conditions	pollution
drunk drivers	slow traffic

Introduction

1. What is the problem you chose? _____

2. Why and how is this a problem? Write sentences that give background information:

_____

_____

_____

3. What two solutions can you suggest for this problem? Write your thesis:

_____

_____

Body Paragraph 1

1. What is your first solution? Write your topic sentence: _____

_____

2. How will this solution work? List ideas:

A. _____

B. _____

Body Paragraph 2

1. What is your second solution? Write your topic sentence: _____

2. How will this solution work? List ideas:

A. _____

B. _____

Conclusion

Why is the problem serious? Remind your reader. What are your solutions? Restate them here: _____

_____

_____

Writing

Write an essay on the topic you chose. Use your ideas from your guided writing. Add or change sentences as necessary. Make sure to include a thesis and topic sentences. Write in your notebook.

Grammar
- *Should have* for Regrets about the Past
- *May have* / *Might have* for Past Possibility
- *Must have* for Logical Conclusions about the Past

Vocabulary

CD 3 TRACK 9 **Match the pictures with the words. Write the numbers. Then listen and check your answers.**

_____ blow off	_____ flashlight	_____ lose power
_____ board up	_____ flood	_____ predict
_____ destroyed	_____ hurricane	_____ stock up on

Weather forecasters think this hurricane will hit the Gulf Coast in 24 hours.

Listening

A CD 3 TRACK **10** **Listen to the conversation. What are the people doing? Check (✓) the correct answer.**

❏ **1.** They have returned to their house a few days after a hurricane and they are checking for damage.

❏ **2.** They were in their basement during the hurricane and they have just come upstairs to check for damage.

❏ **3.** They are cleaning up their neighborhood after a hurricane.

B CD 3 TRACK **11** **Listen again. For each pair of sentences, circle the letter of the sentence that you hear.**

1. a. The wind must be blowing hard.

   b. The wind must have blown it off.

2. a. I shouldn't have that.

   b. I shouldn't have said that.

3. a. It looks like we might have gotten lucky.

   b. It looks like we might be getting lucky.

4. a. We should have stocked up on batteries for the flashlights.

   b. We shouldn't have used all the batteries.

5. a. Oh, they must have opened.

   b. Oh, they must be open.

6. a. Yeah, but they may have lost their power, too.

   b. Yeah, but they may be having power problems, too.

> **Look**
>
> **damage** =. hurt or injure something (a house, car, etc.)

C CD 3 TRACK **12** **Listen again. Check (✓) the sentences that you can infer from the conversation.**

❏ **1.** Many of their windows are broken.

❏ **2.** Other houses in the neighborhood had more damage than theirs.

❏ **3.** They were not at home when the storm started.

❏ **4.** Some of their neighbors refused to evacuate.

❏ **5.** Their neighborhood is the only place where the power is still out.

❏ **6.** The man wants to know when the power will be back on.

Grammar to Communicate 1

SHOULD HAVE FOR REGRETS ABOUT THE PAST

i. Use *should have* + past participle when you express a regret about the past or you criticize what someone else did.	You **should have listened** to the weather report. (= It was a good idea, but you didn't do it.) You **should not have gone** to the beach. (= Going to the beach wasn't a good idea.) I **should have told** you to stay at home. (= I didn't tell you, and I regret it.) I **shouldn't have let** you go. (= I let you go, and I regret it.)
ii. The contracted forms are often used in conversation. *Should've* sounds like /ʃʊdəv/. *Shouldn't have* sounds like /ʃʊdəntəv/.	You **should've** listened to the radio. You **shouldn't have** gone to the beach.
iii. The form of the passive is *should have been* + past participle.	The residents **should have been evacuated**.

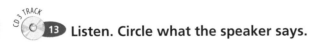

A 13 **Listen. Circle what the speaker says.**

1. You **should've / shouldn't have** come home right away. I was worried.

2. We **should've / shouldn't have** left so late. Look at the traffic.

3. The police **should've / shouldn't have** closed Route 70. It caused a lot of problems.

4. The suitcase **should've been / shouldn't have been** packed last night. We don't have time now.

5. You **should've / shouldn't have** gotten gas yesterday. Now what are we going to do?

6. People **should've been/ shouldn't have been** told where to go. Many people were confused.

B Imagine that you were in a hurricane and you did the wrong thing. Complete the sentences with *should have* and the verbs in parentheses. Add *not* where necessary.

1. You _____*should have gotten*_____ evacuation information. (get)

2. You _____ your cell phone was charged. (make sure)

3. You _____ warnings to evacuate. (ignore)

4. You _____ bottled water. (stock up on)

5. You _____ a flashlight in your home. (have)

6. You _____ the table and chairs in the yard. (leave)

C What should or shouldn't the people have done? Write sentences in your notebook. Use the verbs in the box.

board up	buy	charge	get	not leave ... outside	stock up on

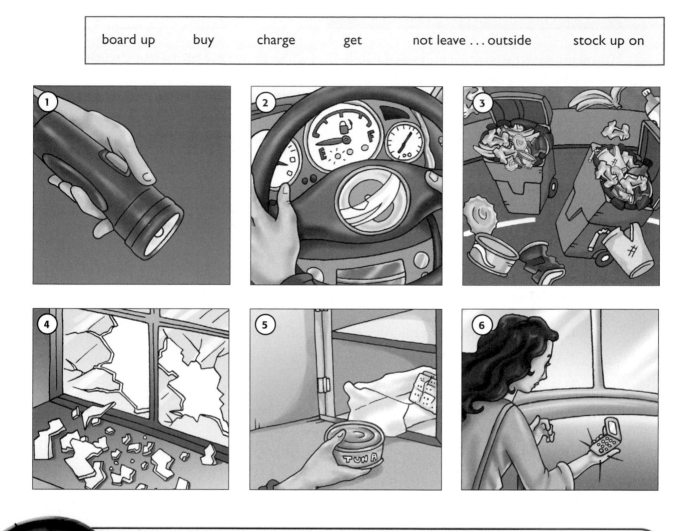

TIME to TALK

GROUPS. Talk about a time when you were not well prepared for an important event. What did you do that you shouldn't have? What didn't you do that you should have? Use the ideas in the box and your own ideas.

birth of a child	holiday	party	trip
exam	hurricane	snowstorm	visitor
heat wave	job interview		

Example:

Last year, I experienced my first snowstorm. I had never driven in the snow before. Everyone told me not to drive, but I didn't listen, and I got into an accident. I shouldn't have driven in a snowstorm. I should have stayed at home, or I should have taken the bus. I should have listened to everyone's advice.

Grammar to Communicate 2

MAY HAVE / MIGHT HAVE FOR PAST POSSIBILITY

i. Use *may have* + past participle or *might have* + past participle to talk about possibilities in the past. They have the same meaning.	There **may have been** a lot of trouble. OR There **might have been** a lot of trouble. (= Maybe there was trouble. I'm not sure.)
ii. For the negative, use *may not have* + past participle or *might not have* + past participle.	They **may not have had** time to leave. OR They **might not have had** time to leave. (= Maybe people didn't have time to leave.)
iii. The passive form is *may have been* + past participle or *might have been* + past participle.	Some houses **may have been** damaged. OR Some houses **might have been** damaged.

A **Match each question with the correct answer.**

_____ 1. Why were people at the hardware store?   **a.** They might not have had flood insurance.

_____ 2. Why did people stay in their homes?   **b.** It may have been too dangerous outside.

_____ 3. Why are people sleeping in the school?   **c.** They may have needed to buy a pump.

_____ 4. Why will repairs cost so much?   **d.** They may not have had to go to school.

_____ 5. Why were kids in the town happy?   **e.** They may have had to evacuate their homes.

B **Rewrite the sentences with *may have*.**

1. Perhaps they didn't know about the problem.

   They may not have known about the problem.

2. Maybe they called the police.

   _____

3. Maybe the storm wasn't predicted.

   _____

4. Perhaps they didn't have enough food in the house.

   _____

5. Maybe they were frightened.

   _____

6. Perhaps they forgot to take extra clothing.

   _____

PAIRS. **Say the sentences above again. Use *might* instead of *may*.**

C Shirley and Mark had to leave their home because of heavy rain and flooding. What might have happened while they were gone? Write sentences with *may* or *might*. Use the passive.

1. (The car / damage)   <u>The car might have been damaged.</u>

2. (Some furniture / get wet) _____

3. (The carpets / ruin)   _____

4. (The house / break into)   _____

5. (The garden / destroy)   _____

6. (Important papers / lose) _____

D CD 3 TRACK **14** Your friends Amy and Paul live in a town that has been flooded. You want to be sure they are fine. Listen and complete the sentences with *may have* or *might have* and the verbs.

A: I'm calling Paul on his cell phone, but there's no answer. I'm really worried about them.

B: They _____ to stay with Paul's family. I think he has relatives nearby.
1. (go)

A: Maybe I should call Amy's mother. Do you know where my address book is?

B: I'm not sure. Did you look upstairs? You _____ it there.
2. (leave)

A: I called the number I had in my address book, but that wasn't Amy's mother who answered.

B: She _____. Check your e-mail. They _____ you a message.
3. (move)   4. (send)

A: I sent them an e-mail yesterday, but they haven't answered.

B: They _____ your e-mail. They _____ their laptop with them.
5. (not / get)   6. (not / take)

TIME to TALK

PAIRS. Look at the newspaper headlines. Talk about what might have happened.

Woman wakes up to car in bedroom: Rolls over and goes back to sleep

Man falls off a 10-story building and survives

Man avoids alligator attack by taping himself to a tree

Grammar to Communicate 3

MUST HAVE FOR LOGICAL CONCLUSIONS ABOUT THE PAST

i. Use *must have* + past participle when you are 95% sure that something about the past is true. (You are not 100% sure.)	Everybody **must have left** the building. There was nobody there when we arrived. (= We think everyone left the building.) People **must not have had** time to take anything. They were standing outside in the cold without coats on. (= We think they didn't have time.)
ii. Do not use *must have* when you are 100% sure.	The building was destroyed. (You could see it.)
iii. The passive form is *must have been* + past participle.	The injured people **must have been taken** to the hospital. When I arrived, there was nobody there.

A Write sentences with the words in parentheses and *must have*. Write in your notebook.

1. People could feel the earthquake 500 miles away.

   (It / be strong)

2. My dog Jasper was acting strangely before the earthquake.

   (He / feel something)

3. There were fires right after the earthquake.

   (The earthquake / start the fires)

4. After the earthquake, people were told not to drive on the bridges.

   (The bridges / be badly damaged)

B Rewrite the second sentence of each conversation with *must have*.

1. **A:** Professor Tomkins predicted the earthquake.

   B: He probably used special equipment. <u>He must have used special equipment.</u>

2. **A:** The students got under their desks when the earthquake happened.

   B: They had probably prepared for one. _____

3. **A:** Sylvia didn't do anything when she felt the earthquake.

   B: It probably wasn't strong. _____

4. **A:** There was a lot of damage to the school.

   B: It probably cost a lot to repair. _____

5. **A:** There was very little damage in my town.

   B: The buildings were probably built well. _____

C **Complete the sentences with the correct form of *must*. Add *not* where necessary.**

A: I remember my first earthquake. First, there was the shaking. Then the lights went out.

B: You _____ frightened.
　　　　　　　　1. (be)

A: I was scared to death. As soon as I got outside, I took a cab to a friend's place.

B: There _____ many cabs on the street.
　　　　　　　　2. (be)

A: No, there weren't. That's strange—I can't remember why I went to John and Margaret's.

B: You _____ to be alone.
　　　　　　　　3. (want)

A: Probably. And they were glad to see me. They were standing at the door when I arrived.

B: They _____ a feeling you were coming.
　　　　　　　　4. (have)

A: Maybe. Anyway, I stayed three days. When I returned home, I saw the door was wide open.

B: You _____ to lock the door.
　　　　　　　　5. (forget)

A: It was amazing that nothing had been stolen.

B: You _____ surprised.
　　　　　　　　6. (be)

A: Actually, I was shocked. But I found a lot of broken things on the floor.

B: You _____ terrible.
　　　　　　　　7. (feel)

A: Are you kidding? I was thankful nothing worse had happened.

TIME to TALK

PAIRS. **Make a short dialogue for each logical conclusion.**

1. You must have been really worried.
2. The hospitals must not have been very prepared.
3. The repairs must have cost a lot of money.
4. They must not have known what to do.
5. They must have been very frightened.

Example:
A: *When I heard about the earthquake on the radio, I tried to call my parents, but the phones weren't working.*
B: *You must have been really worried.*
A: *Yes, I was. For three days I didn't hear anything from them.*
B: *You must not have been able to sleep.*

Review and Challenge

Grammar

Complete the conversation with the words in the box. Be careful. There are several extra words.

be	get	had	have	might not	should
been	~~gotten~~	has	may	must	shouldn't

A: You must have ___gotten___ a big check from your insurance company after the flood.
1.

B: Actually, we knew we _____ have had flood insurance, but we never got any.
2.

A: Flood insurance costs a lot, so you _____ have been able to afford it.
3.

B: True, but we _____ have bought a place near the river if we couldn't afford to
4.

buy insurance.

A: So it _____ have cost you a lot to fix your house. You must not have
5.

_____ able to live in your place for a while.
6.

B: Actually, it took nine months. We stayed with friends. It wasn't easy.

Dictation

CD 3 TRACK
15 **Listen. You will hear five sentences. Write them in your notebook.**

Speaking

GROUPS. **Think of four different situations, one for each sentence below. Then read one situation to the class, but don't read the sentence. Can they guess which sentence goes with the story?**

1. They may have evacuated.   3. They should have evacuated.
2. They must have evacuated.   4. They should not have evacuated.

Example:
You: *There was a flood warning for the neighborhood where my parents live. I called them, but nobody answered.*
Class: *They may have evacuated.*
You: *Yes, that's right.*

220   Unit 16

Listening

A 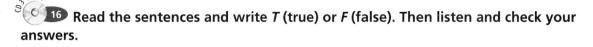 CD 3 TRACK **16** Listen to the TV program. Check (✓) the best title for the show.

❑ **1.** San Carlos: The Sun Shines Again

❑ **2.** San Carlos: One City, One Hurricane, Two Worlds

❑ **3.** Joseph Daniels: A Mayor with a Message

B CD 3 TRACK **16** Read the sentences and write *T* (true) or *F* (false). Then listen and check your answers.

_____ **1.** Hurricane David did a lot of damage.

_____ **2.** This is the first time that the reporter has spoken to the residents of San Carlos.

_____ **3.** Rose Daniels and her husband have decided not to reopen their restaurant.

_____ **4.** The reporter is talking to Mrs. Daniels on the telephone.

_____ **5.** The city of San Carlos received money from the federal government after the hurricane.

_____ **6.** Benito Juarez thinks that he will never get any money from the government.

TIME to TALK

GROUPS. Discuss the questions.

1. What questions do you think the reporter asked the mayor of San Carlos in the next part of the show? What do you think the mayor said?

2. How do you think the two sides of the river in San Carlos might be different?

3. What natural disasters have been in the news recently? What kind of help did people get after the disaster? Did you do anything to help? If not, should you have?

4. Are there hurricanes, earthquakes, floods, or other kinds of natural disasters in your country? Does the government help people rebuild after a disaster? If not, how do people get the money to rebuild?

Reading

Getting Ready to Read

PAIRS. What do you know about Hurricane Katrina? Talk about facts or opinions you have read or heard in the news.

Reading

Read the article. Make a list of questions that you have about the article.

Reading Skill: Asking Questions

When you are reading, ask yourself questions about the text to understand it better. Here are useful questions to ask:

- Who wrote the text?
- Does the writer give facts, opinions, or both?
- Do I agree with the opinions in the text?
- Are the facts correct?
- Is the information complete?

Look

federal = belonging to the national government in Washington, D.C.
sea level = the height of the sea compared to the land

HURRICANE KATRINA

New Orleans has always been famous for its jazz music, spicy food, and the Mardi Gras festival. But on August 29, 2005, New Orleans became famous for another reason—most of the city was destroyed by a hurricane. Hurricane Katrina and the **flooding** after it killed at least 1,836 people and caused about $81 billion in damage. It destroyed not only New Orleans, but also parts of Mississippi and Alabama. It was one of the **deadliest** hurricanes in U.S. history.

New Orleans has always been in danger of flooding because much of the city is below sea level. It is surrounded by the Mississippi River and by two lakes. Special walls, called levees, keep water out of the city. Before Katrina, scientists warned that the *levees* had not been built well enough. They predicted that the levees would not protect the city from a major hurricane. They were right. When Hurricane Katrina hit, the city was flooded. Eighty percent of New Orleans was under water.

Before Hurricane Katrina arrived, New Orleans residents were warned to evacuate.

About 80% of the residents left the city, but others **remained**—mostly the poor, elderly, or sick. The consequences were terrible. Most of the roads out of the city were damaged, and the Twin Span Bridge **collapsed**. There was almost no way out of New Orleans. There were not enough buses or ambulances to take people to safety. There were only two evacuation centers, which were **overcrowded** and dirty. There was not enough water, food, or police security. Some people waited for days on their rooftops before they were rescued.

After the storm, there was much criticism of the federal, state, and city government. People said the government **response** was too slow and came too late. Many people felt the government did not control the **crisis** well or respond to calls for help.

Hurricane Katrina was a deadly, violent hurricane. However, better **planning** before the hurricane would have prevented a lot of the damage. The levees should have been made stronger years earlier. The evacuation order should have been given earlier to give people more time to leave the city. Transportation, food, water, and a clean place to stay should have been provided. Better planning and a faster response could have saved billions of dollars. Most important, hundreds of people's lives might have been saved, and millions of people's lives might not have been ruined.

After You Read

A   Find the boldfaced words in the article. Guess their meaning from the context. Then choose the closest definitions.

1. flooding
    a. when water from a storm covers dry land   **b.** when water is stopped by walls

2. deadliest
    a. strongest   **b.** most fatal

3. remained
    a. refused   **b.** stayed

4. collapsed
    a. fell down   **b.** was not damaged

5. overcrowded
    a. containing too many people   **b.** containing many problems

6. response
    a. complaint   **b.** action

7. crisis
    a. question   **b.** emergency

8. planning
    a. thinking about something in advance   **b.** stopping a problem

B   Read the article again. Write *T* (true) or *F* (false) for each statement.

_____ **1.** Hurricane Katrina destroyed most of New Orleans and Alabama.

_____ **2.** The level of the ocean is higher than the land on which New Orleans is built.

_____ **3.** Scientists did not warn anyone that the city might flood.

_____ **4.** The Twin Span Bridge could not be used after the hurricane.

_____ **5.** There was not enough food or water in the days after the hurricane.

Writing

Read the model essay. Then complete the tasks.

An Unforgettable Day

When I was growing up in Vallejo, California, I thought of earthquakes as a joke, something that only visitors to California worried about. I used to laugh at my teachers when they made us jump under our desks and put our hands over our heads during earthquake drills. Nobody in my family took earthquakes very seriously. But on October 17, 1989, my feelings about earthquakes changed completely.

It was an ordinary day. I was driving toward the Mission District in San Francisco to pick up my daughter from daycare. I was on the freeway, listening to the radio. As I came off the freeway, my car started to shake violently. I thought that I must be driving over broken pavement. I wasn't worried because there were often potholes on the freeway, so I was used to driving on rough roads. But when I got to the daycare center and saw all of the workers and the crying children standing outside, I realized that something was very wrong. I soon discovered that I had not been driving over broken pavement—instead, there had been a major earthquake.

Nothing happened to me that day, so I was very lucky, but many people in Northern California were not. Fifty-seven people died and 4,000 were injured from the earthquake. There was also a great deal of property damage. The Bay Bridge collapsed, and there were fires throughout the city. After experiencing the 1989 earthquake, I made sure I was prepared for another one. I follow all government guidelines in case of an earthquake. I have realized that earthquakes are a serious matter, and everyone needs to be prepared.

1. Circle the thesis in the introduction.
2. Underline the background information in the introduction.
3. Circle the interesting details in the body.
4. Look at the conclusion. Circle the sentence that tells the effect of the story on the writer.

Look

pavement = a paved surface, especially of a road

Prewriting: Using Guided Writing

Choose one of the topics in the box. Then answer the questions. Write in complete sentences or notes.

a natural disaster	the birth of a child
the death of someone close to you	a painful experience

Introduction

1. What is the topic you chose? _____

2. What background information does the reader need to know?

_____

_____

_____

3. Why was this experience powerful or what is your most important idea about this topic? Write your thesis:

_____

_____

_____

Body Paragraph 1

What happened? Write your story in notes:

_____

_____

_____

_____

_____

Conclusion

What effect did the story have on you? How did you change or what did you learn? Write your final idea:

_____

_____

_____

Writing

Write an essay on the topic you chose. Use your ideas from your guided writing. Add or change sentences as necessary. Make sure to include a thesis. Write in your notebook.

Unit 17
In the News

Grammar
- Adverb Clauses: Reason
- Adverbs Clauses: Contrast
- *Because of / Despite / In spite of*

Vocabulary

🔘 **17** Match the pictures with the words. Write the numbers. Then listen and check your answers.

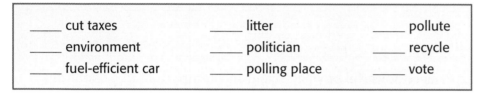

_____ cut taxes	_____ litter	_____ pollute
_____ environment	_____ politician	_____ recycle
_____ fuel-efficient car	_____ polling place	_____ vote

Listening

A CD 3 TRACK **18** **Listen to the conversation. Check (✓) the correct statement.**

❏ **1.** The man and the woman have the same opinions about most topics.

❏ **2.** They have very different opinions.

❏ **3.** They are going to vote for the same person.

B CD 3 TRACK **18** **Read the statements. Then listen again. Who made each statement? Write *W* (woman) or *M* (man).**

____ **1.** "I don't vote because all politicians are the same."

____ **2.** "In spite of their promises at election time, they do whatever they want after the election."

____ **3.** "So although you don't vote, you come in every day and complain about the government."

____ **4.** "But since I don't have the money, I have to keep driving that big old Chevy."

____ **5.** "Even though they're small, they still use gasoline."

____ **6.** "Because of our different schedules."

C CD 3 TRACK **18** **Listen again. Check (✓) the sentences that you can infer from the conversation.**

❏ **1.** The woman and the man have known each other for a while.

❏ **2.** The woman thinks that politics is important.

❏ **3.** The woman thinks that everyone should vote.

❏ **4.** The man doesn't know anything about politics.

❏ **5.** The man often complains about the government.

❏ **6.** The woman is very worried about the environment.

Grammar to Communicate 1

i. Some sentences have a main clause and an adverb clause. An adverb clause begins with a subordinator such as *because*. It is followed by a subject and a verb.	Nick lost his job <u>because business was bad</u>. main clause adverb clause
ii. An adverb clause can come at the beginning or end of a sentence. In conversation, it is more common at the end.	Nick lost his job because business was bad. **Because business was bad**, Nick lost his job.
iii. Adverb clauses that begin with *because* and *since* give reasons. The main clause gives the result.	<u>Since business was bad</u>, Nick was laid off. adverb clause (reason) main clause (result)
iv. In conversation, use *because* (not *since*) to answer a question beginning with *Why?*	A: **Why** did you do that? B: **Because** I needed to find a job. NOT ~~Since I needed to find a job.~~

A   Underline the adverb clause in each sentence.

management

cross the picket line

1. We are talking to management because we want to avoid a strike.

2. We're upset because some of our co-workers are crossing the picket line.

3. We're on strike because we haven't gotten a raise in five years.

4. Since sales haven't been good, we're not able to give a 3% raise.

5. Because I'm out here, I'm not getting paid.

6. I have to go into work today because I have to feed my family.

B Combine the sentences. Use the words in parentheses.

1. Workers and management often cannot agree. There are sometimes strikes. (since)
   Since workers and management often cannot agree, there are sometimes strikes.

2. Workers do not go on strike very often. They are worried about losing their jobs. (since)
   Workers do not go on strike very often since they are worried about losing their jobs.

3. Employers do not pay their workers enough. Strikes are necessary. (because)

   _____

4. Strikes always hurt business. They are bad for the community. (since)

   _____

5. People don't want to make their co-workers angry. They don't cross picket lines. (because)

   _____

PAIRS. Which statements are true about your country? Which statements are false?

C 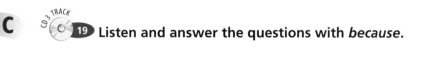 Listen and answer the questions with *because*.

1. According to the man, why did Harry lose his job?
   Harry lost his job because he was too old.

2. According to the woman, why is she paid less than the man?

   _____

3. According to the woman, why did Barbara lose her job?

   _____

4. According to the man, why isn't he getting a raise?

   _____

5. According to the man, why did Bob lose his job?

   _____

GROUPS. Discuss the situations in Exercise C. Do you think they are fair? Why or why not? Are the employers' actions legal in your country?

Example:
In the first situation, Harry didn't get the job because he was too old. I'm not sure if it's fair or unfair. It depends on the kind of job. . .

Grammar to Communicate 2

ADVERB CLAUSES: CONTRAST

i. Some adverb clauses show contrast. They show the opposite of what is expected.	<u>Although traffic is bad,</u> everyone drives. adverb clause main clause
ii. Adverb clauses of contrast begin with *although* and *even though*. The adverb clause can come at the beginning or end of a sentence.	Even though I care about the environment, I do not always recycle. I don't always recycle, even though I care about the environment.
iii. Sentences with adverb clauses of contrast are similar in meaning to sentences with *but*.	The city is polluted, **but** I live here. **Although** the city is polluted, I live here.
iv. Never use *but* in an adverb clause with *although* or *even though*.	**Although** the city is polluted, I live here. NOT ~~Although the city is polluted, but I live here.~~

A Make complete sentences. Circle the correct letter.

1. Although I care about the environment,

   a. I drive a big car.   **b.** I bought a fuel-efficient car.

2. Although paper bags are better for the environment,

   a. I often use plastic bags.   **b.** I often use paper bags.

3. Although my city has a recycling program,

   a. I recycle everything.   **b.** I throw almost everything in the trash.

4. Although people say they like clean streets,

   a. they litter a lot.   **b.** they never litter.

5. Although I have a bike,

   a. I usually ride it to school.   **b.** I usually drive to school.

B Rewrite the sentences. Begin each sentence with *even though*. Write in your notebook.

1. People should use public transportation, but most people drive.
   Even though people should use public transportation, most people drive.

2. Throwing batteries in the trash is bad for the environment, but many people do it.

3. TVs with small screens are more energy-efficient, but people prefer big-screen TVs.

4. There are many fuel-efficient cars on the market, but a lot of people don't buy them.

5. Some people are trying to use less plastic, but most products come in plastic packages.

C Write two sentences about each picture in your notebook. Put the words in the correct order and add *although* or *because*.

1-2
3-4
5-6
7-8

1. have been cut down / there are / the trees / problems when it rains

    Because the trees have been cut down, there are problems when it rains.

2. people / trees / cut them down / are very important

    Although trees are very important, people cut them down.

3. wear masks / a lot of pollution / people / there is

4. wear masks / they / people / still have health problems

5. is polluted / have died / many fish / the water

6. the water / people / is polluted / still go fishing

7. is not safe / is beautiful / it / the beach

8. the water / is not safe / do not swim there / people

TIME to TALK

ON YOUR OWN. **Read the sentences. Check (✓) the sentences that are true about you.**

❏ 1. Although large cars are more comfortable, I drive a small car.

❏ 2. Even though I could take public transportation, I prefer to drive.

❏ 3. I sometimes litter, even though I know it is illegal.

❏ 4. I never litter, even though it's sometimes difficult to find a trash can.

❏ 5. I usually drive to school or work, even though I could walk.

❏ 6. I often walk to school or work, even though driving is faster.

Grammar to Communicate 3

BECAUSE OF / DESPITE / IN SPITE OF

i. We sometimes use phrases to give reasons. Use *because of* + noun to give reasons. Compare *because of* and adverb clauses with *because*.

> Because of the time, we can't go now.
>
> Because it is late, we can't go now.

ii. We sometimes use phrases with *despite* + noun or *in spite of* + noun to show contrast. *Despite* and *in spite of* have the same meaning.

> Despite the time, we can still go.
>
> In spite of his mistakes, we're still going to vote for him.

A Match each phrase with a main clause. Write the correct letter.

_____ **1.** Because of the candidate's promise to cut taxes,

_____ **2.** In spite of the candidate's promise to cut taxes,

    a. he lost the election.

    b. he won the election.

_____ **3.** Despite the candidate's excellent speeches,

_____ **4.** Because of the candidate's excellent speeches,

    a. very few people voted for her.

    b. many people voted for her.

_____ **5.** Because of the high cost of TV ads,

_____ **6.** Despite the high cost of TV ads,

    a. there were a lot more radio ads this year.

    b. there were a lot more of them this year.

_____ **7.** Because of his experience in education,

_____ **8.** Despite his experience in education,

    a. the candidate didn't talk about schools.

    b. the candidate talked a lot about schools.

Look

candidate = someone who is trying to be elected for political office

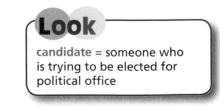

Retired General Wesley Clark was a Democratic candidate for president in 2004.

B Complete the sentences. Use *because of* or *because*.

1. _____ I'm not a citizen, I couldn't vote.

2. _____ the rain, I couldn't get to the polling station.

3. I couldn't get to the polls in time _____ the traffic.

4. I didn't vote _____ I didn't know anything about the candidates.

5. I didn't have time to vote _____ I had to work.

6. I went to the polling station but didn't vote _____ the long line.

7. _____ I was sick on election day, I stayed home.

PAIRS. **Which are good excuses for not voting?**

C Write the sentences in your notebook. Use *despite* and the words in parentheses.

> **Look**
>
> *Despite* and *in spite of* can come before a gerund.
> **Despite having** lost the election, he is still popular in government.

1. (people don't complain / their high taxes)

   ___Despite their high taxes, people don't complain.___

2. (being unhappy about the president's mistakes / people voted for him again)

3. (rising crime in the city / mayor hasn't hired more police officers)

Now write these sentences in your notebook. Use *in spite of* and the words in parentheses.

4. (some people don't vote / having concerns about the country's problems)

5. (people like the Prime Minister / her boring speeches)

6. (her popular tax cuts / she lost the election)

TIME to TALK

ON YOUR OWN. **Do you agree or disagree with the statements? Write *1* (strongly agree), *2* (agree), *3* (disagree), or *4* (strongly disagree).**

_____ 1. Because of a few scandals, people think all politicians are dishonest.

_____ 2. Politicians do not get much respect, in spite of their hard work.

_____ 3. Many politicians win elections only because of their appearance.

_____ 4. Despite their dissatisfaction with the government, many people don't vote.

_____ 5. Most politicians want to be elected because of their desire to help people.

_____ 6. Despite some mistakes, the leaders of my country are doing a good job.

GROUPS. **Compare your answers.**

Review and Challenge

Grammar

Find and correct the five mistakes in the advertisement. The first is corrected for you.

Vote for Al Jimenez

Even though

~~Even~~ you have seen my name a lot in the newspapers and on TV, you probably don't know a lot about me. I'm sending you this letter because of I want you to know who I am. Since I'm a working parent like many of you, I understand your problems. In spite our hard work, we never have enough money at the end of the month. That is because our high taxes. I promise to do something about this problem although we need enough money to take care of our children. Despite of all the taxes we pay, the schools are not getting any better. If you elect me, I promise to improve the schools. But don't vote for me because I make promises. Vote for me because I will get results.

Dictation

 20 Listen. You will hear five sentences. Write them in your notebook.

Speaking

GROUPS. Discuss three problems that are in the news these days. Talk about the causes of the problems and what can be done about them.

Example:

A: *One big problem is global warming. I've heard that the recent hurricanes and other natural disasters are happening because of global warming.*

B: *I've heard that, too. But although I've heard a lot about it, I don't really understand it. Do you?*

Listening

A  CD 3 TRACK **21** Listen to the excerpts from five radio broadcasts. Check (✓) the main topic of each broadcast.

	AGE DISCRIMINATION	A BAD STORM	ELECTION DAY	THE ENVIRONMENT	A STRIKE
1.					
2.					
3.					
4.					
5.					

B CD 3 TRACK **21** Listen again. Write the number of the broadcast next to the speaker. Be careful. There are three extra answers.

_____ **1.** a lawyer   _____ **5.** a radio reporter

_____ **2.** the leader of a workers' union   _____ **6.** a weatherman

_____ **3.** the mayor   _____ **7.** a voter

_____ **4.** a political candidate   _____ **8.** the owner of a large company

TIME to TALK

GROUPS. **Discuss the questions.**

1. In some countries, people don't vote because they think that their vote doesn't really matter. Do you agree or disagree with them? Why?

2. Do people in your country have to vote? Do you think that people should be required to vote?

3. Do you think that strikes are an effective way for workers to protect their rights? Why or why not?

4. What are the problems in your community, city, or country? What can you do to help solve the problems?

Reading and Writing

Getting Ready to Read

Skim the article. What is the general idea?

Reading

Read the article. Did skimming it first help you to understand?

EXTRA INTERNATIONAL EDITION **EXTRA**

RECYCLING DURING WORLD WAR II

Vol. 1   No. 85

Recycling is popular these days throughout the world, from the Netherlands to Senegal. Recycling means that we can **reuse** the same **materials**, such as glass or metal. Most people know that recycling helps the environment, but recycling has also been used for other purposes in **history**, such as the war effort in World War II.

During World War II, the United Kingdom was at war with Germany. In 1940, there was a great **battle** between the countries for control of the skies, the Battle of Britain. Although the British won the battle, the war continued, and Hitler was winning. The British people **realized** that they needed more materials to make more aircraft, such as fighter planes, and weapons, such as guns, tanks, and bombs. Before the war, the British had gotten the metal they needed by ship. However, German **attacks** on the Atlantic Ocean were making it impossible to get enough materials. The British knew that if they did not get the metal they needed to build aircraft and weapons, Germany would **invade** the United Kingdom soon.

Very quickly, the British people began to recycle everything that they could: Glass was saved to build aircraft. Old bedsheets were boiled and made into **bandages** for injuries. The metal from pots and pans and scrap metal, such as old razor blades, was turned into aircraft and tanks. British citizens were encouraged to recycle their toothpaste tubes. Even the metal fences from Buckingham Palace were torn out of the ground, taken away, and recycled to build fighter planes.

World War II was a very hard time for British citizens. German air raids killed thousands of British people and destroyed hundreds of houses and streets. Many British citizens were forced to live underground in subway stations in order to **survive** the air attacks. They also had to make **sacrifices**, such as eating less food, wearing old clothes, and recycling the few things they had. But if they had not recycled, Hitler might have won the war. The British people must have realized it was necessary to make every kind of sacrifice that they could in order to save their country from destruction.

After You Read

A   Look back at the boldfaced words in the article. Guess their meaning from the context. Then circle the best definition.

1. reuse
   a. use again   **b.** not use too much

2. materials
   a. things like airplanes and ships   **b.** things like glass, metal, and plastic

3. history
   a. events that happened in the past   **b.** events that might have happened

4. battle
   a. fight   **b.** argument

5. realized
   a. dreamed   **b.** understood

6. attacks
   a. violence against someone   **b.** taking something away

7. invade
   a. lose a war after a time   **b.** enter a country by force

8. bandages
   a. pieces of cloth to cover injuries   **b.** weapons made of metal

9. survive
   a. continue to live   **b.** change something

10. sacrifice
   a. give away things to friends   **b.** do without something that is important

B   Read the article again. Write *T* (true), *F* (false), or *?* (the information is not in the article and you cannot infer it.)

_____ 1. Recycling is popular today, but it is not new.

_____ 2. Recycling has only been used to help the environment.

_____ 3. The Battle of Britain was a battle fought on the ground.

_____ 4. The fences of Buckingham Palace were made of metal.

_____ 5. Germans did not recycle during World War II.

_____ 6. Recycling helped the British win the war.

In the News   237

Writing

Writing Skill: Supporting an Opinion

In an **opinion essay**, the writer expresses an opinion in the thesis. The writer supports the opinion with facts, examples, and explanations in the body paragraphs.

Read the model essay. Then answer the questions.

Glass Recycling

Most people realize that recycling is very important for the environment and that we should recycle more. We need to think about how we can make less litter and save natural resources. Recycling glass is a good first step. I think recycling glass should not be a personal choice. Instead, the U.S. government can and should require that more glass be recycled or reused.

First, the government should make a law that we must recycle glass. Glass is easy to recycle—you only need to separate the bottles by color. However, not everyone recycles it. In 1998, only 63% of glass was recycled in the United States. We can recycle more glass, and curbside collection will help. Curbside collection means that you only have to put your sorted glass bottles in a box outside your house or apartment building. Then the glass is picked up by trucks and taken to the recycling facility. I think more cities should have this service.

Reusing containers is also important for saving natural resources. The government should make a law that all beverage companies wash and reuse bottles. If beverage companies were required to reuse their bottles, the amount of wasted glass in this country would decrease a great deal. This idea has worked in other places. In Denmark, 90% of beverage containers are reused and refilled and the average bottle is refilled 20 times. Why can't that happen in the U.S.?

Pollution in our environment affects everyone. Deciding whether to protect the environment should not be an individual choice. Instead, the government should pass more laws to protect the environment. Recycling glass is an easy step. It is time for the United States government to follow the example set by countries like Denmark and make the recycling of glass mandatory.

1. **Circle the thesis statement.**
2. **Underline the topic sentence in each body paragraph.**
3. **Circle the facts in the body paragraphs.**

Look

mandatory = required by law

Prewriting: Using Guided Writing

Choose a topic from the box. Then answer the questions. Write in complete sentences or notes.

> Should women be allowed to fight in the military?
>
> Should smoking be illegal in public places?
>
> Should school hours be extended? (longer hours, school in summer)

Introduction

Which topic did you choose? _____

What is your opinion about this issue? Do you think it is a good idea or a bad idea?

_____

_____

_____

_____

Body Paragraph 1

What is your first reason for your opinion? Write your topic sentence:

_____

_____

_____

Body Paragraph 2

What is your second reason for your opinion? Write your topic sentence:

_____

_____

_____

Conclusion

What can you say to convince the reader of your opinion? Explain why he/she should agree and restate your points:

_____

_____

_____

Writing

Write an opinion essay about the topic you chose. Use your ideas from your guided writing. Make sure to include a thesis statement and topic sentences that support your opinion. Write in your notebook.

Unit 18
Money

Grammar
- Present Real Conditionals
- Future Real Conditionals
- *If* and *When*

Vocabulary

CD 3 TRACK **22** Complete the sentences with the words in the box. Then listen and check your answers.

approve	debt	due date	minimum payment	mortgage	pay off

The house I want to buy costs $100,000, so I asked my bank for a 30-year _____ for $90,000. Today the bank decided to _____ my loan! I'm so excited! The mortgage _____ is the first of the month. If I send the check late, I have to pay an extra $25. My _____ will be $600, but I want to pay more than $600. That way I can _____ the loan early, perhaps in 20 years. I don't like to owe money. I hate being in _____.

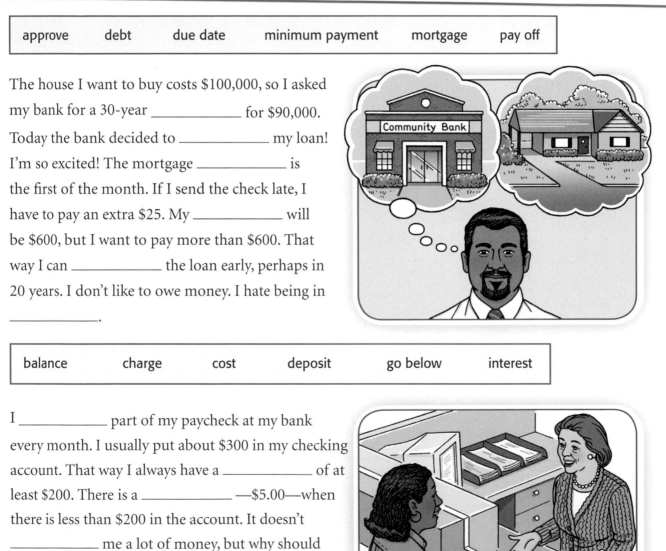

balance	charge	cost	deposit	go below	interest

I _____ part of my paycheck at my bank every month. I usually put about $300 in my checking account. That way I always have a _____ of at least $200. There is a _____—$5.00—when there is less than $200 in the account. It doesn't _____ me a lot of money, but why should I give the bank $5.00? I need the money more than the bank does! Anyway, that's why I always try not to _____ $200. I also get 2% _____ on my money in the bank when I have more than $200.

 Unit 18

Listening

A 

23 Listen to the conversation. According to the woman, what is the man doing wrong? Check (✓) the correct answer.

❏ **1.** He is not paying his bills on time.

❏ **2.** He is paying his bills with a credit card.

❏ **3.** He is paying $50 a month in electricity.

❏ **4.** He is paying his bills with cash.

B **24** Listen again to part of the conversation. For each pair of sentences, circle the letter of the sentence you hear.

1. **a.** If you want to solve your money problems, cut up your credit cards.

   b. If you want to solve your money problems, you won't cut up your credit cards.

2. **a.** If you pay your bills with a credit card, you won't take care of your problem.

   b. When you pay bills with a credit card, you take care of one problem.

3. **a.** If you show me one of your bills, I can tell you.

   b. Show me one of your bills and I'll tell you.

4. **a.** If you pay that bill with cash, how much will it cost you?

   b. When you pay a bill with cash, how much does it cost you?

5. **a.** But what happens when you pay some bills in cash and some with a credit card?

   b. But what happens when you pay the same bill with a credit card?

6. **a.** If you pay off your $50 debt by the due date, you don't pay any interest.

   b. If you pay $50 by the due date, you won't be charged any interest.

C **25** Listen again. Check (✓) the sentences that you can infer from the conversation.

❏ **1.** The man is not very good at managing his money.

❏ **2.** The woman is good at managing money.

❏ **3.** The man went to college.

❏ **4.** The woman went to college.

❏ **5.** The woman works for a credit card company.

Grammar to Communicate 1

PRESENT REAL CONDITIONALS

i. In a conditional sentence, the *if* clause states the condition. The main clause states the result.	**If John doesn't pay the bills on time,** **his wife gets upset.** *if* clause main clause

ii. The *if* clause can come before or after the main clause. The meaning is the same.	The bank pays you interest **if you have a savings account.**
	        main clause *if* clause
	If you have a savings account, the bank pays you interest.
	        if clause main clause

iii. To talk about a general truth or people's habits, use the simple present or present progressive in the *if* clause and the simple present in the main clause.	If you **have** money in your savings account, you **get** interest. If you **are buying** a car, you **need** to compare prices.
iv. To give advice or instructions, use the simple present or present progressive in the *if* clause and the imperative or *should* + verb in the main clause.	If you **want** a loan, **get** an application form. If you **are planning** to buy a car, you **should save** money.

A Read the advice about managing money. Match each *if* clause with the correct main clause.

_____ 1. If you have credit card debt,   **a.** don't buy it.

_____ 2. If you still have money at the end of the month,   **b.** put it in the bank.

_____ 3. If you don't need something,   **c.** pay it off quickly.

_____ 4. If you buy something with a credit card,   **d.** keep a list.

_____ 5. If you don't remember what you spend money on each   **e.** make sure you can
month,   afford it.

B Write sentences. Put the words in the correct order. Add commas where necessary.

Look

Use a comma after an *if* clause when it starts the sentence.
If you like it, I'll buy it for you.

1. doesn't / can't / something / it / she / afford / buy / she

    If _____

2. borrows / he / he / money / pays it back / quickly

    If _____

3. extra money / he / at the end of the year / it / gives / has / to charity / he

    If _____

4. boss / she / asks / needs / money / for a loan / she / her

    _____ if _____

5. she / save / money / worries / a lot / every month / doesn't / she

    _____ if _____

PAIRS. Do any of the sentences describe people you know?

C Complete the expressions about money with the correct form of the verbs.

1. If you _____ "up to your ears in debt," you _____ a lot of money.
   (be)   (owe)

2. If you "_____ ends meet," you _____ able to pay all your bills but you
   (make)   (be)

   _____ any extra money.
   (not / have)

3. If you _____ "broke," you _____ any money at the moment.
   (be)   (not / have)

4. If you "_____ money like water," you _____ money carelessly and quickly.
   (spend)   (spend)

5. If you _____ money aside for a "a nest egg," you _____ the money for a
   (put)   (save)

   special time in your life—for example, for a wedding or retirement.

TIME to TALK

PAIRS. **Student A: Turn to page 295. Look at the money expressions. Read each *if* clause to your partner.**
Student B: Complete Student A's sentences. Make up a main clause for each *if* clause. Now turn to page 297. Read the *if* clauses to your partner.
Student A: Make up a main clause for each *if* clause.

Example:
A: *If you are having trouble making ends meet . . .*
B: *get a loan!*

Grammar to Communicate 2

i. In a conditional sentence about the future, the *if* clause states the condition; the main clause gives the probable result.	**If I need money, I will borrow some.** *if* clause main clause
ii. To make a conditional sentence about the future, use the simple present tense in the *if* clause. Use *will* or *won't* + verb in the main clause.	If I **borrow** money, I **will pay** it back soon. If I **don't have** enough money tomorrow, I **won't go.**
iii. Use *might* + verb in the main clause if the result is possible, but you are not sure that it is going to happen.	If they **don't call** me, I **might call** them. (= I'm not sure.) If they **don't call** me, I'll call them. (= I'm sure.)

A Look at the bank information. Then complete each sentence with the name of the bank.

Checking Account Bank Fees

	Minimum monthly balance	Monthly service charge	Charge per check	Interest rate
Mid Bank	$10	$10	First 20 25¢, then 10¢	0
City Bank	$100	Free*	First 10 free, then 15¢	1.75%
A&M Bank	$1,000	Free**	0	2%

*Free with a checking and savings account at City Bank.
** Below the minimum monthly balance, $8 per month

1. If we open an account at _____ Bank, we'll have to deposit $1,000.

2. There won't be monthly charges if we have a savings and checking account at _____ Bank.

3. We won't get any interest if we have a checking account at _____ Bank.

4. If we don't write a lot of checks at _____ Bank, the checks will be free.

5. If we go below the minimum balance at _____ Bank, it will cost us $8 a month.

6. It will cost us $5 a month at _____ Bank if we write twenty checks a month.

PAIRS. Which bank is the best for you?

B. Complete the sentences. Use the correct form of the verbs.

1. If you _____ $5,000 to buy a car at 8% interest and _____ it back over 4
(borrow)   (pay)
years, you _____ to pay $1802.44. The original $5,000 will cost $6,802.44.
(need)

2. If you _____ $2,000 in a box under your bed every year for 40 years, you
(put)
_____ $80,000. But if _____ $2,000 in the bank every year at 5%
(save)   (deposit)
interest, after 40 years you _____ $267,759.50!
(have)

3. If you _____ a 30-year mortgage for $150,000 at 7% interest, you _____
(get)   (not / pay)
back just $150,000. You will also pay back $359,263 in interest, for a total of $509,263!

C. Write questions with *if*. Write in your notebook. Then ask and answer the questions with a classmate.

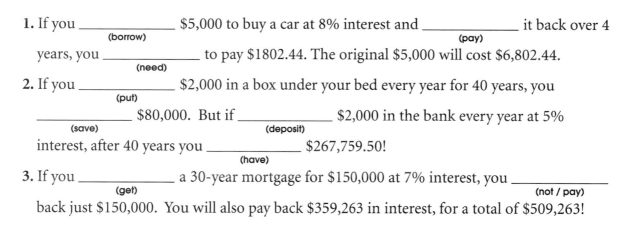

MOBILE I®

• FREE phone, today only
• FREE long distance

$44.00 a month; FIRST 1,000 MINUTES FREE
35 cents each additional minute, North America only

1. use Mobile 1 / how much / I / pay / a month
   If I use Mobile 1, how much will I pay a month?

2. I / get / a free phone / I / sign up / today

3. I / be / in California / how much / cost / to call New York

4. it / be / expensive / I / talk / for 1,500 minutes every month

5. I / be able to call / all over the world / I / have Mobile 1

6. I / make / only long distance calls / how much / it / be

TIME to TALK

PAIRS. Compare cable, telephone, or bank services in your area. Bring in ads from several companies. Ask and answer questions to decide which plan is best for you.

Example:
A: *If I get basic cable service, how much will I pay a month?*
B: *You'll pay $14.95 a month for basic cable service.*

Grammar to Communicate 3

IF AND WHEN

i. Use *if* for events you are <u>not</u> sure will happen. Use *when* for events you <u>are</u> sure will happen.

> **If** I get the money, I'll be happy.
> (= I'm not sure I will get the money.)
>
> **When** I get the money, I'll be happy.
> (= I'm sure I will get the money.)

ii. In sentences about the future, use the <u>simple present</u> after *if* or *when*. Do not use a future verb form after *if* or *when*.

> If you **don't hear tomorrow**, you'll hear in two or three days.
> NOT If you ~~won't hear tomorrow, you~~ . . .
>
> When I **get** the money **next week**, I'll call you.
> NOT ~~When I will get the money next week, I~~ . . .

iii. There are different ways to complete the main clause after *if* or *when*.

> If you get the money, call me.
>   we should save it.
>   we'll pay off our bills.
>   I have a plan.

 A   Complete the conversation with *if* or *when*.

1. **A:** The woman at the bank said that she'll call ___when___ she has news.

2. **B:** Good. _____ the loan is approved, you'll be able to pick up the car.

3. **A:** And _____ it's not approved, will I still be able to get the car?

4. **B:** Well, we can't sell you a car _____ you don't have the money.

5. **A:** Then _____ I don't get the loan, I'll try another bank.

6. **B:** _____ you get the loan, give me a call and I'll make sure the car is ready.

B   Your friend is going to get his first credit card in about a week. Write sentences with *if* or *when*.

1. __When you get your new credit card__ , you won't need to carry a lot of cash.
            (get your new credit card)

2. __If you spend too much__ , you won't be able to pay the bill.
            (spend too much)

3. _____ , someone will be able to use it.
            (not / sign the back of your credit card)

4. _____ , you will need to sign a receipt.
            (use your card)

5. _____ , you should pay it before the due date.
            (the bill come)

6. _____ , the interest will grow quickly.
            (not / pay off your credit card every month)

C Complete the conversations. Add *if* or *when*.

1. **A:** Should I get a second credit card?

   B: I don't think so. *You'll probably spend more money if you get another card.*
   (probably spend more money / get another card)

2. **A:** I get my first paycheck next week.

   B: Good. _____
   (you / get paid / we / be able to pay off / some bills)

3. **A:** How will I know that the loan has been approved?

   B: _____
   (we / call / you / we / get / the approval)

4. **A:** Do you think we should get a new car or a used one?

   B: A used car is probably more affordable. _____
   (we / get / a new car / our monthly payment / be / high)

5. **A:** Will the bank give me a credit card?

   B: _____
   (there / be / no problem / you / have / good credit)

6. **A:** Here's $50.

   B: Thanks so much. _____
   (I / pay you back / I / get / my check)

PAIRS. **Who is talking in each conversation above?**

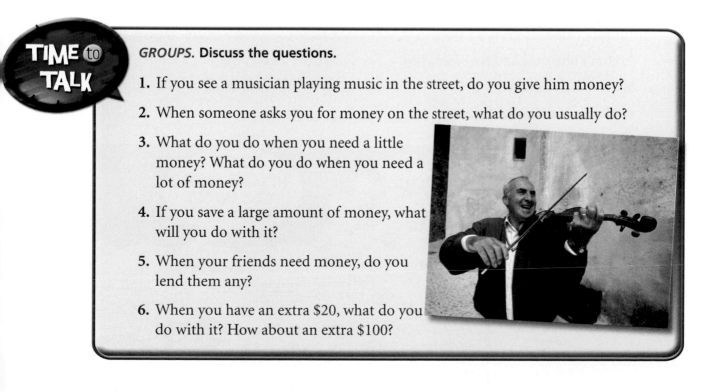

GROUPS. **Discuss the questions.**

1. If you see a musician playing music in the street, do you give him money?

2. When someone asks you for money on the street, what do you usually do?

3. What do you do when you need a little money? What do you do when you need a lot of money?

4. If you save a large amount of money, what will you do with it?

5. When your friends need money, do you lend them any?

6. When you have an extra $20, what do you do with it? How about an extra $100?

Review and Challenge

Grammar

Find the mistake in each sentence. Circle the letter and correct the mistake.

1. If there <u>will be</u> something in a store I like, <u>I</u> <u>buy</u> it.

A   B   C   D

2. When you <u>will get</u> your <u>paycheck</u> tomorrow, <u>be</u> sure to pay the credit card bill.

A   B   C   D

3. If the bank <u>doesn't</u> <u>give</u> me a loan, I <u>don't try</u> again.

A   B   C   D

4. I <u>won't be able to</u> <u>pay</u> you back <u>when</u> <u>I don't get</u> my paycheck next week.

A   B   C   D

5. You <u>will get</u> interest every month <u>if</u> you <u>will</u> <u>keep</u> enough money in your savings account.

A   B   C   D

Dictation

 26 **Listen. You will hear five sentences. Write them in your notebook.**

Speaking

PAIRS. **Look at the expressions about money. What do they mean? Do you have similar expressions in your language? Tell your partner.**

1. Money doesn't grow on trees.

2. Don't bite the hand that feeds you.

3. All that glitters is not gold.

4. Money is the root of all evil.

5. A penny saved is a penny earned.

6. Neither a borrower nor a lender be.

7. There's no such thing as a free lunch.

8. Put your money where your mouth is.

www.cartoonstock.com

Listening

A 🔘 **27** **Listen to the radio report. What is the purpose of the report? Check (✓) the correct answer.**

❑ **1.** to teach people about saving money

❑ **2.** to teach people about credit scores

❑ **3.** to teach people about credit cards

❑ **4.** to teach people not to borrow money

B 🔘 **27** **Check (✓) the sentences that are true, according to the radio report. Then listen and check your answers.**

❑ **1.** When someone applies for a loan, the lender checks his or her school record.

❑ **2.** If you get good scores in school, it will be easier for you to get a loan.

❑ **3.** If you know what to do, it is possible to improve your credit score.

❑ **4.** When you don't pay your bills on time, your credit score goes down.

❑ **5.** If you apply for a loan, the lender will get your credit score from a credit reporting company.

❑ **6.** You will never know your credit score if you don't ask for it.

❑ **7.** If you want to improve your credit score, you should cancel all your credit cards.

❑ **8.** Your credit score will not go down if you pay the minimum on your credit cards each month.

TIME to TALK

GROUPS. Discuss the questions.

1. In your country, is it common for people to get a loan from a bank when they want to buy a car? When they want to buy a house? When they want to go to a university? If loans for these things are not common, how do people pay for them?

2. In your country, how do people pay their bills? In cash? By check? With bank cards? Online? With a credit card? By mail? In person?

3. In your country, do most people have credit cards? At what age do most people get their first credit card?

Getting Ready to Read

PAIRS. **What do you know about buying a home? Discuss.**

Reading

Read the article. Underline seven sentences with *if* clauses.

Buying a home is the largest purchase most people ever make. It's a big decision, and there are a lot of steps.

The first step is to look at your **finances** and decide if you can afford a home. If you already have a lot of debt, it is probably better to rent for now. However, if you have a steady income, a good **credit history**, and some extra money saved for a **down payment**, you may be ready to buy.

The next step is to find out how much you can borrow. Research this on the Internet or go to a bank. The size of the mortgage **depends on** several things. The bank needs to know your **income**, credit history, and current monthly expenses. The bank also considers the down payment, the interest rate, and the time it will take to pay off the mortgage. Compare costs and interest rates at different banks before you choose one.

Now you can start looking for a house. Consider working with a real estate agent. He or she can help you find the house that you want. The agent may also help you **negotiate** the price with the seller. For example, you might make an **offer** of $200,000 for a house. If the seller wants $250,000, the agent may be able to convince the seller to lower his asking price.

The seller may accept your offer. In this case, you are ready to sign the contract. However, be careful! Make sure that the contract says the sale depends on a good home **inspection** report. Then, hire a home inspector. He will look at aspects of the house, such as the basement, the roof, and the electrical system, and tell you whether the house is in good condition or not. If $20,000 or more in repairs are needed, think carefully. Is the house still worth the price?

If the inspector finds something seriously wrong with the house, you have a choice. First, you can **withdraw from** the contract. That means your real estate agent will call the seller and tell him that you are canceling the contract. Your second choice is to renegotiate the price, in this case, offer less money. The seller may still agree.

Buying a home is a difficult, complex process. Having a good real estate agent may help. Most important, don't forget a home inspection. If you buy a house without having it inspected, you may be making an expensive mistake.

Home Realty, Inc.

FOR SALE

215-555-1234

After You Read

A **Find the boldfaced words in the article. Guess their meaning from the context. Then complete the sentences with the words.**

1. If we make a large _____, our mortgage payment will be lower.

2. They wanted to buy a house for $100,000, but they looked at their finances and saw that their _____ wasn't high enough.

3. The seller wants too much money for a house. Let's _____ and try to get a lower price.

4. When you buy a house, you must not forget to do an _____.

5. Whether you can get a mortgage or not _____ your past history with money.

6. People whose _____ are in bad shape can have trouble getting a mortgage.

7. I wanted to _____ the contract after I signed it, but I was afraid I would lose my deposit.

8. Years ago, she had a lot of debts, and she never paid them back. As a result, she has a bad _____ and can´t get a credit card.

9. The real estate agent told us that the house would sell fast, so we made an _____ right away.

B **Which step do you do first to buy a house? Circle _a_ or _b_.**

1. **a.** check if you can get a mortgage   **b.** make an offer

2. **a.** choose a house   **b.** review your finances

3. **a.** make an offer   **b.** ask the owner to lower his asking price

4. **a.** choose a mortgage   **b.** call a home inspector

5. **a.** do an inspection   **b.** sign the contract

Writing

Contrasting means showing differences between two things. For a **contrast essay**, you can talk about the first thing in one body paragraph. Then talk about the second thing in the following paragraph. Try to include three points in each body paragraph.

Read the model essay. Then complete the tasks.

Buying a New or Used Car

Since a car is a major investment, it's a good idea to research your options before you buy one. First you must decide whether to buy a new car or a used one. Deciding between the two will be easier if you first consider some important differences between new and used cars.

There are many good reasons to buy a new car. First, you may feel safer in a new car than a used one. You know the car has never been in an accident or been badly taken care of. Also, a new car will need less maintenance. You probably won't need an oil change, new tires, or any repairs for at least a year. Another advantage is the warranty. Most new cars have a warranty for three to five years. If something goes wrong with the car during that time, the dealership will fix it for free.

On the other hand, there are also excellent reasons to buy a used car. The first reason is the low price. Used cars in good condition cost only about half the price of a new car, for example, $9,000 instead of $20,000. Compared to new cars, they require more maintenance, but you can buy some used cars that are "just like new." Many of these cars have been used by the car dealership only for test drives, so they have very low mileage and are in almost perfect condition. Finally, if you buy a used car through a dealership, they will sometimes offer an extended warranty on the car.

Buying a new or used car may be a difficult decision. It depends on your budget and what is important to you. If you want a reasonable price, a used car is definitely a better choice. However, you may prefer a new car because it is less likely to have hidden problems.

1. **Circle the thesis.**
2. **Underline the topic sentence in each body paragraph.**
3. **Circle supporting points in the body paragraphs.**

> ## Look
>
> **maintenance** = taking care of something
> **warranty** = a guarantee that the (car) maker will make repairs for free in a certain time
> **extended warranty** = a warranty that lasts longer than a regular warranty
> **car dealership** = a company that sells and sometimes buys cars

 Unit 18

Prewriting: Using Guided Writing

Choose one of the topics in the box or your own idea. Then answer the questions. Write in complete sentences or notes.

> differences between cell phones and regular phones
>
> differences between Internet dating and dates arranged by friends
>
> differences between small cars and large cars
>
> differences between take-out meals and home-cooked meals

Introduction

1. What are you contrasting? Differences between _____ and

_____

2. What can you say about this topic to make your reader interested?

_____

_____

3. What is your most important idea about this topic? Write your thesis:

_____

Body Paragraph 1

What are good points about the first thing? List them.

A: _____

B: _____

C: _____

Body Paragraph 2

What are good points about the second thing? List them.

A: _____

B: _____

C: _____

Conclusion

What is your final idea about this topic?

_____

_____

Writing

Write an essay on the topic you chose. Use your guided writing. Add or change sentences as necessary. Make sure your thesis statement clearly tells what two things you are contrasting. Write in your notebook.

Unit 19
Decisions and Dilemmas

Grammar
- Present Real and Unreal Conditionals
- Making Wishes: Present and Future
- Past Unreal Conditionals

Vocabulary

28 Complete the sentences with the words in the box. Then listen and check your answers.

| can't think straight | listen to my heart |
| is up to you | make up your mind |

I know we need to make a decision, but I
_____. I'm very confused.
When I _____, I'm sure we
should buy the house. But then my head tells
me we can't afford it, so it _____.
You make the decision. When you
_____, tell me your decision.

approve of	out of your hands
break up with	proposed
broke her heart	

Liz went out with Jack for 6 months. But
Jack was 15 years older than Liz, so her
parents didn't _____ him.
Then he _____. They didn't
want her to marry him, so they made her
_____ him. They said, "It's not
your decision. It's _____." It
_____ and she cried for days.

Listening

A CD 3 TRACK 29 **Listen to the conversation. Why is Ana crying? Check (✓) the correct answer.**

❏ **1.** Ana's boyfriend, Evan, has just told her that he is going out with another woman.

❏ **2.** Ana wants to marry Evan, but she can't because her mother doesn't approve of him.

❏ **3.** Ana expected Evan to propose to her, but he told her he didn't love her.

❏ **4.** Mark asked Ana to marry him, but she refused because she loves Evan.

B CD 3 TRACK 30 **Listen again. Complete the sentences with the words from the box. (Be careful!, there are three extra words.)**

break	did	have	meet	were
broken	had	I'd	met	would

Oh Jenny, why did I ever meet Evan? If we'd never _____, I wouldn't have
                                                        1.

_____ up with Mark. And Mark would never _____ broken my heart,
        2.   3.

I'm sure of it! I should have listened to my mother. If _____ listened to her,
                                                                4.

none of this would have happened. And Mark and I _____ be married right
                                                            5.

now . . . I wish Mark _____ here. If I _____ another chance with him,
                            6.   7.

I'd never let him go.

C CD 3 TRACK 31 **Listen again. Check (✓) the sentences you can infer from the conversation.**

❏ **1.** Ana met Mark before she met Evan.

❏ **2.** Mark didn't ask Ana to marry him.

❏ **3.** Ana's mother didn't approve of Mark.

❏ **4.** Ana's mother doesn't approve of Evan.

❏ **5.** Evan is going to marry someone else.

Grammar to Communicate 1

PRESENT REAL AND UNREAL CONDITIONALS

i. Real conditional sentences can show true situations. Unreal conditional sentences show imaginary situations.	REAL: If Paul **gets** the place, he **will be** happy. (= I think Paul might get the place.) UNREAL: If Paul **got** the place, he **would be** happy. (= I don't think Paul will get the place.)

ii. In unreal conditional sentences, use the simple past in the *if* clause and *would* + verb in the main clause.	If I <u>had the money, I would buy a house.</u>
	    if clause main clause
	 (= I don't have it, so I'm not buying a house.)
	
	 If I <u>didn't have kids, I would live</u> downtown.
	    if clause main clause
	 (= I have kids, so I don't live downtown.)

iii. When you use the verb *be* in the *if* clause of an unreal conditional, use *were* for all subjects.	If I **were** rich, I wouldn't live here. (= I am not rich, so I live here.) If he **were** here, he would help us. (= He is not here, so he doesn't help us.)

A **32** The Hong family is moving. Listen to the Hong family and their neighbors. Circle the correct verbs.

Look

We often use *if you were me. . .* OR *if I were you. . .* to ask for and give advice.

A: **What would you do if you were me?**
B: **If I were you, I'd move.**

1. If it were up to us, we **would / wouldn't** move.

2. If it were up to me, we **would / wouldn't** buy a house in the country.

3. If it were up to me, we **would / wouldn't** get another apartment in the city.

4. If it were our decision, they **would / wouldn't** stay right here.

5. If it were my decision, they **would / wouldn't** live with us.

6. If it were my decision, he **would / wouldn't** live so far away.

B   **Write advice to the people. Write in your notebook.**

1. Jill is divorced with one child. Should she rent an apartment or buy a small house?

   If I were her, I'd buy a small house. OR _If I were her, I'd rent an apartment._

2. Ann is 20. She can't make up her mind. Should she stay with her parents or get her own place?

3. Your best friend has decided to move back to the city. If it were up to you, what would you do? Get a place in the city or stay in the country?

4. Hal just lost his job. He's upset and can't think straight. Should he get a roommate or move to a cheaper apartment?

5. Sam needs a place right away. He can't decide whether to go to a real estate agent or look for a place online.

PAIRS. **Compare your sentences. Did you give the same advice?**

C   **Luis and Elba have to move but can't make a decision. Complete the sentences.**

1. We want to buy a house, but houses in the city aren't cheap.

   If they ___were___ cheaper, we ___would buy___ a house.

2. We would like to move into the building next door, but the rent is so high.

   If the rent _____ so high, we _____ into the building next door.

3. I'm pregnant, so we have to move.

   We _____ to move if I _____ pregnant.

4. We need to live downtown because we don't have a car.

   We _____ to live downtown if we _____ a car.

5. My mother won't be able to babysit because we don't live close to her.

   If we _____ close to my mother, she _____ to babysit.

TIME to TALK

PAIRS. **Discuss the questions.**

1. If you had the choice between living in a big beautiful house in the country or a small apartment in the city, which would you choose?

2. If you could change one thing about your city, what would it be?

3. If you could change one thing about your current living situation, what would it be?

4. Where would you live if you could live anywhere in the world?

5. If you could redecorate one room of your home, how would you change it?

Grammar to Communicate 2

MAKING WISHES: PRESENT AND FUTURE

i. Use *wish* when you are not happy about a situation. You want the situation to be different.	I **wish** I had enough money for a new car. (= You don't have enough money, and you're not happy about it.)
ii When you use *wish* to talk about the present or future, the verb in the noun clause is in the past.	I **wish** (that) I **didn't have** to go to the party in this old car. I **wish** (that) I **were** driving a new car.
iii. When you use the verb *be* in the noun clause after *wish*, use *were* for all subjects.	I **wish** (that) I **were** rich. We **wish** (that) we **were** rich.
iv. Do not confuse *wish* and *hope*. Use *wish* when you want something, but you know that it won't happen. Use *hope* when you want something, and you think that it might happen.	I **wish** I had enough money for college. I'm upset that I don't. I **hope** I can save enough money for college. I'm doing my best.

A Complete the sentences about the picture. Write *Sue* or *Ann*.

1. _____ wishes she didn't live alone.

2. _____ wishes she lived in a mansion.

3. _____ wishes she had servants.

4. _____ wishes she had a large family.

5. _____ wishes her house weren't so quiet.

6. _____ wishes her house weren't so noisy.

PAIRS. Which lifestyle would you prefer?

B **Dora has money problems. What does she wish? Complete her sentences.**

Dora's Reality

Dora's Wishes

1. I don't make enough money.

_____ I wish I made _____ more money.

2. I have a lot of debt.

_____ so much debt.

3. Our credit card bills are high.

_____ so high.

4. I can't make ends meet.

_____ ends meet.

5. We can never save any money.

_____ some money.

6. I often need to borrow money from friends.

_____ so often.

C **Complete the letter. Use *wish* or *hope* and the correct form of the verbs.**

United Bank

Dear Mrs. Reilly:

I _____ I _____ to give you better news, but I'm afraid we cannot
   (1. hope / wish)   (2. be able)

approve the college loan for your daughter. Of course, we _____ we never
                                                              (3. hope / wish)

_____ turn down any applications. However, because of your credit history, we
(4. have to)

cannot give you a loan at this time. I _____ I _____ the power to help
                                          (5. hope / wish)   (6. have)

you, but the decision is out of my hands. I _____ you _____ my difficult
                                               (7. hope / wish)   (8. understand)

position, and I _____ your daughter _____ successful in college.
                  (9. hope / wish)   (10. be)

Seymour Marx

Assistant Loan Officer

TIME to TALK

PAIRS. **Talk about your present situation. Then talk about your hopes and wishes. Use the verbs and the ideas in the chart.**

HAVE	BE	LIVE
children	tall	alone
a brother / sister	thin	with _____
an interesting job	a _____ (profession)	in _____ (place)

Example:

A: *I don't have any children, but I wish I did. I hope that I will have children in the future.*
B: *I have three sons. I wish that I had a daughter. . .*

Grammar to Communicate 3

i. Past unreal conditional sentences tell about a situation that was not true in the past.	She **would have married him** if he **had proposed.** (=She didn't marry him because he didn't propose.)
ii. Use the past perfect in the *if* clause and ~~*would have* + past participle in the main~~ clause.	If I **had married her**, I **would have been happy.** *if* clause main clause (= I didn't marry her, so I was not happy.) If I **hadn't married her**, I **wouldn't have been happy.** *if* clause main clause (= I married her, so I was happy.)
iii. The contracted form *would've* sounds like / wʊdəv /. *Wouldn't have* sounds like / wʊdandəv /.	If you'd come, we **would've** had a good time. If you'd been there, I **wouldn't have** left early.

A   Read the sentences. Then answer the questions. Write *Y* (yes) or *N* (no).

1. If Jim and Lena hadn't lived next door, they wouldn't have met.

    a. Did Jim and Lena live next door? ____   **b.** Did they meet? ____

2. If Jim had taken a job in a different city, he would have been far away from Lena.

    a. Did Jim take the job? ____   **b.** Was he far away from Lena? ____

3. If Jim hadn't proposed to Lena, she would have proposed to him.

    a. Did Jim propose to Lena? ____   **b.** Did Lena propose to him? ____

4. Lena wouldn't have married Jim if her parents hadn't liked of him.

    a. Did Lena marry Jim? ____   **b.** Did her parents like him? ____

5. They would have lived with her parents if they hadn't bought their own house.

    a. Did they live with her parents? ____   **b.** Did they buy a house? ____

B   🎵 CD 3 TRACK **33** Five people talk about bad decisions they made in the past. Listen and complete the sentences.

1. If I'd listened to my mother, I _____ wasted ten years of my life.

2. If she hadn't gone out with a co-worker, she _____ had to quit.

3. If we hadn't lived with my in-laws, we _____ avoided a lot of arguments.

4. If I had listened to my heart, I _____ broken up with her.

5. If I'd been smart, I _____ stayed with Alex.

C   **Complete the sentences. Use the correct form of the verbs in parentheses.**

1. I didn't study enough in high school. If I (study) _____ enough, I would have gotten a scholarship.

2. If I (get)_____ a scholarship, I would have gone to college.

3. If I (go) _____ to college, I would have majored in engineering.

4. If I had majored in engineering, I (get) _____ a job as an engineer.

5. If I'd gotten an engineering job, I (be) _____ well-paid and saved money.

6. If I'd saved money, I (be able to) _____buy a house.

7. If I (be able to) _____ buy a house, Sandra (marry) _____me.

D   **Read about the choices Sally made. How would her life have been different if she had made different choices? Write conditional sentences.**

1. "Chris was the man of my dreams, and I fell madly in love with him."
   If Chris hadn't been the man of her dreams, she wouldn't have fallen in love with him.

2. "I listened to my heart and said yes when he proposed."
   _____

3. "Our parents didn't approve of our marriage, so they refused to help us."
   _____

4. "We didn't have enough money to pay for college, so we got jobs."
   _____

5. "We both worked very hard, so we were able to go to college."
   _____

6. "Our parents didn't help us, so we learned how to help ourselves."
   _____

PAIRS. **Talk about things that you did (or didn't do) in the past few years. Use the ideas in the box. What would have happened if you had made a different decision?**

attended / didn't go to college	had / didn't have a child
got / didn't get married	moved / didn't move
graduated / didn't graduate from high school	worked / didn't work

Example:
A: *I didn't go to college. If I'd gone to college, I would have majored in business.*

Review and Challenge

Grammar

Find the mistake in each sentence. Circle the letter and correct the mistake.

1. If it <u>were</u> up to me, <u>I</u> <u>will</u> <u>do</u> things differently. But I'm not the boss.
   A   B   C   D

2. My parents don't like my boyfriend; I <u>wish</u> <u>that</u> <u>they</u> <u>approve</u> of him.
   A   B   C   D

3. We're going on a picnic tomorrow. I <u>wish</u> <u>it</u> <u>doesn't</u> <u>rain</u>.
   A   B   C   D

4. Al needs a long time to make decisions. <u>If</u> he <u>made</u> up his mind quickly, we <u>will</u> all <u>be</u> happy.
   A   B   C   D

5. You shouldn't work and go to school at the same time. I <u>would</u> <u>stop</u> working <u>if</u> I <u>am</u> you.
   A   B   C   D

6. Jack wanted to leave early. If it <u>was</u> up to me, I <u>would</u> <u>have</u> <u>stayed</u> longer.
   A   B   C   D

Dictation

 34 Listen. You will hear five sentences. Write them in your notebook.

Speaking

ON YOUR OWN. **Complete the sentences.**

1. If I had enough money, _____

2. If I had more free time, _____

3. If I could have any job in the world, _____

4. If I found a wallet with a thousand dollars in it, _____

5. I wish that my house (or apartment) _____

6. If I were a man (a woman), _____

7. If I were (weren't) married, _____

8. I wish I lived _____

9. If I were in _____ (name of city) right now, _____

10. If I could meet a famous person, _____

11. I hope that _____

GROUPS. **Discuss your answers.**

Example:
A: *If I had enough money, I would quit my job and study full time.*
B: *What would you study?*

Listening

A CD 3 TRACK **35** Listen. What kind of radio program is this? Check (✓) the correct answer.

❏ **1.** Parents call in and talk about how to raise a child.

❏ **2.** People call in and talk about their personal lives.

❏ **3.** Young people call in and talk about their career choices.

B CD 3 TRACK **35** Listen again. Complete the sentences with the correct form of the verb. Use *not* where necessary.

1. If Roger's father _____ a dentist, Roger _____ to dental school.
                  (be)   (go)

2. If Roger _____ his heart, he _____ an architect.
            (listen)   (become)

3. Roger wishes that he _____ a dentist.
                            (be)

4. Roger thinks that he _____ happier today if he _____ an architect.
                        (be)   (be)

5. If Beth and her husband _____ to accept their son's marriage, their son
                                   (refuse)

_____ speaking to them.
(stop)

6. The host hopes that Beth's son _____ her.
                                 (call)

7. According to the host, if Beth's son _____ her, he _____ his decision.
                               (call)   (regret)

TIME to TALK

GROUPS. Discuss the questions about the listening.

1. If Roger were your friend, what advice would you give him? If you were Roger, what would you do?

2. If Beth were your friend, what advice would you give her? If you were Beth, what would you do?

3. If you were Beth's son, what would you do? If you were Beth's daughter-in-law, what would you do?

4. Do you know anyone who has had an experience like Roger's or Beth's? If so, tell your group about it.

Reading

Getting Ready to Read

PAIRS. **What were you like as a child? Were you a good child? Were you difficult child? Talk with a partner.**

Reading

Read the article. Are the parent-child relationships similar to those in your family or different?

My Clever Three-Year-Old

There are so many wonderful things about young children. They're curious, **clever**, and have an **endless** amount of energy. Sometimes, however, I wish I had known how hard it is to be a parent. At times my son Olek drives me so crazy that I can't think straight.

First there is the dinnertime battle. Olek, who is 3, can't make up his mind about what he wants to eat. First he wants a cheese sandwich, but then he wants spaghetti. I bring him the spaghetti, but no, now he wants chicken soup. If it were up to him, I would make food for him all day long. He is also a very **picky** eater. Every time I think I have found a food he likes, he changes his mind. By the time "dinner" is over, I haven't eaten anything. Neither has Olek.

Then there's bedtime. We read a story and get on Olek's Superman pajamas. I manage to brush his teeth. But then he wants to eat! He wouldn't eat at dinnertime, but now, at 10 P.M., he says he's hungry. I don't approve of late-night snacks. However, I'm afraid that Olek doesn't eat enough so I heat up his spaghetti. Of course, he doesn't eat it. It's **obvious** that he's just trying to avoid bedtime. When I tell Olek it's time for bed, he says, "No." He is now standing on the table with his little hands on his stomach, watching me with a **naughty** smile.

At this point, I complain to my husband who is reading the newspaper. I say, "Andrij! Do something!" Without looking up from his newspaper, he answers, "Why?"

"What do you mean?" I say. "You're his father!" Andrij looks at me and responds, "I would put him to bed if I thought it would work. But he's just going to get up again. He always does. What's the point?" He starts reading his newspaper again.

Maybe Andrij is right. Maybe we can't control Olek's bedtime. But that's not the way I was **raised**. My parents **laid down the law**. They always told us what to do. Sometimes I wonder what my mother would think of us as parents, if she were still alive. Maybe she would say, "Now you know what I **went through** with you! Even if you had ten Oleks, they would never be as bad as you were!"

After You Read

A   **Find the boldfaced words in the article and guess their meaning from the context. Then complete the sentences with the words.**

1. Tomek and his wife _____ a lot of hard times, but now things are better.

2. My parents were strict and never let me stay out late. They always _____.

3. We fight all the time. Our arguments are _____.

4. I was _____ by my grandmother in the city. We always lived in small apartments when I was growing up.

5. It takes her hours to decide what to wear. She´s _____ about her clothes.

6. Dogs are very _____. If they get lost, they can find their way home.

7. She is a very good child, but her little brother is very _____.

8. It's _____ that he's smart because he always gets the best grades in the class.

B   **Check (✓) the statements you can infer from the article.**

_____ 1. The writer loves her son, but she gets frustrated sometimes.

_____ 2. Olek usually goes to bed early.

_____ 3. Olek loves to eat.

_____ 4. Olek's parents have trouble controlling him.

_____ 5. The writer always did what her mother told her to do.

_____ 6. The writer has only one child.

C   **What is the author's tone in the article? Circle the best answer.**

a. angry   **b.** humorous   **c.** sad

PAIRS. **Discuss why you chose your answer.**

> **Reading Skill:**
> **Recognizing Tone**
>
> **Tone** is the way a writer decides to talk about a topic: For example, serious, humorous (funny), angry, or sad.

Writing

Writing Skill: Writing Conclusions

An essay ends with a **conclusion**. The conclusion tells the reader that the essay is coming to an end and gives a final idea. Sometimes it repeats the idea in the thesis with different words. In a narrative essay, the conclusion tells the effect of the story on the writer.

Read the model essay. Then complete the tasks.

Magda's Difficult Decision

My neighbor Magda Kaminski has lived in the Detroit area her whole life. Her parents came from Poland to Hamtramck, a small city close to Detroit. Magda's father worked for General Motors. Now Magda is married with her own children and they live right down the street from her parents. Last year, Magda and her husband had to make a very difficult decision. It was a painful decision to make but she thinks they made the right choice.

Magda's husband, Joe, lost his job a couple of years ago. He had worked for General Motors, too, and his factory closed. It was very hard for him to find a good job because the Michigan economy is bad. He was out of work for six months and it got more difficult to pay the bills. Then one day, they got a call from Joe's friend, Ryan, who lives in Norfolk, Virginia. Ryan said he could get Joe a job there in the shipping industry.

Magda and Joe talked about moving. If they moved to Norfolk, Ryan's boss would give Joe a job. If that didn't work out, there would be many other jobs in Norfolk in shipping and manufacturing. Finally, they decided that they would move there if Magda's parents agreed to move with them. Unfortunately, her father, Pavel, didn't want to go. He said, "I've lived in this house since I came from Poland 30 years ago. I have everything just the way I want it, even my garden with my apple tree that I planted the year after we arrived. I'm not moving!"

As a result, Magda and Joe had to make a hard decision—move to Norfolk or stay in Detroit. If they moved, they would have more job security, but they would be far from the family. At last, they decided not to leave. They didn't want to take their children so far away from their grandparents. It has been a year since they made that decision. Since then, Joe has found a part-time job. They think they will stay in Detroit, but he will probably have to retrain for a different job. It was a difficult decision, but they feel they have made the best choice for now.

1. Underline the thesis in the introduction.
2. Look at the conclusion. Circle the sentence that repeats the idea in the thesis.

Prewriting: Using Guided Writing

Interview a relative, friend, classmate, or neighbor about a difficult decision he or she made. Answer the questions in complete sentences or notes.

Introduction

1. What is the name of the person you interviewed? Who is this person in relation to you?

_____

_____

2. What is a difficult decision this person had to make?

_____

_____

Body Paragraph 1

What background information is important to know? What was the person's situation before the decision?

_____

_____

_____

_____

Body Paragraph 2

What decision did the person have to make? Explain it fully. Tell when it happened, where, and who was involved or affected by it:

_____

_____

_____

_____

Conclusion

What was the final effect of this decision on the person's life? How did it change his or her life? Did he or she make the right choice?

_____

_____

_____

Writing

Write an essay about the person you interviewed. Use the ideas from your guided writing. Add or change sentences as necessary. Make sure to include a thesis. Write in your notebook.

Vocabulary

36 Match the pictures with the words in the box. Write the numbers. Then listen and check your answers.

_____ call off

_____ call on

_____ do over

_____ figure out

_____ hand in

_____ look up

_____ run into

_____ take someone out

Listening

A  CD 3 TRACK **37** **Listen to the conversation. Who is Dr. Johnson? Check (✓) the correct answer.**

> **Look**
>
> a freshman = a student in the first year of high school or college

❏ **1.** One of Hannah's professors.

❏ **2.** A close friend of Hannah and her parents.

❏ **3.** A school counselor that Hannah goes to see.

B CD 3 TRACK **37** **Read each sentence. Does it describe Hannah's high school experience or her college experience? Write _H_ (high school) or _C_ (college). Then listen and check your answers.**

_____ **1.** She hands her homework in late.

_____ **2.** She hands in her homework on time.

_____ **3.** She does her assignments over several times before she hands them in.

_____ **4.** She gets up early.

_____ **5.** She can't think straight when the teacher calls on her.

_____ **6.** She puts all her papers away.

_____ **7.** She never throws anything away.

C CD 3 TRACK **37** **Listen again. Check (✓) the sentences that you can infer from the conversation.**

_____ **1.** Hannah is getting good grades in college.

_____ **2.** Hannah is not used to having problems in school.

_____ **3.** Being a high school student is very different from being a college student.

_____ **4.** Hannah's professors like her.

_____ **5.** Hannah is going to take a semester off from college.

Grammar to Communicate 1

PHRASAL VERBS: TRANSITIVE AND INTRANSITIVE

i. Phrasal verbs have two or three words. The first word is a verb. The second (and third) word is a particle—for example, *along, down, forward, into, to, up, with.*	I **gave up** calling Liz because she never returned my calls. I was ready to **break up with** her anyway.
ii. The meaning of a phrasal verb is usually different from the meaning of a verb by itself.	She **broke down** when she heard the bad news. (broke down = became upset or started crying) She **broke** the glass. (broke = broke into pieces)
iii. Phrasal verbs are either transitive or intransitive. Transitive phrasal verbs take an object. Intransitive phrasal verbs do not take an object.	object I **ran into** <u>Jane</u> at the subway station last week. I hadn't seen her in a while. Jane and I used to **get along**. Now we fight all the time.
iv. Use a preposition after some phrasal verbs.	Linda **broke up** <u>with</u> George a week ago.

A Underline the phrasal verbs. Mark the verbs *T* (transitive) or *I* (intransitive).

Oscar and I started going out last year. We got along well in the beginning, but there was always one problem. I could never count on him. He was late when we had a date, and sometimes he didn't show up at all. Last summer we had a big fight about it and didn't talk to each other for a month. Then we made up. But the same thing happened again in November. I couldn't put up with the situation any more, so we broke up. It was hard at first, but I'm getting over it. I'm almost ready to move on and find someone new.

B Write the phrasal verbs from Exercise A next to the correct meanings.

1. _____ know that someone will be there when you need him or her

2. _____ arrive at the place where someone is waiting for you

3. _____ become friends with someone again, after you have had an argument

4. _____ accept a bad situation or a problem with a person without complaining

5. _____ feel better after a bad experience

6. _____ make positive changes in your life

7. _____ date someone

8. _____ have a good relationship with someone

9. _____ stop dating or being married to someone

C "Ask Alice" is an advice column in a newspaper. Complete Alice's sentences. Use the phrasal verbs from the box.

break down	get along	make up	run into
break up	get over	put up with	

1. If you can't count on your boyfriend, you should _____ with him.

2. If you don't _____ with your husband, you should see a marriage counselor.

3. If you can't _____ your wife's friends, don't go out with them.

4. You broke up two years ago. Stop crying and _____ it.

5. Many couples have fights and then _____. You will too.

6. Don't worry about it. If you _____ your ex-wife on the street, be friendly.

7. When you lose someone you love, it is normal to _____. Crying can make you feel better.

PAIRS. Do you agree with all of the advice?

PAIRS. **Make up a story. Use at least four of the phrasal verbs in the box. Then read your story to the class.**

call off	get over	give up	grow up	move on	run into

Grammar to Communicate 2

PHRASAL VERBS: SEPARABLE AND INSEPARABLE

i. Transitive phrasal verbs are separable or inseparable. The object of a separable phrasal verb can follow the verb or the particle.

> object
> I'm going to pay **my debts** off soon. OR
> object
> I'm going to pay off **my debts** soon.
>
> object
> Don't throw **the bills** away. OR
> object
> Don't throw away **the bills**.

ii. If the object of a separable phrasal verb is a noun with three or more words, we usually do not separate the verb and the particle. We put the object after the particle.

> object
> I'm going to pay back **the neighbor who lent us the money.**
> NOT I'm going to pay the neighbor who lent us the money back.

iii. The object of an inseparable phrasal verb must follow the particle.

> object
> I ran into **Maria** the other day.
> NOT I ran Maria into the other day.

A CD 3 TRACK 38 **Listen. Circle the letter of the correct meaning of the phrasal verbs.**

1. It was hard to **bring** my kids **up** alone.

  a. take care of a child until he or she is an adult **b.** become an adult

2. I almost **gave** my job **up**.

  a. stopped hoping for something   **b.** stopped doing something you usually do

3. We never had any money, so we had to **cut down on** a lot of things.

  a. use less of something   **b.** get things at a lower price

4. By the end of each month, we had usually **run out of** money.

  a. use all of something, so nothing is left   **b.** leave a place

5. I had to **go over** our budget all the time.

  a. spend more money than you should   **b.** look at or think about something carefully

6. When I applied for a loan, the bank **turned** me **down**.

  a. said *no*   **b.** said something nice

B **Write the phrasal verbs from Exercise A in the correct list.**

Separable: _____ , _____ , _____

Inseparable: _____ , _____ , _____

C Look at the pictures. Write sentences about the changes in Max's life in two ways. Write in your notebook.

1. pay off my debts   **2.** give up smoking   **3.** pay back my friends

4. put aside money   **5.** take up yoga   **6.** fill out / mortgage form

D Carol is going to move. Circle the phrasal verbs and underline the objects. Check (✓) the sentences that can be rewritten. Look at page 289 for help.

❏ **1.** I'm going to clean out my attic.   ❏ **4.** I want to give away old clothes.

❏ **2.** I want to throw away old papers.   ❏ **5.** I need to pick up some boxes.

❏ **3.** I need to pack up books.   ❏ **6.** I have to put some things away.

Rewrite the sentences you checked. Write the sentences in your notebook.

> *Example:*

1. I'm going to clean my attic out.

TIME to TALK

PAIRS. Ask and answer the questions. Then tell the class about your partner.

1. Do you usually throw your old bills away, or do you keep them?

2. Is your home neat or messy? Do you usually put things away?

3. When you have things that you don't need anymore, do you give them away?

4. When was the last time you cleaned out your closets?

Grammar to Communicate 3

PHRASAL VERBS WITH PRONOUNS

i. When you use a pronoun (*me, you, it, him, her, us,* or *them*) with a separable phrasal verb, you must put the pronoun <u>between</u> the verb and the particle.

> I hope I can **figure it out.**
> NOT ~~I hope I can figure out it.~~

ii. When you use a pronoun with an inseparable phrasal verb, you must put the pronoun <u>after</u> the particle.

> I **called on him** and he knew the answer.
> NOT ~~I called him on and he knew the answer.~~

iii. Most phrasal verbs with three words are inseparable. Put the pronoun after the second particle.

> I can't **put up with them** anymore.
> NOT ~~I can't put them up with anymore.~~

A **Match the sentence and the response.**

_____ **1.** I tried to guess the meaning, but I couldn't.

_____ **2.** I was sick and didn't finish my homework.

_____ **3.** I don't understand this grammar.

_____ **4.** I've made mistakes on the application form.

_____ **5.** Why do you think the teacher doesn't like you?

a. You can hand it in tomorrow.

b. Look it up.

c. Try to figure it out.

d. He never calls on me.

e. Get a new one and do it over.

PAIRS. Underline the phrasal verbs. Write *S* (separable) or *I* (inseparable).

B **Answer the questions. Use a pronoun in your answers.**

1. **A:** Did your teacher go over the homework?
   B: Yes, he <u>went over it.</u>

2. **A:** Did you hand in your homework assignment?
   B: Yes, I _____ yesterday.

3. **A:** Did you look up the words in your new dictionary?
   B: No, I _____ in my old one.

4. **A:** Did you figure out the meaning with your partner?
   B: No, I _____ by myself.

5. **A:** Did Ms. Coleman call on Jane?
   B: Yes, she _____ at the beginning of class.

C Complete the advice from a teacher. Use the phrasal verbs in the box and a pronoun. Be careful. There is an extra phrasal verb.

call on	do over	figure out	go over
hand in	look up	put off	put up with

1. When you don't know the meaning of a word, first try to _figure it out_ from context.

2. If you can't guess the meaning of the new word, _____ in a dictionary.

3. Start studying a week before a test. Don't _____ until the night before.

4. If you finish a test early, don't _____ right away.

5. If you have extra time on a test, go back to the difficult parts and _____ carefully.

6. If you make a lot of mistakes on your homework, _____. That way, you will learn from your mistakes.

7. When teachers _____, always try to answer, even if you are not sure.

PAIRS. Do you agree with the advice? Do you usually do these things?

D TRACK 39 **Listen and complete the conversations.**

1. **A:** Are you going to start college in September?

   B: No, I'm going to _____ for a year. I need time to put more money aside.

2. **A:** What happened at your interview? Did you like the company?

   B: Yes, very much. If they offer me a job, I'm not going to_____.

3. **A:** What are you going to do with your books at the end of the course?

   B: I'm going to _____!

4. **A:** What are you going to do with *your* books at the end of the course?

   B: I'm going to _____ in a safe place.

5. **A:** Are you going to keep your job?

   B: No, I'm going to have to _____. I don't have time to work and study.

6. **A:** Should we give the teacher a good-bye gift?

   B: No, let's _____ for a meal.

TIME to TALK

PAIRS. **Look at the pictures on page 268. Tell the stories.**

Review and Challenge

Grammar

Complete the conversation with the words in the box. Be careful. There are several extra words.

| along | ~~give~~ | her over | it off | off it | up |
| away | her into | into her | look | over her | with |

A: Why do you want to _____give_____ up this beautiful apartment?
1.

B: I can't put up _____ the noise. There's traffic all night long.
2.

A: But why now? It's not your neighbors, is it?

B: No, I get _____ with them just fine. It's really just the noise. And Sue lives in the
3.

neighborhood, and sometimes I run _____. That makes me uncomfortable, too.
4.

A: But you two broke _____ over a year ago. You haven't gotten _____ yet?
5.   6.

B: Sure, I have. I've wanted to move for a long time, but I've kept putting _____.
7.

Now's the time.

A: Well, if you're giving any of your furniture _____, let me know.
8.

Dictation

CD 3 TRACK 40 **Listen. You will hear five sentences. Write them in your notebook.**

Speaking

ON YOUR OWN. **Check (✓) the statements that are true about you. If a statement is not true about you, change it to make it true.**

❑ **1.** I go over my budget a few times a year.

❑ **2.** I don't run out of money at the end of the week because I'm very careful.

❑ **3.** I need to cut down on some of my expenses.

❑ **4.** People can count on me.

❑ **5.** I never show up late.

GROUPS. **Compare your answers. Which two members of the group are the most similar? Which two are the most different?**

Listening

A 🔘 **41** **Listen. Who is speaking? Check (✓) the correct answer.**

❏ **1.** Someone who is learning English.

❏ **2.** One of the writers of this textbook.

❏ **3.** Someone who gave up trying to learn English.

B 🔘 **42** **Listen again. What advice does the speaker give? Complete the sentences with the correct phrasal verbs.**

1. Take responsibility for your own learning. Don't wait for the teacher to _____ you.

2. Don't get frustrated, and don't _____.

3. Don't _____ every new word in your dictionary.

4. Practice _____ the meaning of new words from the context.

5. Try to _____ new vocabulary for about ten or fifteen minutes before you go to sleep.

6. Never _____ a first draft of a paper. Rewrite it several times.

7. Don't _____ your work _____ to the last minute.

8. Finish your assignments early so that you have time to _____ them before class.

GROUPS. Discuss the questions.

1. Are you going to keep on studying English after this course? Why or why not?

2. Are you satisfied with the progress that you have made in this course? Why or why not?

3. If you could go back to the beginning of the semester and take English again, what would you do differently?

4. What advice would you give to someone who is going to take an English course next semester?

Reading

Getting Ready to Read

GROUPS. Talk about a perfect school, either an elementary or high school. What does it have? What doesn't it have?

Reading

Read the article. Highlight important points. Compare your work with a partner. Did you highlight the same points?

The right school

One of the most important decisions parents must make is choosing where to send their children to school. Many years ago, most Americans simply sent their children to the public school in their neighborhood. These days, however, there are many different possibilities. It can be challenging to find the best school for your child. Once you have chosen a school, it's not always easy to figure out how your child can **get in**.

The easiest thing, of course, is to **sign** your child **up** at the nearest public neighborhood school. This has definite advantages. First, the local school must accept all of the children who live nearby, so there is no problem with **enrolling**. Also, your child will not have to spend hours every day on a school bus commuting to a school that is far away.

Sometimes, however, there are problems with the neighborhood school. It might be crowded, or have a high number of students who **drop out**, or maybe you just think that your child would do better in a different environment. If that is the case, it might be possible to choose another public school in a neighborhood nearby.

Another possibility might be a magnet school, which you can find in most large American cities. A magnet school often has a **specialty**, like the performing arts (music, drama, dance) or auto repair. Students apply through a **lottery** system, and the schools **fill up** quickly, so you need to hand in your application on time.

A third possibility is a **private** school. Unlike public schools, private schools are not paid for by taxes. Therefore, private schools charge **tuition**. Sometimes these schools are very expensive. However, your child might be able to get financial aid.

It is important to do as much research as you can before you choose a school. In many big cities, public schools have a report card that you can look up on the Internet. The report card gives facts about the school, such as how well its students do on **standardized tests** and how many are **reading at grade level**. Finally, it is very important to visit schools. If possible, talk to the principal, parents, and students. Does the school make a good impression on you? Do the students enjoy coming to school? Most important, is the school right for your child?

After You Read

A   **Find the boldfaced words in the article and guess their meaning from the context. Then complete the sentences with the words.**

1. My son wasn't doing well in public school, so I put him in a _____ school.

2. That school has good English teachers. The students are doing very well with their reading. They are all _____.

3. If you want to send your child to that school, you put his name in a _____ and your child gets a number. If the computer chooses his number, he can go to the school.

4. I want to lose weight. I'm thinking about _____ in an exercise class.

5. He never finished high school because he was bored. If he had been in a magnet school, perhaps he wouldn't have decided to _____.

6. I bake good bread, but my real _____ is cakes. Everyone says that my cakes are the best they have ever had.

7. She wanted to go to the state college, but she didn't have high enough grades to _____.

8. Remember to apply to the schools early. The best ones _____ quickly.

9. I want to _____ my daughter for Camp Regesh this summer. I'll send in the deposit today.

10. Students take _____ in the fourth grade to check their reading levels.

11. The _____ at that school is so expensive. Then we also have to pay for books, uniforms, and some after-school activities.

B   **Read the article again. Write _T_ (true), _F_ (false), or _?_ (The information is not in the text and cannot be inferred).**

_____ 1. Children apply for public schools through a lottery system.

_____ 2. There is more than one school in some neighborhoods.

_____ 3. Magnet schools are good for children who have a specific interest.

_____ 4. If you apply for financial aid from a private school, you will get it.

_____ 5. The Internet has information about how safe schools are.

Writing

Read the model essay. Then complete the tasks .

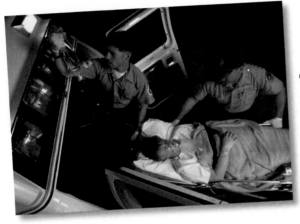

When I was growing up, I always wanted to be an emergency medical technician (EMT). It was one of the most important jobs that I could imagine. Now that I have become an EMT, I know that I was right. As an EMT, you help people with all kinds of emergencies. For example, once my partner and I saved a mother and her five-year-old child when their car turned over in a car crash. The child was stuck under the car. We were able to pull the little girl out and take her to a hospital in time. This is what is so great about being an EMT: saving people's lives.

To be an EMT, you need to have special skills and training. You have to know how to lift and carry sick and injured people. You have to think quickly. You need to recognize the patient's condition immediately. Then you need to move the patient quickly and safely to the hospital. You also need to use special equipment. In terms of training, you need to have at least a high school diploma and a certificate before you can become an EMT.

The working conditions can be difficult. First of all, the work hours can be long or irregular, because emergencies happen all of the time. For example, you might work 24 hours and then have 48 hours off. Also, the pay is not very good, especially when you start out. Then the conditions can be bad. You have to stand on your feet a lot, sometimes in bad weather. The work can be tiring, also. You come across life and death situations all of the time. Sometimes people die before you can get them to the hospital.

Even though the working conditions can be difficult, I'm satisfied with being an EMT. My satisfaction comes from helping people in the worst of times. As an EMT, I have the chance to get people to the hospital in time for doctors to save them.

1. **Underline the thesis and the topic sentences.**
2. **Look at the conclusion. Underline the sentence that gives a final idea about the topic.**
3. **Write a title above the essay. Compare your title with a partner's.**

Prewriting: Using Guided Writing

Think of a career that you are interested in and research it on the Internet. Then answer the questions in complete sentences or notes.

Introduction

1. What is the career you are interested in? Why?

_____

_____

_____

2. Why is this career important or special to you? Write your thesis:

_____

_____

Body Paragraph 1

What are the requirements for this career? (For example, skills, education, training, certifications.) Write your topic sentence:

_____

_____

_____

Body Paragraph 2

What are the responsibilities of this career? OR What are the work conditions? Write your topic sentence:

_____

_____

_____

Conclusion

What final idea do you want to tell your reader about this career? You can summarize your main points, or restate your most important idea:

_____

_____

_____

_____

Writing

Write an essay about the career that you chose. Use your ideas from your guided writing. Add or change sentences as necessary. Make sure to include a thesis, topic sentences, and a final idea in your conclusion. Write in your notebook.

Grammar Notes

The Grammar Notes below contain additional material on selected grammar points.

UNIT 1 Fun and Entertainment

Present Perfect and Simple Past (1)
- Use *how long* to ask about the length of time from the past until now.

    A: How long **have** they **been** married?
    B: For six years. (=They are married now.)

  You can also use *how long* to ask about the past.

    A: How long **were** they married?
    B: For six years. (=They are not married now.)

Present Perfect and Simple Past (2)
- Use the simple past with questions with *when*. Do not use the present perfect.

    A: When **did you go** there?   B: Last year.
    NOT When have you gone there?

UNIT 2 Health and Fitness

Present Perfect Progressive and Present Perfect (1)
- For both the present perfect progressive and the present perfect, the contracted forms (*'ve* and *'s*) are very common. Be careful: *'s* = *has*, not *is*.

UNIT 3 Crime

Past Perfect
- Use the past perfect in expressions with *in a long time* and *never…before*.

    There hadn't been any crime in the town in **a long time**.
    We had **never** been afraid **before**.

Past Perfect and Simple Past
- The time clause can come at the beginning or end of the sentence. Use a comma when the time clause comes at the beginning of the sentence.

    When the police got to the house, the woman had already died.
    The woman had already died **when the police got to the house**.

UNIT 4 Moving In

Generic Nouns
- When you use a generic noun, it stays generic for the whole conversation. It does not become definite the second time you talk about it.

    I don't like **apartments.** I prefer **houses.**
    Apartments are too noisy. **Houses** are quieter.
    NOT I don't like apartments. I prefer the houses. The apartments are too noisy. The houses are quieter.

UNIT 5 New on the Job

Tag Questions
- Be careful! Don't forget to include the auxiliary in responses to negative statements.

    A: You **don't live** around here, **do you?**
    B: **Yes, I do**. (=I live around here.) OR
    B: **No, I don't**. (=I don't live around here.)

- Don't answer with *yes* or *no* to respond to polite requests with a tag question.

    A: You can't help me with the photocopier, can you?
    B: Sure. What's the problem? OR Sorry, I don't know anything about it.

So / Too / Either / Neither
- Use *so*, *too*, *either*, and *neither* to talk about similarities between two things or people.

    I work here **and so does Tom**.=
    I work here **and Tom does too**.
    I'm not full-time **and Pam isn't either**. =
    I'm not full-time **and neither is Pam.**

- In conversation, we often say *Me too* or *Me neither* instead of sentences with *I*.

    A: I'm hungry.   A: I'm not tired.
    B: **Me too**.   B: **Me neither.**

UNIT 6 Food

Passive and Active
- Do not use *by* in a passive sentence if it is clear who does an action.

    Potatoes **are cooked** in different ways. (It is clear that people cook potatoes.)

UNIT 7 Safety

Present Perfect Passive
- The passive, including the present perfect passive, is often used to report news.

    The country's food supply **has been destroyed** by floods.

UNIT 8 Advertising

Adjectives with *so* and *such*
- We often leave out *that* in conversation.
  > The bike is so old **I don't ride** it anymore.
  > (= I don't ride the bike because it is old.)
- *So* and *such* are similar in meaning to *very* and *really*, but we use *so* and *such* when thinking about a result.
  > The book is **very interesting**.
  > (=The book is **really interesting**.)
  > The book is **so interesting**.
  > (=Result: You should read it.)

UNIT 9 Gadgets

Subject and Object Relative Pronouns
- Do not repeat the subject when *that*, *who*, or *which* is the subject of the adjective clause.
  > The appliance that heats food quickly is called a microwave oven.
  > NOT ~~The appliance that it heats food quickly is called a microwave oven.~~
- Do not repeat the object when *that*, *who*, *whom*, or *which* is the object of the adjective clause.
  > The gadget I bought last week is fun to use.
  > NOT ~~The gadget I bought it last week is fun to use.~~
- When the object of the relative clause is a person, we use *whom* in formal, written English. However, in everyday conversation we use *who* or *that*. We can also omit *who* or *that*. There is no change in meaning.
  > The technician **whom we know** will be able to take care of the problem.
  > The technician **who we know** will be able to take care of the problem.
  > The technician **that we know** will be able to take care of the problem.
  > The technician **we know** will be able to take care of the problem.

Adjective Clauses: Objects of prepositions
- In everyday conversation, we put the preposition at the end of the adjective clause. However, in formal English, we put the preposition at the beginning of the adjective clause. We use *whom* or *which*, not *who* or *that*.
  > The inventor **about whom I know the most** is Thomas Edison.
  > The invention **for which Thomas Edison is best known** is the electric light bulb.

UNIT 10 Shopping

Noun Clauses: *If / Whether*
- Use *or not* with *whether* in two different positions in a sentence.
  > I wonder **whether or not** the store sells children's clothing.
  > I wonder **whether** the store sells children's clothing or not.
- Use *or not* with *if* in only one position in a sentence.
  > I wonder **if** the store sells children's clothing **or not**.
  > NOT ~~I wonder if or not the store sells children's clothing.~~
- You do not need to include *or not* in noun clauses with *if* or *whether*.

UNIT 11 Interviews

Reported Speech: Statements
- We can use *that* at the beginning of the noun clause, but it is not necessary.
  > Rick **said that he** got a lot of information.
  > Rick said **he got** a lot of information.
- It is not necessary to change the form of the verb in the noun clause if reporting a general truth.
  > "Students **take** different courses."
  > She said students **take** different courses.
- Do not change the form of the verb if the reporting verb in the main clause is in the simple present or present perfect.
  > "The interview **is** short."
  > She **says** the interview is short.
  > "We've hoped for a change."
  > He **says** they'**ve hoped** for a change.

UNIT 12 Psychology and Personality

Gerunds as Subjects
- Use the plural form of the verb after two or more gerunds.
  > Pronouncing new words and spelling them are hard.
- Gerunds and the present participle of verbs look the same. They both end in *–ing*.
  > VERB (present participle)
  > Tom and Jack are **taking** an art class.
  > GERUND
  > **Taking** an art class is expensive.

Gerunds as Objects of Prepositions
- Use a possessive adjective (*my, your, his, her, its, our, their*) when the subject of the gerund is different from the subject of the sentence.
  > I am sick of **your** talking all the time.
  > (I am sick of it. You talk all the time.)

Verb + Infinitive or Gerund

- Some verbs take either an infinitive or gerund but with a difference in meaning. After *stop*, *forget*, and *remember*, the gerund refers to something that happened before the action of the main verb. The infinitive refers to something that happened after the action of the main verb.

    He **stopped looking** for an apartment in the city.
    (= He was looking for an apartment in the city. Then he stopped.)
    He **stopped to look** for an apartment in the city.
    (= He stopped what he was doing. Then he looked for an apartment in the city.)

Suggestions and Offers: *Let's / Let me / Why don't we / Why don't I*

- To respond positively to a question with *Let's* and *Why don't we*, use one of these answers:

    A: Let's go to the park. OR
       Why don't we go to the park?
    B: **That's a good idea.** OR
    B: **That sounds good.** OR
    B: **OK.** OR
    B: **All right.**

    To respond negatively to a question with *Let's* or *Why don't we*, say *I'd rather not*.

    A: Let's go to the park.
    B: **I'd rather not. It's cold outside.**

Preferences: *Would rather / Would prefer*

- Be careful! Use *prefer* + infinitive or *prefer* + gerund to talk about general preferences.

    A: Which do you enjoy more, swimming or running?
    B: I prefer **swimming**. = I prefer **to swim**.

- Don't repeat the verb when it is the same in both positions.

    Would you rather have chicken or fish?
    NOT ~~Would you rather have chicken or have fish?~~

Polite Requests: *Would you mind*

- Don't repeat *would you mind* before a second gerund.

    Would you mind calling Mimi and **telling** her I can't come?
    NOT ~~Would you mind calling Mimi and would you mind telling her I can't come?~~

Should / Ought to / Had better

- *Had better* is usually contracted (*'d*). *Had better* is not used in questions.

    You**'d better fasten** your seatbelt.
    (=If you don't fasten your seatbelt, you'll get a ticket.)

Have to / Be supposed to / Can

- *Must* also means "to be necessary." However, in spoken American English *have to* is more common.

    You **must be** on time. = You **have to be** on time.

    Be careful! The negative *must not* does not mean the same thing as *not have to do*.

    You **must not park** there.
    (=You can't park there because it's forbidden.)
    You **don't have to park** there.
    (=It's not necessary to do it, but you can if you want to.)

May have/ Might have for Past Possibility

- There are no contracted forms for *may have* or *might have*.

    There may have been people in the building.
    NOT ~~There may've been people in the building.~~

Must have for Logical Conclusions about the Past

- Be careful! Do not confuse *may have* or *might have* and *must have*. You are not very sure when you use *may have* or *might have*. You are very sure when you use *must have*.

    She **may have been** tired. That's why she was in a bad mood.
    She **must have been** tired. She didn't sleep all night.

Adverb Clauses: Reason

- An adverb clause can come before or after the main clause. Notice the difference in punctuation.

    Because the election is next week, the candidates are very busy.
    The candidates are very busy **because the election is next week.**

- You can also use *since* to give a reason. *Since* is more formal than *because* and usually comes at the beginning of the sentence. *Since* usually tells the listener information he or she already knows.

  Since people are starting to get sick from the pollution, we have to do something about it.
- Be careful! *Since* is also used at the beginning of adverb clauses of time.

  Since I started my new job, I have gotten promoted twice. (since = time)

  Since I've done good work, I have gotten promoted twice. (since = reason)

Because of / Despite / In spite of
- Phrases with *because of, despite,* or *in spite of* can come at the beginning or at the end of the sentence. Notice the difference in punctuation.

  In spite of the bad weather, most people voted.

  Most people voted **in spite of the bad weather**.

UNIT 18 Money

Present Real Conditionals
- The *if* clause can come before or after the main clause. Notice the difference in punctuation.

  ADVERB CLAUSE (condition)   MAIN CLAUSE (result)

  If you pay by check**,** you have to show identification.

      MAIN CLAUSE (result)   ADVERB CLAUSE (condition)

  You have to show identification **if** you pay by check.

Future Real Conditionals
- You can use the *if* clause to answer questions about future events. Remember to use the present form of the verb in the *if* clause.

  A: Are you going to buy a car?

  B: Yes, if the bank **gives** me the loan.

UNIT 19 Decisions and Dilemmas

Present Real and Unreal Conditionals
- An unreal conditional states a condition that is not true or probably not true. Unreal conditional sentences refer to the present or future. However, we use the simple past in the *if* clause and *would* + verb in the main clause.

  If I **had** the time today, I **would go** with you.

  (=I don't have time today, so I won't go with you.)

  If I **didn't have to work** next week, I **would visit** my family. (= I have to work next week, so I won't visit my family.)

- In everyday conversation, people sometimes use *was* in the *if* clause of unreal conditional sentences.

  If I **was** you, I wouldn't do that.
- Use *could* + verb in the main clause when you talk about possibility.

  If I had a lot of money, I **could move**.

  (= It would be possible for me to move.)

  If I had a lot of money, I **would move**.

  (= I would definitely do this.)

Making Wishes: Present and Future
- In everyday conversation, people sometimes use *was* after *wish*.

  I wish (that) she **was** here.
- We often use the simple present with *hope*.

  We **hope** (that) they **come** tomorrow.

  Sometimes we use *will* after *hope*.

  We **hope** (that) they **will come** tomorrow.

Past Unreal Conditionals
- If it was possible for something to happen in the past but it did not happen, use *could have* + past participle in the main clause.

  If you had been on time, we **could have taken** the bus.

  (=It was possible for us to take the bus but we didn't, because you weren't on time.)

UNIT 20 Moving On

Phrasal Verbs: Transitive and Intransitive
- Some phrasal verbs have more than one meaning.

  After the fight, we **made up** quickly.

  (= became friends again)

  The actress **made up** her face before the performance. (= put on lipstick, etc.)

  The little boy always **makes up** stories. (= invents)

  The teacher usually **makes up** classes when he is absent. (= reschedules)

Charts

Irregular Verbs

Base form	Simple Past	Past Participle	Base form	Simple Past	Past Participle
be	was	been	make	made	made
become	became	become	meet	met	met
buy	bought	bought	pay	paid	paid
catch	caught	caught	put	put	put
come	came	come	read	read	read
cost	cost	cost	ride	rode	ridden
cry	cried	cried	ring	rang	rung
cut	cut	cut	run	ran	run
do	did	done	say	said	said
drink	drank	drunk	see	saw	seen
drive	drove	driven	sell	sold	sold
eat	ate	eaten	send	sent	sent
feel	felt	felt	shine	shone	shone
find	found	found	sit	sat	sat
fly	flew	flown	sleep	slept	slept
forget	forgot	forgotten	speak	spoke	spoken
get	got	gotten	spend	spent	spent
give	gave	given	stand	stood	stood
go	went	gone	steal	stole	stolen
have	had	had	swim	swam	swum
hear	heard	heard	take	took	taken
hit	hit	hit	teach	taught	taught
hold	held	held	think	thought	thought
hurt	hurt	hurt	try	tried	tried
know	knew	known	wake	woke	woken
leave	left	left	wear	wore	worn
lose	lost	lost	win	won	won
			write	wrote	written

Common Stative Verbs

Senses	Possession	Likes	Needs	Mental States	Measurement	Description
feel	belong	hate	need	agree	cost	be
hear	have	like	want	believe	weigh	look
see	own	love		forget		seem
smell				know		
sound				remember		
taste				think		
				understand		

Verb + Gerund

acknowledge	consider	enjoy	justify	prohibit	risk
admit	delay	escape	keep (*continue*)	quit	stop
advise	deny	explain	mention	recall	suggest
appreciate	detest	feel like	mind (*object to*)	recommend	support
avoid	discontinue	finish	miss	regret	
can't help	discuss	forgive	postpone	report	
celebrate	dislike	give up (*stop*)	practice	resent	
	endure	imagine	prevent	resist	

Verb + Preposition + Gerund

adapt to	approve of	be into	consist of	engage in
adjust to	argue (with	blame for	decide on	forgive (someone)
agree (with	someone) about	care about	depend on	for
someone) on	ask about	complain (to	disapprove of	
apologize (to	believe in	someone) about	discourage (someone)	
someone) for		concentrate on	from	

Verb + Infinitive

agree	choose	hesitate	need	promise	want
appear	consent	hope	neglect	refuse	wish
arrange	decide	hurry	offer	request	would like
ask	deserve	intend	pay	rush	
attempt	expect	learn	plan	seem	
can't afford	fail	manage	prepare	volunteer	
can't wait	help	mean (*intend*)	pretend	wait	

Verb + Object + Infinitive

advise	encourage	hire	persuade	tell
allow	expect	invite	promise	urge
ask	forbid	need	remind	want
cause	force	order	request	warn
choose	get	pay	require	would like
convince	help	permit	teach	

Verbs Followed by the Gerund or the Infinitive

begin	continue	hate	love	remember*	stop*
can't stand	forget*	like	prefer	start	try

* These verbs can be followed by the gerund or the infinitive, but there is a difference in meaning.

Time Word Changes in Indirect Speech

Direct Speech		Indirect Speech
now	⟶	then
today	⟶	that day
tomorrow	⟶	the next day OR the day after
yesterday	⟶	the day before
this week / month / year	⟶	that week / month / year

Common Expressions Followed by Noun Clauses

Statements	Questions
I don't know . . .	Do you know . . .?
I don't understand . . .	Do you understand . . .?
I wonder . . .	Can you tell me . . .?
I'm not sure . . .	Can you explain . . .?
I can't remember . . .	
It doesn't say . . .	
I'd like to know . . .	
I want to understand . . .	
I'd like to find out . . .	

Common Reporting Verbs

acknowledge	complain	say
add	demand	shout
admit	explain	state
advise	invite	suggest
announce	mean	tell
answer	order	want to know
argue	promise	warn
ask	repeat	whisper
believe	reply	wonder
claim	report	write
comment	respond	yell

Transitive Phrasal Verbs (Separable)

ask someone over	hand something in	put something together
bring someone or something back	hang something up	send something back
	help someone out	start something over
bring someone up	lay someone off	take something away
call someone back	leave something off	take something/someone back
call something off	leave something on	take something off
check something out	let someone down	take someone out
clean something out	look something up	take something up
close something down	make something up	talk something over
cut something up	move something around	think something up
do something over	pass something out	throw something away/out
drop someone off	pay someone back	try something on
figure something out	pay something off	turn someone down
fill something out	pick someone / something up	turn something on/off
find something out	pick something out	use something up
give something away	put something away	wake someone up
give something back	put something off	work something out
give something up	put something on	write something down

Transitive Phrasal Verbs (Inseparable)

break up with someone	go along with something
call on someone	go out with someone
come up with something	go over something
count on someone / something	keep up with someone / something
cut down on something	look after someone / something
drop out of something	look over someone / something
follow through with something	make up with someone
get along with someone	miss out on something
get off (a bus)	put up with someone / something
get on (a bus)	run into someone
get over something	run out of something
get through with something	think back on something
give up something	watch out for someone / something

Intransitive Phrasal Verbs

break down	make up
get along	move on
go out	show up

Partner Activities

From Time to Talk, page 37

DETECTIVE JENKES GAME

INSTRUCTIONS

1. Act out the investigation of Oscar Snodgrass's murder. Choose one student to be Detective Jenkes, and the other students to be his assistants or suspects.

2. The suspects meet and decide who the murderer is, and how the murder happened. While they are meeting, the detectives discuss which questions they will ask the suspects.

3. Begin the investigation. The detectives ask the suspects questions.

4. When the detectives think they have found the murderer, Detective Jenkes will arrest him or her.

Example:

Detective: *So Ms. Hodges, please tell me how you found the body of Mr. Snodgrass.*
Ms. Hodges: *I had been out doing errands for Mr. Snodgrass all day . . .*

A.
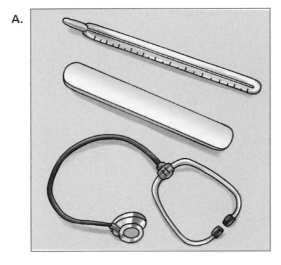

B.

C.
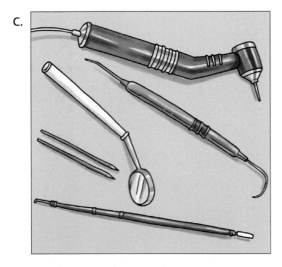

D.

E.
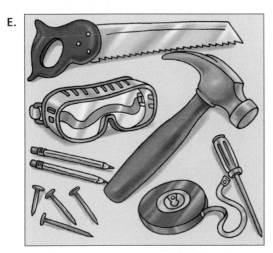

F.
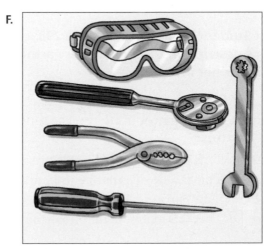

Student A: Write descriptions of these inventions. What were they made for? Where and when were they made?

A.

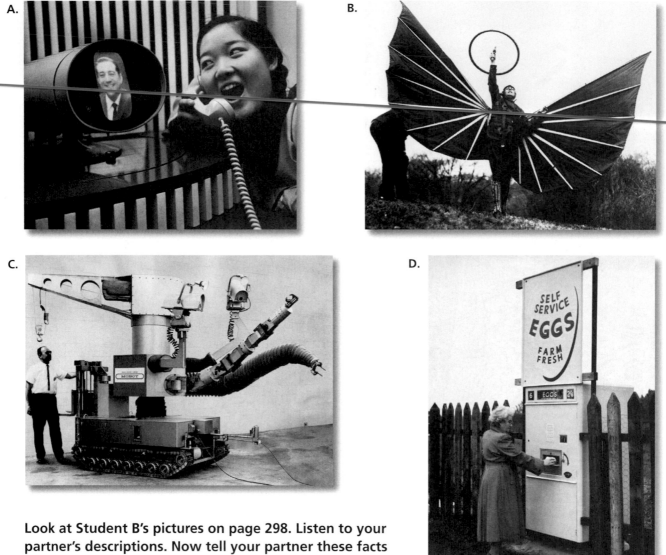

B.

C.

D.

Look at Student B's pictures on page 298. Listen to your partner's descriptions. Now tell your partner these facts about his or her inventions:

Picture A: These are robots that make music. They were made in Paris, France around 1954.
Picture B: This is a device that scares rats and mice. It was made in Japan around 1963.
Picture C: This is a device that helps people eat spaghetti. It was made in the United States around 1955.
Picture D: This is a machine that treats hair. It was built in England in the 1930s.

From Time to Talk, PAGE 147

Questions that you asked at a job interview:

1. When will I get my first paycheck?

2. What kind of health insurance is available?

3. How many sick days will I get during the first month?

4. How much overtime will I be able to work?

5. When will I get a raise?

6. How soon can I take a vacation?

From Time to Talk, PAGE 149

HILLSIDE COLLEGE

Has it all!

HILLSIDE COLLEGE

SPORTS	HILLSIDE COLLEGE
Sports/recreation center	✓
Basketball team	✓
Soccer team	–
Football team	✓
Sports scholarships	✓

ARTS	
Orchestra	✓
Chorus	✓
Theater	✓
Dance studio	✓
Fine arts	✓

ACADEMIC	
# of libraries	3
Academic resource center	✓
Computer labs	5
Number of students	20,000
Rate of graduation	90%
Student / teacher ratio	100 / 1

OTHER	
% of international students	5%
Male / female ratio	40 / 60
On-campus housing	✓
Student health center	✓
Work study program	✓
Evening / part-time program	–

From Time to Talk, PAGE 243

1. If you are having trouble making ends meet . . .

2. If you´re up to your ears in debt . . .

3. If you want to build a nest egg . . .

From Time to Talk, PAGE 95

Look at the picture. Answer the building inspector's questions about your building.

carbon monoxide detector

boiler

Now you are the building inspector. Ask the landlord questions. What has the landlord done or not done on your list?

CHICAGO DEPARTMENT OF BUILDINGS
220 N LaSalle Street
Chicago, IL. 606601

LIST OF REPAIRS FOR LANDLORD

TO DO BY 2/1

1. Make sure heat is 68 degrees from 8:30 A.M.-10:30 P.M.

2. Remove graffiti from building.

3. Add door security alarm system.

4. Replace cracked windows.

5. Call painter. Repaint fire escapes.

Questions that you were asked at a job interview:

1. Who are you married to?

2. What health department rules are you familiar with?

3. Where did you go on vacation last year?

4. What babysitting arrangements do you have for your children?

5. What kind of car do you have?

6. What is important to make a supermarket attractive to customers?

Providing for All of Your Needs

MCC
Midway Community College

SPORTS	MIDWAY COMMUNITY COLLEGE	ACADEMIC	MIDWAY COMMUNITY COLLEGE
sports / recreation center	--	# of libraries	1
basketball team	--	academic resource center	✓
soccer team	✓	computer labs	5
football team	--	number of students	5,000
sports scholarships	--	rate of graduation	70%
		student / teacher ratio	50 / 1
ARTS		**OTHER**	
orchestra	--	% of international students	20%
chorus	✓	male / female ratio	50 / 50
theater	✓	on-campus housing	--
dance studio	✓	student health center	✓
fine arts	✓	work study program	✓

From Time to Talk, PAGE 243

1. If you are broke . . .

2. If your husband spend money like water . . .

3. If you want to save for a rainy day . . .

From Time to Talk, PAGE 95

You are a building inspector. Ask the landlord questions. What has the landlord done or not done on your list?

 CHICAGO DEPARTMENT OF BUILDINGS
220 N LaSalle Street
Chicago, IL. 606601

LIST OF REPAIRS FOR LANDLORD

TO DO BY 2/1

1. Fix boiler and turn up heat.
2. Install carbon monoxide detectors.
3. Repair broken elevator.
4. Call plumber. Install new pipes.
5. Fix cracks in walls outside building.

Now you are the landlord. Look at the picture. Answer the building inspector's questions about your building.

Student B: Write descriptions of these inventions. What were they made for? Where and when were they made?

A.

B.

C.

D.

Look at Student A's pictures on page 292. Listen to your partner's descriptions. Now tell your partner facts about his or her inventions.

> Picture A: This is a picturephone that lets you see the people you are calling. It was made by AT&T in the United States around 1964.
>
> Picture B: This is a wingsuit that was made to help people fly. However, these wingsuits did not work. This wingsuit was probably made in Europe in the 1930s.
>
> Picture C: This is a robot that does dangerous jobs. It was built by the Hughes Aircraft Company in California in 1965.
>
> Picture D: This is a vending machine that sells eggs. It was made in England around 1960.

Answers to Exercise A, page 76

1. Food <u>wasn't</u> first canned in the 20th century. The idea of canning food started in 1795. Nicolas Appert, a French candy-maker and baker, preserved food in glass jars for Napolean's army. In 1810, Peter Durand, an Englishman, preserved food in tin cans. The first canning factory opened in 1813.

2. Pepsi® <u>was</u> invented by a pharmacist. Caleb Bradham of North Carolina, like many pharmacists at the time, had a soda fountain in his drugstore. He created "Brad's drink" in 1893. He later renamed it Pepsi-Cola® for the pepsin and cola nuts used in the recipe.

3. Pasta <u>wasn't</u> created by Italian chefs. No one knows exactly where and when pasta first came from. It was probably first brought to Sicily, in southern Italy, by Arabs in the 8th century. Some people thought Marco Polo brought it from China in 1295, but this is incorrect.

4. The first cookbook <u>wasn't</u> written in 1940. There is evidence of recipes being written down in 1500 B.C. in Bablyon. These recipes did not look like modern cookbooks. The first cookbook was printed in Italy in 1485.

5. Tomatoes <u>weren't</u> eaten until the mid-1700s in England. Tomatoes were grown in England for many years before that. However, in 1597, a famous expert in plants, John Gerard, wrote that tomatoes were poisonous. As a result, the English did not eat tomatoes for over 100 years, until the mid-1700s.

6. The first sandwiches <u>were</u> eaten in England by the Fourth Earl of Sandwich. These sandwiches looked like sandwiches of today. They were made with toasted bread and salted meat. The idea of a sandwich is even older. Some people say that Hillel the Elder, a Jewish rabbi in Jerusalem made a "sandwich" of matzah and bitter herbs for Passover in the 1st century B.C.

Audioscript

Unit 1: Fun and Entertainment

Listening, A, B, and C, page 3

Bruce: Hey, Tina. Have you tried out for the school play yet?

Tina: No. I'm not going to this year. I tried out last year and I didn't get a part.

Bruce: Ah, come on! That was last year. This year there are a lot of parts.

Tina: But I haven't acted before.

Bruce: So? You've performed in lots of dance competitions.

Tina: Dancing is completely different from acting.

Bruce: It's not so different. They're both performing.

Tina: Well . . .

Bruce: Come on. We've never been in a play together, and this is our last chance.

Tina: All right, I'll try out, but on one condition.

Bruce: Sure, anything.

Tina: Well, since we started high school, I've danced with every guy in our class . . . except you. We've known each other for three years, but in all that time, you've never asked me to dance. In fact, I don't think I've ever seen you dance.

Bruce: No . . . no . . .

Tina: If you want me to try out for the play, you have to dance with me at graduation.

Bruce: No way! Nobody's ever seen me dance because I've never danced in my life.

Tina: I'll teach you. I've taught lots of people how to dance.

Bruce: Uh-uh . . .

Tina: Come on. Have you forgotten already what you told me a minute ago? That dancing and acting aren't so different?

Grammar to Communicate 1, C, page 5

A: Look at this picture of Wanda Simpson.

B: Boy, she's gotten old.

A: I know. And it says here that she hasn't made a movie in a year.

B: Is she still with Jimmy Peace, or have they broken up?

A: They're still together. They've been together for years.

B: Well, he's gorgeous. He always has been. His brother is too. Have you seen this picture of Jimmy and his brother together?

A: No, I haven't. He *is* good-looking. What movies has he been in?

B: He's not an actor. He's a dancer.

Grammar to Communicate 3, A, page 8

Steve: So . . . it says here that we should talk about something fun that we've done in the past year.

Miranda: Hmm . . . something fun . . . OK, I'll start. I've learned how to dance.

Steve: Finally!

Yvonne: So Steve, tell us, what's the most fun you've had?

Steve: Fun? I haven't had much time for fun. I've been too busy. I opened my own business a few months ago.

Miranda: Oh that's right. I forgot. Robert, it's your turn.

Robert: Well, I joined the basketball team. It's been a lot of fun. Since I joined my team we've won two championships.

Steve: Really? I didn't know you were on the team.

Dictation, page 10

1. How long have you been an actor?
2. I've acted in movies since I was a kid.
3. Have you ever been in a show?
4. Yes, I was in a play two years ago.
5. But I haven't done any work in the theater since then.

Listening, A and B, page 11

Reporter: This is Ty Bradley, with this week's entertainment report. So, think carefully—when was the last time you watched a movie in a movie theater? Not on TV, not on DVD, not on your computer, but in a real movie theater? If you can't remember, you're not alone. A recent report on the movie industry has found that since 2001, ticket sales at most movie theaters have fallen. And that has begun to make some people in Hollywood very nervous. So, why have so many of us stopped going to the movies? Have we gotten bored with Hollywood? Have ticket prices become too expensive? Has technology made movie theaters a thing of the past?

Let's consider the questions one-by-one. First of all, has the public lost interest in the same old Hollywood stories? Many people think so. And because technology has given people more entertainment choices, going to the movies is no longer the only thing to do on a Saturday night. At the same time, many of us have less free time, so we have become more careful about how we spend it. And speaking of spending, what about ticket prices? Has the cost of a movie become too expensive? With ticket prices as high as $15 at some theaters, the answer seems obvious. Going out to the movies has simply become too expensive for a lot of people.

Finally, what effect has technology had? If you can rent a DVD for a few dollars and watch it at home on your widescreen TV, why would you drive to a movie theater, stand in line for a $15 ticket, spend $20 on a soda and a bag of popcorn—just to sit next to some guy talking on his cell phone?

So, what do you think? Has the golden age of Hollywood finally come to an end? And if so, is that a good thing or a bad thing? Call us now and join the conversation.

Unit 2: Health and Fitness

Listening, A, B, and C, page 17

Secretary:	Good morning, Dr. Morgan's office, may I help you?
Mrs. Roberts:	This is Alice Roberts. I haven't been feeling very well lately, and I'd like to make an appointment to see the doctor.
Secretary:	Are you a patient at this office?
Mrs. Roberts:	Yes, of course. I'm Alice Roberts. I've been Dr. Morgan's patient since the day he finished medical school!
Secretary:	Oh, I'm sorry Mrs. Roberts—you haven't visited us in a long time. Now…you said you haven't been feeling well—what's been bothering you?
Mrs. Roberts:	Well, my arthritis has been acting up, I haven't been sleeping very well, and I don't have much of an appetite. And I'm losing weight—I've noticed that some of my clothes don't fit me anymore.
Secretary:	How long has this been going on?
Mrs. Roberts:	Oh, for about a month.
Secretary:	Hmmm . . . Unfortunately, we're all booked today and tomorrow. Let's see . . . our next opening is on Friday, with Dr. Freeman.
Mrs. Roberts:	Dr. Who? I told you, Dr. Morgan is my doctor.

Secretary:	Dr. Freeman has been working with Dr. Morgan since September, and I promise you that he's an excellent doctor.
Mrs. Roberts:	Hmph! Well, I want Dr. Morgan. He's known me for years.
Secretary:	OK, Mrs. Roberts, but his next appointment isn't until next Wednesday at 11:00.
Mrs. Roberts:	I'm not going anywhere. I can wait.
Secretary:	Now, you know we've moved, right? We're in the same building, but on the second floor, room 256.
Mrs. Roberts:	You've moved? What? Where?
Secretary:	Yes, that's right. Just one floor up from the old office—second floor, room 256.

Grammar to Communicate 1, A, page 18

Doctor:	How long have you been dieting?
Patient:	I've been dieting for about a month.
Doctor:	And have you been exercising?
Patient:	Yes. I've been working out every day.
Doctor:	And what have you been eating?
Patient:	I've been trying to eat healthy food. I've been eating a lot of vegetables, and I haven't been having dessert.

Grammar to Communicate 2, A, page 20

1. Ella's been talking to the doctor for half an hour.
2. Ella has talked to the doctor.
3. He has been reading an article about diabetes.
4. He has read several articles about diabetes.
5. The surgeon has operated on many patients today.

Grammar to Communicate 2, C, page 21

Dr. Simon:	So how long have you been ill?
Betty:	I haven't been feeling right for about week. But over the past two days I've gotten worse and worse, and I haven't been sleeping much.
Dr. Simon:	Have you taken any pain killers?
Betty:	Yes. I've been taking Pain Away every four hours.
Dr. Simon:	And has it helped?
Betty:	No, not really.
Dr. Simon:	How has your appetite been?
Betty:	Not very good.
Dr. Simon:	Well, you haven't had a blood test since last year so I'll give you one now. Have you had anything to eat in the past three hours?
Betty:	No, but I've drunk a cup of tea.

Dr. Simon: That's all right. Wait here and I'll be right back.

Dictation, page 24

1. I've been feeling lousy for the past couple of weeks.
2. Has your asthma been acting up again?
3. No, but I've had a terrible headache for days.
4. Have you taken any pain medication?
5. Yes. I've tried several different kinds, but nothing has worked.

Listening, B and C, page 25

Reporter: Good afternoon, this is Michelle Miller reporting for Health Watch. Today, we're going to take a look at health trends worldwide. The information in this report comes from the World Health Organization and the United Nations.

Just how healthy are we? Well, the news is mixed. During the last 50 years, life expectancy has improved by almost 20 years overall, from 46.5 years to 65.2 years. But that's only if you include the life expectancy of people in all countries, including the richest countries, for example Japan and the United States. Sadly, in some African and Eastern European nations, life expectancy, especially for men, has been falling recently.

Worldwide, the death rate for children under the age of 5 has been going down. In 1970 approximately 17 million children under age 5 died worldwide. In 2002, that number was 10.5 million. However, the situation has not improved everywhere—in 14 African countries, the child death rate has gone up since 1990.

Cancer rates worldwide have been rising steadily. Health officials have predicted a sharp increase in new cases, from 10 million in the year 2000 to 15 million in the year 2020. According to a recent report, causes of the predicted increase include a world population that has been getting older, as well as continued high rates of smoking.

Worldwide, the number of smokers has been going up. However, there is a big difference between the richer, more developed countries, and the poorer, less developed nations. In the poorer countries of the developing world, the number of smokers has increased a lot.

In contrast, smoking rates have been falling since the 1960s in the richer countries of the developed world. This drop is mainly due to a decrease in male smokers. Interestingly, in many of the richer developed nations, the number of female smokers has been going up over the past ten years.

For Health Watch, this is Michelle Miller.

Unit 3: Crime

Listening, A, B, and C, page 31

Officer: So, Ms. Snodgrass, tell us what you were doing this evening between the hours of 8 and 10.

Ms. Snodgrass: Well, I had been shopping all day, so I was tired.

Officer: What time did you get home from shopping?

Ms. Snodgrass: At around 8:15. As I said, I was pretty tired when I got home, but little Fluffy hadn't eaten yet . . .

Officer: Who's Fluffy?

Ms. Snodgrass: Fluffy's my dog . . . As I was saying . . . she hadn't eaten, so I fed her. While she was eating, I called my friend Bernie. He'd been away, and we hadn't talked in a while. We talked until Fluffy started to bark . . . She wanted her walk.

Officer: What time was this?

Ms. Snodgrass: Well, I didn't look at the clock . . . oh, but wait a minute . . . yes, I had been listening to the radio, and the 10 o'clock news had just come on . . . So it was 10:00 when we left the house.

Officer: Go on.

Ms. Snodgrass: Well, we had just started our walk when we heard a scream. It was coming from the garage. I had never heard a scream like that before, except in movies. I grabbed Fluffy and ran back into the house.

Officer: So you called the police.

Ms. Snodgrass: Uh, no.

Officer: You had just heard a terrible scream, but you didn't call the police?

Ms. Snodgrass: Well, when I got in the house, the phone was ringing. It was my neighbor . . . Mrs. Dobbs. She wanted to know if I had heard the scream. She said that she would call the police . . .

Grammar to Communicate 2, A, page 34

1. As soon as I opened the door, I knew someone had been in the house.
2. I had checked out every part of the house when the police arrived.
3. My neighbors and I were surprised because there hadn't been a break-in in the neighborhood in years.

4. By the time the police caught the thief, he had broken into three more houses in the neighborhood.

Dictation, page 38

1. How long had you been waiting when the police arrived?
2. I hadn't been there long.
3. Had the manager already gone home?
4. Yes, he had left a few minutes before.
5. There hadn't been any customers all night, so he closed the store early.

Listening, A and B, page 39

Reporter: And now, it's time for our weekly round-up of the world's stupidest criminals. This week, we have two bank robberies for you. The first one happened in Virginia. The robbery started out pretty well. The robber walked into a bank and handed the teller a note. Within minutes, he was on his way to the getaway car with the money. But then he realized that he had left the demand note in the bank. He rushed back, got the note, and ran to his car. But this time he had forgotten his car keys.

Somehow, he was able to get away on foot, and make it to his apartment. But he had borrowed his roommate's car, and the car was at the bank. . . . he told the roommate that someone had stolen the car. Naturally, the roommate called the police to report the stolen car. Less than 20 minutes later, several police officers who were investigating the robbery saw the parked car a block from the bank. When the robber's keys fit the lock, they knew that they had found their man. The police officers ran a check on the car's license plate. Within an hour, they had arrested the bank robber. How did they know his address? Because the roommate had reported his car stolen. At first, the police thought that the roommate had lied about his stolen car. They were sure that he was the real robber. But after they interviewed him and found out that he had loaned his car to his roommate, they believed him. After all, the real robber wasn't hard to find. He was busy counting his money in the next room . . .

Unit 4: Moving In

Listening, A, B, and C page 45

Mr. Dufy:	Hello. You must be Mr. and Mrs. Lang. I'm Andrew Dufy. Please, have a seat.
The Langs:	Thank you.
Mr. Dufy:	So, I see here that you're looking for a two-bedroom apartment in the $750-$1,000 range.
Mr. Lang:	That's right. We're in a one-bedroom now. We love the apartment, but we're having a baby and it's too small for three.
Mr. Dufy:	Congratulations! When's the baby due?
Mrs. Lang:	In four months. So we need to find an apartment soon.
Mr. Dufy:	Don't worry. I'm sure we can find you a nice place.
Mrs. Lang:	Oh, that's great.
Mr Dufy:	So let's talk about what's important to you in an apartment.
Mr. Lang:	Location, definitely. We want to live in a safe neighborhood, close to public transportation.
Mrs. Lang:	And laundry facilities are very important. With the baby coming, there's going to be a lot of laundry.
Mr. Dufy:	Do you mean you want a washer and dryer right in the apartment? That might be difficult to find in your price range. Most buildings just have laundry facilities in the basement.
Mrs. Lang:	Oh, that's fine. As long as there's a laundry room in the building.
Mr. Dufy:	And do you need parking?
Mr. Lang:	No, we don't have a car.
Mr. Dufy:	Excellent. That makes things a lot easier— and cheaper. OK, so let me see. . . I have several 2-bedrooms that we can look at today. The first one is right around the corner. It's in a wonderful building with excellent security. And the landlord takes great care of the property. There's also a park with a playground right next door. And the utilities are included.
Mr. Lang:	It sounds perfect.
Mr. Dufy:	Great! I'll get the keys.

Grammar to Communicate 3, A, page 50

1. Parks are great, but other things are more important.
2. Public transportation is important. We don't have a car.
3. Safety is important. I live alone.
4. Good weather is important. I like to walk outside.
5. Schools are not very important to us. We don't have kids.
6. Good restaurants are not very important. We hardly ever eat out.

Dictation, page 52

1. Is there a trash chute on this floor?
2. Yes, but you need a key for it.
3. Where do I get the key?

4. Ask the building manager.

5. He gives new tenants their keys.

Listening, A and B, page 53

Reporter: This is Jeremy D'Alessandro for Culture Watch. When you move to a new country, you may find that many customs are different. However, you expect that some things will be the same. Take, for example, finding a place to live. People all over the world rent apartments and buy houses, right? So how different could the customs be from one modern country to another? Today we are going to compare housing in two countries: Greece and the United States.

First of all, how long are rental leases in each country? In the United States, where people move a lot, a lease is usually for one year. In Greece, a landlord can't rent an apartment for less than two years, but most tenants and landlords prefer three-year leases.

Our next question is: What appliances are there in most apartments? In the United States, apartments almost always come with a stove, an oven, and a refrigerator. In Greece, however, tenants have to buy their own kitchen appliances. And in the United States, the rent sometimes includes utilities such as heat, water, and electricity; but in Greece, tenants always pay for their own utilities.

Now let's talk about how many people own their own homes. In the United States today, about 68% of families are homeowners. How about in Greece? Approximately 80% of Greeks own their own homes. That is one of the highest rates of any European country.

And are the kinds of housing that people buy the same in the two countries? In the United States about 66% of all housing units are single-family homes. Only about 12% of Americans live in buildings with 10 or more apartments. The situation is very different in Greece, which is much more crowded than the United States. Single-family homes are not very common. Instead, most people live in apartment buildings; they buy their own apartment, but share the building facilities and costs with the other apartment owners.

Tomorrow, we will take a look at housing in Buenos Aires.

Unit 5: New on the Job

Listening, A, B, and C, page 59

Mr. Torres: Now let's talk about Townsend.

Mr. Wilson: I was there for three years. I started as a sales clerk. After six months, I was promoted to supervisor.

Mr. Torres: So you were doing well there, right?

Mr. Wilson: Absolutely.

Mr. Torres: Then why did you decide to leave?

Ms. Wilson: I wanted to become a manager, but there weren't any openings. You're familiar with the policies at Townsend, aren't you?

Mr. Torres: No, I'm not.

Ms. Bauer: Neither am I.

Mr. Wilson: Oh, I'm sorry, I thought . . . anyway, most of their managers have been there for years. I felt that I was ready to move up, and so did my boss. But there were no openings.

Ms. Bauer: So, when we call your former boss, what will he say about you?

Mr. Wilson: That's an interesting question . . . I think he'll tell you that I'm a very hard worker. When I say I'll do something, I do it.

Mr. Torres: And the people that you supervised?

Mr. Wilson: They'll say that I expect a lot, but I'm fair.

Mr. Torres: OK, that's all for me. Grace, you don't have any other questions, do you?

Ms. Bauer: No, that's fine.

Mr. Torres: We'll make our decision either this week or next. Neither Ms. Bauer nor I will be in the office tomorrow, but you can call my assistant with the names of your references.

Mr. Wilson: I'll do that. Thank you very much for your time.

Mr. Torres: And thank you for coming in.

Mrs. Bauer: You know your way out, don't you?

Mr. Wilson: Yes, no problem. Thanks again.

Mr. Torres: So, what did you think?

Ms. Bauer: I liked him.

Mr. Torres: I did too. And he's got both the qualifications *and* the personality we need.

Grammar to Communicate 1 A, page 60

1. (*checking information / rising intonation*) She has the right qualifications, doesn't she?

2. (*expecting agreement / falling intonation*) His performance hasn't improved, has it?

3. (*checking information / rising intonation*) You're familiar with our policies, aren't you?

4. (*expecting agreement / falling intonation*) It was quiet here last week, wasn't it?

5. (*expecting agreement / falling intonation*) You're not from around here, are you?

6. (*checking information / rising intonation*) You didn't check her references, did you?

Dictation, page 66

1. Val and Tom have worked here for a long time, haven't they?
2. Val has been here for three years, and so has Tom.
3. Has either Val or Tom moved up?
4. No, neither Tom nor Val has gotten a promotion yet.
5. But both Val and Tom are very hard workers.

Listening, A and B, page 67

CONVERSATION 1

Man: You don't work here, do you?

Woman: Yes, in fact, I do.

Man: Really? I haven't seen you around before.

Woman: I just started last week. I'm Gloria.

Man: Nice to meet you Gloria. I'm Paul Tierney. I work in human resources.

Woman: Nice to meet you, too. I'm in the accounting department. Ummm . . . You don't have a minute, do you?

Man: Sure, what do you need?

Woman: Well, I can't seem to turn on the air conditioner in my office.

Man: Oh, yeah, these new air conditioners are a little tricky, aren't they? I couldn't figure out how to work mine at first, either . . .

CONVERSATION 2

Man: I'm going to grab something to eat. You don't need anything, do you?

Woman: No, thanks. I've already eaten. You haven't forgotten the meeting at 2:00, have you?

Man: What meeting?

Woman: You're kidding, aren't you?

Man: Of course I'm kidding. Would you please relax? Everything is going to be just fine . . .

CONVERSATION 3

Woman: You know why you're here, don't you?

Man: Ummm . . . well, I have some idea, yes.

Woman: Your supervisor tells me that you've either arrived late or left early every day this month.

Man: Really? It hasn't been every day, has it?

Woman: Yes, it has. I checked your time card.

Man: Well . . . You see, my wife is working now too, so I need to drop the kids off at day care. We're not from around here, so we don't have any family to help out. You have kids, don't you?

Woman: No, I don't. I'm sorry that you're having a hard time, but this situation cannot continue. You need to find a way to handle both your personal life and your work life. Have you talked to someone in human resources about our employee daycare center?

Man: There's an employee day care center? I didn't see any information about that in either the employee handbook or the newsletter.

Woman: Really? It's either in the handbook or on the employee bulletin board. Now, let's get back to . . .

Unit 6: Food

Listening, A, B, and C, page 73

Angela: Hi, Ben. What are you reading?

Ben: A really interesting article about food. It has a lot of cool facts.

Angela: Like what?

Ben: Well, for instance, where certain types of food are and aren't eaten, and when certain kinds of food were first eaten. Did you know that beef is not eaten in many parts of India?

Angela: Of course I did. Everyone knows that cows are considered sacred in India. In Hinduism, one of the major religions of India, it's not permitted to hurt or kill a cow.

Ben: Well, I didn't know that. Did you know that pork isn't eaten in many parts of the world?

Angela: Oh, come on! You were never taught that?

Ben: OK, if you're so smart, let's see if you can answer this food quiz.

Angela: Sure! Go ahead.

Ben: Let's see . . . Here's a good question: What kind of food was used to pay the workers who built the Pyramids in Egypt?

Angela: That's easy—bread!

Ben: Right . . . What other kinds of food were used instead of money in human history?

Angela: Actually, many different kinds of food have been used as money. Salt and pepper are two more examples.

Ben: Right again. Hmmm . . . here's a harder one. Where was coffee first served?

Angela: I think that the first coffee shops appeared in the Middle East.

Ben: And who introduced coffee to Europe?

Angela: Hmmm . . . Oh, yeah, coffee was brought to Europe by the Dutch.

Ben: Amazing! You really do know your food facts, don't you?

Angela: I guess so.

Ben: OK, one last question—tomatoes—vegetables, right?

Angela: Yes, and so?

Ben: Hah! Wrong! Tomatoes are fruit.

Angela: You're kidding.

Ben: No, I'm not. Look, it's written right here.

Angela: Let me see that . . . hmmm . . . interesting . . .

Dictation, page 80

1. Ice cream is eaten all over the world.
2. Many years ago it was eaten only by rich people.
3. Ice cream cones were invented a long time ago.
4. Ice cream cones are made with flour and sugar.
5. More ice cream is consumed in the United States than in any other country.

Listening, A and B, page 81

Host: This is Jessica Chambers with Food for Life. On today's program, we are happy to welcome Dr. Hilary Xin, an expert on the use of food for medical purposes. Welcome.

Dr. Xin: Thank you. It's nice to be here.

Host: Today's topic is "food as medicine." Dr. Xin, if you could choose just three kinds of food for your medicine bag, what would they be?

Dr. Xin: Hmmm . . . That's a difficult question. There are so many different types of food that can be used as medicine… and of course the choice depends on what the medical problem is . . . but ginger, garlic, and honey would have to be at the top of my list.

Host: What makes those three so special?

Dr. Xin: Well, all three are used for very common health problems. For example, ginger can be taken for stomachaches or nausea. That is why pregnant women with morning sickness are often told by their doctors to drink ginger tea.

Host: Interesting…so is that why children are often given ginger ale to drink for a stomachache?

Dr. Xin: Yes, probably.

Host: What about the second thing on your list, garlic?

Dr. Xin: Garlic is considered by many health experts to be the oldest known health food. Among other benefits, it's believed to be a natural blood thinner; that is, it makes it easier for the blood to move through the body. Patients who have heart problems are often advised to consume garlic, usually in pill form. However, a word of warning: while many health experts are convinced of garlic's positive effects, the health benefits have not been scientifically proven. And of course you should always ask your doctor before you take any kind of dietary supplement.

Host: And what is known about the health benefits of the last item on your list, honey?

Dr. Xin: When honey is eaten regularly—a little every day—it can help prevent allergies to the plants that grow in your area. But only if you eat local honey—that is, honey that is made by bees in the area where you live. Honey has also been used for centuries to clean and soften the skin. It can be used safely on any type of skin. Actually, that's something that ginger, garlic, and honey all share. They have been used safely for medical purposes for many thousands of years.

Unit 7: Safety

Listening, A, B, and C, page 87

Owner: Has the lock to the laundry room been changed?

Super: Uh . . . no, not yet.

Owner: Oh come on! You've been told more than once! It needs to be done today! And what about the batteries in the smoke detectors on the third floor? Have they been replaced?

Super: Yes, I replaced them all last week.

Owner: And what's going on with the sprinkler system? Have you been given an installation date?

Super: I called them last week, but they haven't gotten back to me yet.

Owner: So call them again!

Super: Yes, sir.

Owner: Now, how about the safety locks on the windows . . . have they been installed yet?

Super: They're being installed tomorrow.

Owner: Good. And the front stairs? Have they been repaired? We've been lucky that no one has fallen, but sooner or later it's going to happen.

Super: I'm sorry, but I haven't had a chance to take care of that yet.

Owner: Well, it needs to be done this week. And a warning sign needs to be posted.

Super: I've already posted one. And the stairs will be fixed tomorrow. I promise.

Owner: Don't promise—just do it! And have you called the fire department?

Super: The fire department?

Owner:	Oh, come on. Don't tell me you've forgotten! I just spoke to you about it the other day. The elevators need to be inspected by the end of the month.
Super:	Yes, of course. I'll get on it right away.
Owner:	Well, don't leave it until the last minute, like you usually do.

Grammar to Communicate 1, A, page 88

Reporter: And this news just in. . . The search for the black bear that escaped from Metroparks Cleveland Zoo is over. The bear has been found. . . A man has been injured in a hunting accident. . . Several cats on the north side of town have disappeared. . . A little girl has been rescued from Lake Erie. . . A fire has been reported at an old paint factory on 143nd Street. . . an ambulance has been sent to the scene. . . Stay tuned for more details.

Dictation, page 94

1. What happened to the stop sign on the corner?
2. It disappeared last night.
3. So it´s been stolen again! It's those kids next door.
4. Maybe. Anyway, the sign is being replaced right now.
5. Something needs to be done about those kids.

Listening, A and B, page 95

Alex Martinez: This is Alex Martinez with today's headlines. Good news in Larchmont tonight, as police report that the search for 7-year-old Matthew Perry has ended. Perry, missing since Sunday, has been found in the woods just two miles from his house. Apparently, the young boy had been playing in the woods on Sunday when he lost his way. Young Perry appears to be fine—just hungry and scared. Now, let's go to Dorothea for the evening traffic report.

Dorothea Dixson: Thanks, Alex. This is Dorothea Dixson. An accident is being cleared from the northbound side of Route 55. Traffic is backed up for about 2 miles in both directions. Just the usual slowdowns downtown, but remember that the Charlestown Bridge has been closed for repairs. For Channel 7, this is your rush hour traffic report.

Alex Martinez: Thanks, Dorothea. And this news, just in: A three-alarm fire has been reported at the Belmont Office Park. Fire crews are being sent to the scene, and the roads into the office park have been closed. According to a witness, all of the offices have been safely evacuated, and no injuries have been reported. We will keep you informed as more information comes in...Now, here's Dana Roth with the community safety report. So, Dana, what's the word on the street?

Dana Roth: Good evening, Alex. Well, there's good news and bad news. The good news is that the potholes on Brewster Road are finally being filled, and we've been told by the mayor's office that new street lights are being installed in North Park this weekend. However, residents say they've been promised the same thing several times before. So we'll need to wait and see. And remember the repairs that were done on the city's swimming pools last year? Well, all of the work needs to be done—again. Apparently the repairs were not done correctly and the pools have been declared unsafe—again. So for the second summer in a row, the city's residents will need to find other ways to stay cool. For Community Safety, I'm Dana Roth, reporting . . .

Unit 8: Advertising

Listening, A, B, and C, page 101

Advertiser: Are you tired of high gasoline prices? Worried about the environment? Embarrassed about that big car you've been driving around, but disappointed in the hybrid vehicles on the market? Well, the hybrid you've been waiting for has finally arrived at your local Topline dealer. But don't believe me...Listen to what some of our satisfied customers have said:

Customer 1: I love sports cars. High performance is so important to me that I had never considered buying a hybrid vehicle. But my wife finally convinced me to take the Topline Slalom out for a test drive; I was amazed. I had such a great time! And even more importantly, my wife and I have finally found a car that we can agree on!

Customer 2: It's a little embarrassing to say this, but when I buy a car, the most important thing to me is the way it looks. Of course I'm concerned about the environment too, so as soon as I saw the Topline Elant, I knew that I had found the car of my dreams. It's a comfortable efficient automobile...and it looks great, too.

Customer 3: I have three small children, so I need a large, safe vehicle. But gas prices are so high now that I had to sell my van. I wasn't even thinking about a hybrid. They're so expensive that only rich people can afford them, right? Wrong! I got a great deal on my Topline Adventure. And every time I go to the gas pump, I'm amazed at how little I spend.

Advertiser: Topline Hybrids… The future is now. Don't delay! Test drive one today!

Grammar to Communicate I, A, page 102

1. So why wait! Enjoy a refreshing Tepsi today!
2. Hungry? Have some Snap, the satisfying snack.
3. Play it now . . . Run for Your Life! The most exciting game of the year.
4. You don't need to feel depressed anymore. Talk to your doctor today!
5. You'll be amazed at your savings at the gas pump.
6. Try Grow Back. We guarantee you won't be disappointed.

Dictation, page 108

1. Your car is amazing.
2. Really? It's so old that I don't want it anymore.
3. Are you interested in selling it?
4. Why do you want to buy such an old car?
5. To you it's old, but to me it's a great little car.

Listening, A and B, page 109

Annie Chow: This is Annie Chow with the Business Report. Today's topic is false advertising. I am delighted to welcome back Jeffrey Douglas from the Better Business Bureau.

Jeffrey Douglas: Thanks, Annie.

Annie Chow: So, what exactly *is* false advertising?

Jeffrey Douglas: Let's start with two basic rules. First, advertisers must tell the truth. Second, they must be able to prove that what they say about their products or services is true.

Annie Chow: They're such clear simple rules that it must be easy to follow them.

Jeffrey Douglas: The rules *are* simple. But it's amazing how difficult it can be to use the rules in specific situations.

Annie Chow: Well, let's take some calls . . . Joe? Go ahead.

Joe: Yes, good afternoon. I own a furniture store. Six months ago, the owner of a furniture store down the street put up a sign that said "Going out of business! Everything on sale!" However, every time I go in there, he has new furniture out. I'm sure he's not going out of business, but what can I do? Is this kind of advertising legal?

Jeffrey Douglas: The only time a business can advertise a going out of business sale is when the business is actually closing. This definitely sounds like false advertising to me. You should report him to your state Attorney General's office.

Joe: Thanks. I'll do that.

Annie Chow: Our next caller is Christine.

Christine: Well, I own a dry cleaning business. Yesterday, I saw an ad for another dry cleaners. I was shocked to see the name of my business with my price list, right next to their price list.

Jeffrey Douglas: Were the prices correct?

Christine: Well. . . yes . . . but . . .

Jeffrey Douglas: Then there is nothing you can do. If the information is correct, comparative advertising—that is, advertising that compares two products or businesses—is completely legal.

Christine: But the ad also says that they have better service.

Jeffrey Douglas: Better how?

Christine: It says "Better prices, better service." That's all.

Jeffrey Douglas: "Better" is not a specific claim—it's an opinion. Customers can decide for themselves whose service is better. It's not false advertising.

Christine: But that's so unfair!

Jeffrey Douglas: Maybe, but it isn't illegal.

Annie Chow: What if the ad said, "The service at Chris's Drycleaners is terrible." That's an opinion, too.

Jeffrey Douglas: You're right, it is an opinion. However, if the opinion is about *the other* business, you need to be able to prove it, or it's false advertising. And "terrible" is such a difficult word to prove.

Annie Chow: Now I see what you meant about using the rules. It *is* confusing. . .

Unit 9: Gadgets

Listening, A, B, and C, page 115

Customer 1: Excuse me? What's this?

Salesman: It's a baby monitor.

Customer 1: What's it used for?

Salesman: It's similar to a walkie talkie—except you use it to listen, not talk. People who have newborn babies put one in the baby's room. They keep the other one with them. That way, they will know if the baby wakes up and starts to cry.

Customer 1:	I'm looking for a gift for a neighbor who just had a baby.
Salesman:	That would be perfect.
Husband:	Honey, they probably already have one. Why don't we check first?
Customer 1:	Hmmm . . . I guess you're right. Thanks anyway.
Salesman:	You're welcome.
Salesman:	Can I help you find something?
Customer 2:	I'm not sure. I'm looking for a gadget I saw on TV.
Salesman:	We have a lot of gadgets. What's it called?
Customer 2:	That's the problem. I don't remember. It's an appliance that you can use to cut all kinds of food.
Salesman:	Oh, you mean the Chef's Helper—We don't carry it. It's one of those gadgets sold only on TV.
Customer 2:	OK, thanks.
Salesman:	You're welcome. Is there anything else that I can help you with today?
Customer 2:	No, thanks.
Customer 3:	Excuse me? I'm looking for that thingamajig that was advertised in today's paper.
Salesman:	Well, we advertise a lot of "thingamajigs."
Customer 3:	Oh, you know, that thing you can use to clean places that are hard to reach, like ceilings and small corners?
Salesman:	Oh, the Magic Duster.
Customer 3:	Yes, that's it!
Salesman:	I'm sorry, but we're sold out.
Customer 3:	But I called this morning and the man that I spoke to said there were plenty.
Salesman:	There were, but by 11:00 we had sold out. It's a very popular item.
Customer 3:	Hmphhh.
Salesman:	You have a lovely day, ma'am.

Dictation, page 122

1. Look at this great new clock I bought yesterday.
2. That's the one I was looking at last week.
3. I like it because it has the green light that shows the date.
4. Oh, the clock I saw didn't have a date.
5. Yes, the woman who was helping me said this was the newest model.

Listening, A and B, page 123

Michelle Marks: This is Michelle Marks with Spotlight on Technology. It's time to hear what you have to say. Here's an e-mail that we received from a frequent listener. I think it expresses a point of view which many of our listeners will understand, even if they don't completely agree.

John Parker: Dear Michelle: I always listen to your program with pleasure. I enjoy learning about technology, especially new gadgets and tools that will save me time, or improve my life in some other way. However, more and more often these days, I find that the gadgets that are coming out on the market do not, in fact, simplify our lives at all. Instead, they add more stress to the lives of people who already have too much stress.

An example that immediately comes to mind is the remote control. Now don't get me wrong—when the television remote was invented, I was one of the first people in my neighborhood who had one. And those early remotes definitely improved my life. When an advertisement that annoyed me came on, I could just change the channel. However, as I am sure your listeners will agree, remote controls are no longer the simple devices that they once were. They have become so complicated to operate that you need to be a technician to program one. And even if you are lucky enough to know someone who can program your remote for you, what happens when the cat steps on it and presses the wrong button? Well, forget about watching TV that night! What I want to know is, if we can send a man to the moon, why can't we design a remote control that is easy to use?

Another invention that was originally a good idea but has become a nightmare is the cell phone. Nowadays, it's impossible to buy a cell phone that doesn't sing, dance, and make your bed in the morning! What was wrong with the old cell phones that used to just make calls? Why do we need cell phones that take pictures and play movies on a screen that most people over 30 can't even see?

Are there other people out there who feel the same way that I do? And if there are, is there anything we can do about it?
John Parker

Michelle Marks: So, do you agree with Mr. Parker? Is technology making your life easier, or more difficult? Let us know what you think . . .

Unit 10: Shopping

Listening, A, B, and C, page 129

CONVERSATION 1

Customer 1:	Excuse me, could you tell me where the bookstore is?
Tom:	Better Books? I'm afraid they closed last month.
Customer 1:	Oh, no! I loved that bookstore. Do you know whether they've opened another store?
Tom:	Sorry, but I have no idea where they went. I'm not even sure if they're still in business. I heard that they were having trouble.
Customer 1:	Ah, well. Thanks anyway.
Tom:	You're very welcome.

CONVERSATION 2

Customer 2:	Excuse me? Do you happen to know if there's an ATM machine around here?
Tom:	There's one on this floor, next to the jewelry store, and there's one on the first floor...oh, but wait a minute, I'm not sure if that one is working. Try the one next to the jewelry store first.
Customer 2:	Thanks.
Tom:	No problem.

CONVERSATION 3

Tom:	Are you OK, ma'am?
Customer 3:	I've lost my little boy!
Tom:	Please, calm down… Now, can you tell me how long he's been missing?
Customer 3:	Just a few minutes . . . I was looking at a sweater, and when I looked up, he was gone!
Tom:	How old is he? Can you tell me what he was wearing?
Customer 3:	He's only three! I don't remember what he was wearing!
Tom:	Please, try to calm down, and think. Are you sure that you don't remember?
Customer 3:	Oh, yes, he was wearing blue shorts and a red T-shirt.
Tom:	Good. And could you tell me what his name is, please?
Customer 3:	Danny Burton.
Tom:	OK, wait one moment. [*on intercom*] May I have your attention please. . . If anyone has seen. . .
Danny:	Mommy?
Customer 3:	Danny! Thank goodness! Where have you been! I've been looking all over for you!

Dictation, page 136

1. Can you see what size this is?
2. No, but I don't think it will fit you.
3. Do you know where I can try it on?
4. I'll find out whether there is a fitting room on this floor.
5. Can you ask if there's a restroom too?

Listening, A and B, page 137

Host:	Good afternoon. This is Nick Parnell with Spotlight on Business. Bonnie Caldwell, president of the Northeast Small Business Association, is here today to talk about the effect that large chain discount stores, or superstores, is having on traditional family-owned businesses. Welcome, Ms. Caldwell.
Ms. Caldwell:	Thank you.
Host:	So, is it true that the small Mom and Pop stores of our childhood are a thing of the past?
Ms. Caldwell:	Well, luckily, no—not yet. However, there is a danger that in the near future, small businesses such as your corner pharmacy or family-owned neighborhood restaurant will disappear. That's why we formed the Northeast Small Business Association. We want to make sure that small businesses remain an important part of our economy.
Host:	But don't superstores offer their customers exactly what they want—low prices? It's a fact that small businesses cannot afford the discounts that large chain stores can. And we all want low prices. I'm not sure why that's a problem.
Ms. Caldwell:	When you describe it that way, it doesn't sound like a problem. However, the reality is not so simple.
Host:	Could you give us an example of what you mean?
Ms. Caldwell:	Yes, certainly. Imagine that a large supermarket chain wants to open a superstore in your town. However, the town already has a supermarket— a small business that has been owned by the same family for many years. What does the chain store do? They build their superstore and offer large discounts during the first year that they are in business. The small store can't compete with such large discounts, they lose customers, and have to close. Now there is no competition, so the

superstore can raise prices. By the time the townspeople realize what has happened, it's too late.

Host: I'm not sure if I understand. Explain to me how the superstore can afford to offer such low prices without losing money.

Ms. Caldwell: They do lose money . . . at first. But they can afford to lose money at one store for a while—after all, they have many stores. And they can be almost sure that the small supermarket will not last very long. They know that the owners will not be able to lower their prices enough to keep their customers. Sooner or later they will have to close.

Host: Is that legal?

Ms. Caldwell: Not really—but it isn't easy to prove exactly what happened, and large chain stores can afford to hire the best lawyers.

Host: Interesting. OK, let's bring some callers into the conversation.

Unit 11: Interviews

Listening, A, B, and C, page 143

Myrna: How did your interview go?

Tony: Terrible. It was a disaster!

Myrna: What happened?

Tony: Well, first of all, I was 15 minutes late.

Myrna: How did that happen?

Tony: Well, I called the day before the interview and asked if there was parking available. They told me that there would be plenty of spaces available on the street.

Myrna: And?

Tony: Well, I got there early, but there were no parking spaces. I finally managed to find a spot—10 blocks away. By then I was late, so I had to run. When I got to the building, the doorman told me that the elevator was out of order! So I had to walk up eight flights of stairs. By the time I got to the reception area, I was 15 minutes late.

Myrna: Oh, no! Did they ask you why you were late?

Tony: No, the receptionist didn't say anything. She just called the interviewer and told her that I had arrived. Then I had to wait 30 minutes.

Myrna: So how many people interviewed you?

Tony: There was just one interviewer—Mrs. Doe. First she asked me if I was working. When I told her

that I was, she asked me why I was looking for another job.

Myrna: And?

Tony: I said that I needed to make more money.

Myrna: That's all you said? What about the answers we practiced?

Tony: I was so nervous that I forgot everything that we had talked about.

Myrna: So what did she say?

Tony: She seemed surprised at my answer . . . Then she said that she couldn't discuss salary with me at the first interview. If they called me in for a second interview, the department manager would discuss salary and other details. But I knew what she was thinking.

Myrna: What?

Tony: That I would never get a second interview!

Grammar to Communicate 2, A, page 146

A: Why did you leave your other job?

B: I only worked there part-time. I needed more hours.

A: When will you be able to start?

B: In two weeks. I've already given my notice.

A: Who can we call for a reference?

B: My references and their phone numbers are on my résumé.

A: What are your salary requirements?

B: That's difficult to say. At my last job I made $14 an hour.

A: What kind of experience do you have?

B: I've done this kind of work for five years.

A: How long have you been working at your present job?

B: For a year and a half.

Grammar to Communicate 3, B, page 149

A: Well, first of all, are they going to give you any financial aid?

B: I was too embarrassed to ask if they were going to give me financial aid.

A: Too embarrassed??!! Well, how about the dorms? Do you have to live on campus?

B: I forgot to ask whether I had to live on campus.

A: Can you take classes in the evening?

B: I never asked if I could take evening classes. I forgot.

A: What about the number of students? Are the classes big?

B: I didn't ask whether the classes were big, and he didn't mention it.

A: Do they accept many international students?

B: I asked if they accepted a lot of international students, but he never answered.

A: Well, do you think he liked you?

B: I don't know! I didn't ask him whether he liked me!

Dictation, page 150

1. First, the woman asked what I did for a living.
2. I told her that I had a job in a store, but that I was going to give my notice.
3. She asked me if I was looking for another job.
4. I told her that I had decided to go back to school.
5. At the end of the interview, she asked whether I had any questions.

Listening, A and B, page 151

CONVERSATION 1

Man: How was the interview?

Woman: Strange.

Man: Strange? What do you mean?

Woman: Well, the interviewer made me uncomfortable. He asked a lot of personal questions.

Man: Like what?

Woman: Well, first of all, he looked at my wedding ring, and asked me how long I had been married. When I told him that I was a newlywed, he asked me if I was planning on having children.

Man: Really? Did you answer him?

Woman: Yes . . . what else could I do? I told him that we wanted children, but not for a few years. I think he was trying to find out if I would get pregnant. . . maybe he was worried that I wouldn't stay very long.

Man: Hmmm. I didn't think that employers were allowed to ask those kinds of personal questions.

Woman: Yeah, I asked my teacher if it was legal, and she said no. She gave me a telephone number to call and report him.

Man: And are you going to do it?

Woman: I don't know. I told her that I'd think about it.

CONVERSATION 2

Woman: So Andy, your Mom told me that you had your first interview yesterday. How did it go?

Andy: Good, I think. The interviewer was a really nice woman.

Woman: What kinds of questions did she ask you?

Andy: First she asked me if I had any questions for her. That was a little uncomfortable because I hadn't prepared anything.

Woman: Why not?

Andy: I didn't know that I needed to ask questions. I just thought that I'd need to answer them.

Woman: Oh, no. You should always prepare some questions to ask in an interview. So what did you do?

Andy: I said that I didn't have any questions because the college's Web site was so clear.

Woman: That was a good answer.

Andy: Yeah . . .

Woman: So what else did she ask you?

Andy: Oh, you know, the usual questions about which subjects in high school were my best, and what I was planning to major in. She also asked a lot of questions about what I did in my free time.

Woman: And what was the most difficult question?

Andy: She asked me why they should accept me.

Woman: Interesting. How did you answer?

Andy: I told her that I would be the first person in my family to go to college. So I felt a responsibility not only to myself, but to my whole family, to do my best.

Unit 12: Psychology and Personality

Listening, A, B, and C, page 157

Alex: Hey, Jackie, what're you doing?

Jackie: I'm taking a personality quiz. The career counselor at school gave it to me.

Alex: A personality quiz? How is that going to help you choose a career?

Jackie: It will help me find out what I'm good at doing.

Alex: Hmmm . . . Now I'm curious. What kinds of questions do they ask?

Jackie: Well, in one section they give you three statements, and ask you to choose the one that describes you best. For example:
a. I avoid being alone.
b. I can spend hours alone without getting bored.
c. Being alone doesn't bother me, but spending time with people is more interesting.

Alex: What was your answer? Wait a minute—let me guess. You answered a.

Jackie: Wrong! I answered c.

Alex: Really? I don't think you're capable of spending more than a few minutes alone! You spend all of your free time socializing!

Jackie: Yes, but I don't *avoid* being alone. I just enjoy spending time with other people. How about you? What's your answer?

Alex: Definitely b. I'm not good at socializing; I feel more comfortable being alone.

Jackie: So you *avoid* socializing?

Alex: No . . . I'm just not interested in being with people a lot of the time . . . Ask me another question.

Jackie:	OK, here's a true/false one. I'll read you the statement, and you say whether it's true or false for you.
Alex:	Go ahead.
Jackie:	"I have trouble concentrating when my desk is messy."
Alex:	That's a good one for you!
Jackie:	What do you mean?
Alex:	Oh, come on, Jackie! Your desk is always a mess!
Jackie:	So what? Being messy isn't the worst thing in the world. I never have any trouble studying.
Alex:	That's true . . .

Grammar to Communicate 2, A, page 160

1. Visual learners learn best by looking at pictures, diagrams, and charts.
2. Verbal learners learn best by reading and discussing things.
3. Physical learners learn best by doing things with their hands and bodies.
4. Aural learners learn best by listening.
5. Logical learners learn best by thinking about things.

Grammar to Communicate 2, B, page 160

1. Lynn is interested in reading books about many subjects. She´s very curious about a lot of different things.
2. Robert is very good at doing things with his hands. He can look at a picture and understand exactly what he has to do.
3. Sammi takes great pride in doing things on time. She's capable of staying up all night if she has to finish something.
4. Claudia believes in learning by doing. She is not interested in reading instruction manuals.

Dictation, page 164

1. Talking to people I don't know well is hard for me.
2. I'm not good at socializing either.
3. I keep trying to meet new people, but I can't.
4. I have a hard time meeting new people too.
5. I can't help thinking we have a lot in common.

Listening, A and B, page 165

Professor: Last week, we discussed three types of learning styles: visual, verbal, and logical. This week, we are going to discuss two other learning styles: aural and physical. In many ways, aural and physical learners have the most difficulty in a traditional classroom. That's because most teachers are visual, verbal, or logical learners. And as I said last week, teachers teach the way that they learn.

First, let's look at aural learners. Aural learners learn by listening. They often remember things by the way they sound. For example, remembering voices is usually easier for aural learners than remembering faces. And aural learners often understand something better by reading it out loud. That's because they have to hear something to learn it.

Aural learners can improve their school performance by sitting where they can hear clearly. As a teacher, you can help the aural learners in your classes by reading instructions out loud. Aural learners can help themselves by reading new material out loud, and then asking a friend to ask them questions about what they have understood. Finally, studying and listening to music at the same time can help some aural learners remember things better.

Now let's discuss physical learners. As the name suggests, physical learners learn best by using their bodies. They prefer touching, moving, building, or drawing to reading or listening. They are good at remembering things that they have *done*, but have more difficulty remembering what they have seen or heard. Most physical learners use their hands when they talk, and they often have a hard time sitting still for very long.

Being a successful student is not easy for many physical learners. This is not because they are less intelligent than other types of learners. They are just as capable of learning as anyone else. It is because most classrooms are not designed for them. And many teachers have difficulty teaching students who can't sit still. So how can you teachers help physical learners succeed? Whenever possible, let your students move around in the classroom. Also, tell students who have trouble sitting still that when they study at home, they should walk around, rock in a chair, tap their pencils, or hold onto something. Using a computer is also helpful for many physical learners, because typing involves moving and touching. And taking short breaks to get up and move around is important for physical learners.

Unit 13: Looking Back

Listening, A, B, and C, page 171

Man:	What are you looking at?
Woman:	Just some old photos.
Man:	Can I see?
Woman:	Sure.
Man:	Is that you?
Woman:	Yeah. It was taken at our farm when I was about 6.
Man:	You used to live on a farm?
Woman:	I grew up there. We didn't move to the city until I was in high school.

Man: Really? Was it hard for you to get used to the city?

Woman: Yes, of course. At first I didn't think that I would ever get used to being around so many people. I was used to spending most of my time with my horses. And it was really hard to get used to being inside all day. Actually, I'm still not used to it! If I don't manage to spend some time outside every day, I feel terrible.

Man: Tell me about the farm. Did you have to work a lot?

Woman: No . . . I was the youngest and the only girl. My older brothers were expected to do most of the work, so I had a lot of freedom. I spent most of my time riding my horse and pretending to be a cowboy.

Man: You know how to ride horses?

Woman: Yeah, I used to be a good rider. But I haven't ridden in years.

Man: But isn't riding a horse something you never forget?

Woman: Not exactly. If you haven't ridden in a while, you have to get used to being on a horse all over again.

Man: It sounds like you really miss riding. Have you ever considered taking it up again?

Woman: No . . . Riding is something that I used to do. It's like these pictures—I used to be that little girl, but not anymore. That's something I learned from my Mom—she taught me never to look back, only forward.

Grammar to Communicate 2, A, page 174

1. I wasn't the greatest student at first. I hated to do homework, so I never knew the answers when teachers called on me. I hated reading too. I hardly ever went to the library. I didn't study, but I managed to pass the tests. I started to do better in ninth grade. That's when we moved, and I started going to a new school.

2. I was scared a lot in school. I used to avoid raising my hand because I didn't want people to laugh at me. I pretended to be sick when we had a test because I was afraid I was of doing badly. I stopped being so afraid when I learned to relax.

3. I wasn't a very nice student. I never offered to clean the board, and I refused to work in a group with the other students. I kept getting into trouble because I didn't want to listen to the teacher. I don't know how the teachers and other students could stand being around me.

Grammar to Communicate 3, A, page 176

When I was teenager, my parents were very strict. They expected me to come home right after school and do my homework. They didn't allow me to go out with my friends during the week. Saturday was the only night that they allowed me to go out. My parents also encouraged me to get a good education and they taught me to work hard. They *really* wanted me to succeed. When I have kids, I will teach them to work hard too, but I'm not going to be as strict as my parents were. I would like my kids to have more freedom than I did, it's important for children to obey their parents, but I think it's also important for children to have fun.

Dictation, page 178

1. Did your family expect you to stay here for a long time?
2. No, because I used to move around a lot.
3. What convinced you to stay?
4. I managed to start my own business.
5. I'm used to working for myself now and I love it.

Listening, A and B, page 179

Host: Our guest today is Isabel Muñoz Thomas. She's just written a book called *Half and Half* about her life in Ecuador and the United States. Welcome to the show.

Isabel: Thank you.

Host: Now your father was Ecuadorian, and your mother was American, right?

Isabel: Yes, that's right. When my mother was 19, she spent a year studying Latin American culture and history in Quito, Ecuador. My father was an engineer. His best friend had just gotten married to an American woman. She was having a very hard time getting used to living in a new culture—so she used to have a lot of parties and invite all of the Americans she knew. My mom and dad met at one of her parties.

Host: And was it love at first sight?

Isabel: For my mom and dad, yes, but not for my father's family. They didn't approve of the relationship at all. They wanted my dad to marry a nice Ecuadorian girl. They tried to convince him not to marry my mother, but he refused to listen. He was the only son, so he always managed to get what he wanted. And he wanted my mom. They got married six months later, and moved into his parents' house. The honeymoon didn't last very long. My mom was used to having the freedom to do whatever she wanted. But my grandmother and aunts expected her to behave like a proper Ecuadorian wife. That meant staying at home and taking care of the house and family. The outside world was a man's world. My mom was really in love with my dad, so she tried very hard to get used to her new life. For a long time, she pretended to be happy. But three years after I was born, she stopped pretending. She wrote to her parents and asked them to send her three plane tickets home. When the tickets arrived, she convinced my father to go to the United States on a long vacation. She promised to return to Ecuador within six months. In fact, it would be six years before we finally returned. And that was the way I grew up—moving back and forth every few years.

Host: What an interesting childhood. We have to take a short break, but don't go away. We'll be right back with more from Isabel Muñoz about growing up "Half and Half" . . .

Unit 14: Socializing

Listening, A, B, and C, page 185

Tom: Would you mind getting the door?

Gilda: Oh sure, no problem.

Tom: Thanks.

Gilda: Are you moving into Mrs. Andrews' place?

Tom: Yes, that's right.

Gilda: I'm Gilda. I'm in the building next door . . . Here, let me get that for you…

Tom: Thanks. I'm Tom.

Gilda: Nice to meet you Tom. Hey, I'm having a few neighbors over later for a potluck. At about 4:00? Why don't you stop by and meet everyone?

Tom: That's very nice. I'd love to come . . . but I don't think I'll be able to cook anything. Everything is in boxes…

Gilda: Oh, don't worry about it! There will be plenty of food.

Tom: As long as you're sure it's OK . . .

Gilda: Of course . . . I'm in Building 3, apartment 6B.

Tom: Great . . . I'll see you at 4:00.

Later that day

Gilda: Tom, please, come in. Here, let me take your coat. . . OK, let's go meet the neighbors . . . Hey, everybody, come meet Tom. He's just moved into Mrs. Andrews' apartment.

Guests: Hey Tom. Great to meet you. Welcome. Welcome to the neighborhood.

Paul: I'm Paul, in 4C, across the hall from you. This is my wife, Rita.

Rita: Hi, Tom. Welcome.

Tom: Hi, thanks. It's nice to meet you.

Rita: How about something to drink? There's juice, soda, coffee, and tea. Which would you prefer?

Tom: Coffee please. Thanks.

Rita: Honey, would you mind getting Tom some coffee?

Paul: Sure . . .

Tom: There are three chairs over there. Why don't we go and sit down?

Rita: Good idea.

Tom: So, have you lived here long?

Rita: Only about a year.

Tom: And how do you like it?

Rita: Paul loves it, but to tell you the truth, I'd prefer to live in a house. It's a little noisy here.

Paul: Actually, I'd rather not live in an apartment either, but who has time to take care of a house?

Tom: You can say that again . . .

Grammar to Communicate 1, A, page 186

1. **A:** Let me take your coat.
   B: Thanks.
2. **A:** Let's order some Chinese take-out.
   B: Mmmm. That sounds good.
3. **A:** Why don't we take a break?
   B: Great idea.
4. **A:** Why don't I get the door?
   B: I'd really appreciate that.

Grammar to Communicate 3, A, page 190

1. **A:** Would you mind taking the suitcases?
   B: No problem.
2. **A:** Would you mind doing me a favor?
   B: Sure. What is it?
3. **A:** Would you mind looking at the stove?
   B: Not at all.
4. **A:** Would you mind getting the door?
   B: Of course not.
5. **A:** Would you mind going to the store?
   B: Sure. What do you need?
6. **A:** Would you mind getting take-out?
   B: No, not at all.

Dictation, page 192

1. Why don't we plan a get-together for next Sunday?
2. Sounds good, but would you rather have people over or go out to a restaurant?
3. Let's get take-out and stay here.

4. I'd prefer to have a potluck. How about 6:00?

5. Good idea, but I'd rather do it in the afternoon.

Listening, A and B, page 193

Prof. Rivers: Our guest lecturer tonight is Professor Don Bryant from the University of Eldridge. Professor Bryant has been teaching English for over 30 years, and is the author of numerous English textbooks that are used all over the world. Please join me in welcoming Professor Bryant.

Prof. Bryant: Good evening, and thank you . . . Professor Rivers, when you called a few months ago to ask me to speak tonight, you left this message:

Prof. Rivers: "Hello, Don? It's Roberta. I'm planning a lecture series called *Real English For Real Life* for the advanced English learners in our program, and I have a favor to ask... Would you mind giving a short lecture for the series? You could talk about your latest book—or if you'd rather talk about something else, that's fine too. Call me."

Prof. Bryant: I guess I didn't mind. And that brings me to the topic of my lecture: Polite—and not so polite—requests: What can we learn from them?

Let's consider Professor Rivers' message. Professor Rivers uses the expression "Would you mind," which, as you have probably learned, is used for polite requests. And in fact Professor Rivers' request *was* polite. In your textbook, you study polite requests. You practice with your classmates. You pass the test. So now you have learned polite requests . . . right? . . . Not so fast . . . Consider this:

The day after the test, you're on a crowded bus. A teenager is lying down across two seats. A woman gets on the bus, looks at the teenager, and says "Would you mind?"

Clearly, studying grammar, although important, is not enough. The context—the way we say something, who we say it to, and when and where we say it—is just as important as the words.

So...should you throw away your grammar books? Stop going to class? Of course not. As you heard in Professor Rivers' message, "would you mind" *is* used to make polite requests . . .

So, what can you do? Well, first of all, remember that even the best books and teachers can only open the door to the language—you need to walk through the door. How? Take

the grammar with you when you leave the classroom. Listen to native speakers. When they use the grammar you have studied, pay attention to the context. Build on what you have studied in class. In this way, you will be *learning* the language—not just studying it—and you will learn much more quickly.

Unit 15: On the Road

Listening, A, B, and C, page 199

Susan: Tim, what's wrong? You look terrible!

Tim: I just failed my road test!

Susan: Oh no! What happened?

Tim: Everything went wrong. First of all, I forgot that I wasn't supposed to wear flip-flops. I had to go home to change my shoes. So then I was late. I was supposed to be there at 9:00, but I got there at 9:05. The driving examiner wasn't too happy.

Susan: Uh-oh . . . That wasn't a very good way to start!

Tim: Really . . . Anyway, we got in the car, and he told me to back up. You know how you're always supposed to look over your right shoulder? Well, I forgot.

Susan: Did he say anything?

Tim: No, not in words, but . . . Then, I had to parallel park. And you know how good I am at that! . . . Anyway, after about 15 minutes, I finally parked the car. Now came the best part—driving in traffic. I pulled out and turned left at a traffic light. Suddenly he told me to pull over and stop the car. Then he asked me, "What do you have to do whenever you make a turn?"

Susan: Oh, no, don't tell me you forgot to use your turn signal!

Tim: That's right! Well, that was the end of the test.

Susan: When can you take it again?

Tim: I have to wait at least two months. And he told me that I'd better not be late the next time. He also said I'd better practice parallel parking.

Susan: You know, you really ought to go to driving school. Look how it helped me. I passed the road test with no problem.

Tim: Yeah, maybe I ought to do that . . .

Grammar to Communicate 1, A, page 200

1. You'd better slow down. There's a police car behind you.

2. You shouldn't talk to the driver.

3. That boy ought to give the old woman his seat.

4. Should we stop and look at a map?

5. You'd better not park there. You're too close to the fire hydrant.

Grammar to Communicate 2, A, page 202

1. Max Lee: How old do I have to be to take the test?

Ann Yu: You have to be at least 16.

2. Sue Pike: Can I take the test today?

Ann Yu: No. You're supposed to wait three months. Then you can take it.

3. Mr. Kay: Are we supposed to pay today?

Ann Yu: No. You don't have to pay until the day of the test.

4. Ms. West: Does my daughter have to go to a driving school?

Ann Yu: No, she doesn't. She can learn from you.

Grammar to Communicate 3, A, page 204

1. Mae had to wait a long time for the bus on Monday.
2. The bus was supposed to come at 7:30 on Tuesday. It came at 7:55.
3. Mae didn't have to pay for the bus on Wednesday.
4. On Friday Mae's bus was supposed to stop in front of her office, but the driver forgot.
5. Mae didn't have to work on Saturday, so she didn't have to take the bus.

Dictation, page 206

1. You'd better let that pedestrian cross the street.
2. But she's supposed to wait for the walk signal.
3. Yeah, but you aren't supposed to hit her!
4. Great! Now I have to wait for *him*, too.
5. Maybe I ought to drive next time.

Listening, A and B, page 207

Host: Good evening. This is Rachel Mannheim with Focus on Youth. Today, Captain Jim Thompson of the highway patrol is here to discuss teen driving safety. Captain Thompson, my daughter is going to get her license next month. What should I know?

Captain: Well, first of all, has your daughter taken driving lessons? Because if she hasn't, she really ought to.

Host: She has taken driving lessons.

Captain: And do you think that she should be driving now?

Host: Well, she definitely knows the rules of the road.

Captain: Understanding the laws is important, but it's just the first step. People, especially teenagers, often know what they are supposed to do, but do they do it?

Host: That's a very good point. So what should parents do to keep their children safe?

Captain: This is not a very popular opinion, but I honestly believe that most teenagers cannot handle the responsibility of driving. You can, and should, teach them how to drive. They have to get as much practice as they can. But if you ask me, most teenagers ought to wait until they are at least 18 years old to drive a car alone.

Host: Really?

Captain: Yes. Safe driving involves making good decisions—and teenagers are not very good at that. When you were a teenager, did you always do what you were supposed to do?

Host: No . . .

Captain: Did you do things that you were not supposed to do?

Host: Hmmm . . . I'd better not answer . . . my daughter might be listening. OK, I understand your point. However, the reality is that most teenagers *do* drive. In fact, many of them have to drive to get to their jobs or school.

Captain: You're absolutely right. So . . . here's my advice: First, a teenage driver should never have more than one friend in the car. In my experience, more than two teenagers in a car is trouble. They are much more likely to forget what they are supposed to do. Second, they have to have a cell phone with them at all times. However, they should *never* use it while they are driving. If they have to make a call, they should pull over and stop the car. Third, they have to wear their seatbelts. Period. No argument. Tell them they'd better do it, or else! And finally, they have to understand that they can never drink and drive. If they do, take away their car keys—forever . . .

Unit 16: Natural Disasters

Listening, A, B, and C, page 213

Man: Are you ready?

Woman: No . . . but let's go. Wow . . . Look at this mess. The storm must have been worse than they predicted.

Man: Oh my gosh—what happened to Rick's house? Look at the roof!

Woman: Unbelievable. The wind must have blown it off.

Man: And look at all this broken glass. I told you that we should have boarded up the windows.

Woman: There wasn't any time to board up the

windows! Are you saying that we shouldn't have evacuated?

Man: I'm sorry, honey. I shouldn't have said that. I'm just upset . . . actually, it looks like we might have gotten lucky. At least the roof is still on.

Woman: Have you noticed how quiet it is? Everyone must have obeyed the order to evacuate.

Man: Probably. Come on, let's go take a look around inside. Ready?

Woman: You go first . . .

Man: I can't believe it. . . There's almost no damage except for the windows.

Woman: Incredible!. . . Let's go take a look at the backyard.

Man: Something doesn't look right.

Woman: Hmmm . . . Oh, I know! The picnic table and benches are gone. And the dog house is gone too! The wind must have blown them all away.

Man: Well, we've been really lucky, if that's the worst that happened . . . Did you try the lights?

Woman: Yeah—there's no power. The clocks are all stopped at 6:00. The electricity must have gone out almost as soon as the storm started.

Man: We should have stocked up on batteries for the flashlights.

Woman: I'll go to the hardware store and pick some up.

Man: Do you think they're open?

Woman: Oh they must be open. The storm was two days ago.

Man: Yeah, but they may have lost their power too.

Woman: Well, I'll go and see.

Man: I'll call the electric company. Have you seen my cell phone?

Woman: No, but check the car. You might have left it there.

Grammar to Communicate 1, A, page 214

1. You should've come home right away. I was worried.
2. We shouldn't have left so late. Look at the traffic.
3. The police shouldn't have closed Route 70. It caused a lot of problems.
4. The suitcase should've been packed last night. We don't have time now.
5. You should've gotten gas yesterday. Now what are we going to do?
6. People should've been told where to go. Many people were confused.

Grammar to Communicate 2, D, page 217

A: I'm calling Paul on his cell phone, but there's no answer. I'm really worried about them.

B: They may have gone to stay with Paul's family. I think he has relatives nearby.

A: Maybe I should call Amy's mother. Do you know where my address book is?

B: I'm not sure. Did you look upstairs? You might have left it there.

A: I called the number I had in my address book, but that wasn't Amy's mother who answered.

B: She may have moved. Check your e-mail. They might have sent you a message.

A: I sent them an e-mail yesterday, but they haven't answered.

B: They may not have gotten your e-mail. They might not have taken their laptop with them.

Dictation, page 220

1. I'm worried about driving. The roads may have flooded.
2. We should've left yesterday.
3. You're right. We shouldn't have stayed.
4. I didn't see Tom and Sue's car. They must have left town.
5. Or they might have put their car in the garage.

Listening, A and B, page 221

Host: This is Christine Chung. Welcome to this week's edition of "Channel 20 Investigates." It has been exactly one year since Hurricane David almost completely destroyed the city of San Carlos. Last week, reporter Luisa Mendes returned to San Carlos to check in on some of the residents that she interviewed a year ago. And you might be surprised at what she found.

Luisa Mendes: At the time of the hurricane, Rose Daniels and her husband had owned a restaurant in San Carlos for over 25 years. Hurricane David destroyed not only their restaurant, but also their home. So, Rose, when we last spoke, you said that you would never reopen the restaurant. It looks like you must have changed your mind.

Rose Daniels: Yes, that's right. A year ago we were sure that this day would never come. But here we are. With the money we received from the government, we have managed to rebuild not only the restaurant, but also our home.

Luisa Mendes: And it looks like business is good.

Rose Daniels: Oh, yes. It's never been better.

Luisa Mendes: But not all of the residents of San Carlos have been as lucky as Rose. Benito Juarez also lost his home in the hurricane, but he has received no money from the government. Benito, what's happened since we spoke to you last year?

Benito Juarez: What's happened? Nothing, that's what! The politicians all came in after the hurricane with their TV cameras and promises to help. I must have convinced myself they were telling the truth because I *wanted* to believe them. I shouldn't have been so stupid. I should have known that they would forget about us as soon as the cameras were turned off.

Luisa Mendes: But didn't the city receive money from the federal government to rebuild?

Benito Juarez: Well, the city might have received the money, but I never saw one penny of it—and neither has anyone else on this side of the river.

Luisa Mendes: On this side of the river?

Benito Juarez: Yeah, that's right. You must have noticed all of the building on the other side of town—but none here.

Luisa Mendes: And why do you think that is?

Benito Juarez: Why don't you ask the mayor?

Host: So, what is going on in San Carlos? Why did some residents receive money to rebuild, while others did not? When we come back, we'll show you Luisa's surprising interview with the Mayor of San Carlos, Joseph Daniels.

Unit 17: In the News

Listening, A, B, and C, page 227

Woman: Did you hear the President's speech last night?

Man: What speech? I didn't know there was a speech. Anyway, I hate politics.

Woman: You know, I'm sick of that attitude. The country's in a mess because of people like you!

Man: Whoa! Wait a minute. You're kidding, right?

Woman: No, I'm not. Do you vote?

Man: Well, since you asked, no, I don't vote. I don't vote because all politicians are the same. It doesn't matter who gets elected. In spite of their promises at election time, they do whatever they want after the election.

Woman: So although you don't vote, you come in every day and complain about the government. I just don't understand that attitude.

Man: It's a free country. I have the right to complain if I want to.

Woman: Of course you do. And do you know why it's a free country? Because people fought and died for the right to vote!

Man: Oh, please. Politics just isn't my thing.

Woman: So what *do* you care about?

Man: Well . . . the environment, for one thing.

Woman: Really? That's interesting. So . . . you drive that big car?

Man: For your information, I'd love to be able to afford a new, energy efficient car. But since I don't have the money, I have to keep driving that big old Chevy. And by the way, how many cars do you have in your family?

Woman: Well . . . umm . . . three.

Man: So you have three cars for three people?

Woman: Yeah, but they're all small cars.

Man: Oh, please! Even though they're small, they still use gasoline. Why do you need so many cars?

Woman: Because of our different schedules.

Man: Why don't you take public transportation to work?

Woman: Because . . . You know what? Let's change the subject. I'm tired of arguing with you.

Man: Oh, *now* you're tired of arguing?

Grammar to Communicate 1, C, page 229

1. **Man:** I heard that Harry Jackman lost his job.
   Woman: Really? Why?
   Man: I guess he was too old.
   Woman: What makes you think that?
   Man: Well, they hired a much younger guy to replace him.

2. **Woman:** Why is it that the men in this company make more money than the women?
   Man: Oh come on. That's not true.
   Woman: Really? How much do you make?
   Man: Fourteen dollars an hour.
   Woman: You see? I only make $12.
   Man: But I've been here longer.
   Woman: Hmph!

3. Man: Where is Barbara? I haven't seen her in a few weeks.

Woman: She doesn't work here anymore.

Man: Why not?

Woman: I'm not sure. I know she told the boss she was pregnant, and he wasn't happy about it.

Man: She's going to have a baby. That's great.

Woman: Yeah, but she doesn't have a job.

4. Woman: Did you get a raise?

Man: No, my boss told me that since business is bad, there won't be any raises this year. But I don't believe him.

Woman: Why not?

Man: I'm pretty sure Barney got a raise.

Woman: So why did your boss tell you that?

Man: Because he doesn't like me.

5. Woman: I haven't seen Bob lately. What happened to him?

Man: He doesn't work here any more. He lost his job.

Woman: How come?

Man: He didn't get along with anybody. He was always causing problems.

Woman: Yeah, I never liked him very much.

Dictation, page 234

1. Because of the election, the candidates are giving a lot of speeches.
2. Although I don't know much about the candidates, I'm going to vote.
3. I listen to the candidates' speeches even though they are sometimes boring.
4. Since one candidate promised to cut taxes, the others had to, also.
5. Despite their promises, I don't believe that they will really cut taxes.

Listening, A and B, page 235

1. Good morning. I was hoping to have better news for you today, but unfortunately, although we worked through the night, we were not able to reach an agreement with the city. Because of the mayor's refusal to consider a pay increase, a strike of all city transportation workers will begin tomorrow morning at 6:00 A.M. Now I'll take your questions. . .
2. Please, if you do not need to be on the roads, stay at home. Although city workers are doing their best to keep the roads clear and safe, this is a very large storm, and it is going to continue for a while. So even though the roads in your neighborhood might look safe now, please do not go out unless it is an emergency.

3. Natalie has spent the day going from polling place to polling place, talking to voters. Natalie, how is the voter turnout?
   In spite of the rain, voter turnout has been high all day, Chet. Voters on both sides are saying that because of the clear differences between the two candidates, they felt it was a very important election. So even though the weather is bad, there are long lines at most polling places.
4. Since we use more oil than any country in the world, we have a special responsibility to work harder to protect the environment. However, what does our government do? Raise taxes on gasoline? Build better public transportation? Encourage people to buy smaller, more energy-efficient cars? No.
5. Have you had trouble finding a job because of your age? Have you lost a job because your employer thought that you were too old? Although age discrimination is illegal, it can be very difficult to prove. We at Sloane and Sloane are here to help you. If you believe that you have been the victim of age discrimination, contact our office at 1-800-533-2626

Unit 18: Money

Listening, A, B, and C, page 241

Man: Look at these bills—college loans, the mortgage, my credit card . . . How am I going to pay them all?

Woman: If you want to solve your money problems, cut up your credit cards.

Man: Cut up my credit cards?

Woman: Yes.

Man: But if I don't have a credit card, how will I pay my bills?

Woman: You pay your bills with a credit card? Oh dear, things are worse than I thought.

Man: What do you mean?

Woman: When you pay bills with a credit card, you take care of one problem…

Man: Exactly!

Woman: Yes, but you will have a much bigger problem later. What's the interest rate on your credit card?

Man: I have no idea.

Woman: If you show me one of your bills, I can tell you.

Man: Here.

Woman: It's 15%.

Man: And?

Woman: Let's say your electric bill is $50. If you pay that bill with cash, how much will it cost you?

Man:	$50?
Woman:	Exactly. But what happens when you pay the same bill with a credit card? Are you still paying $50?
Man:	Yes . . .
Woman:	No, you're not. You aren't really *paying* anything. You're *borrowing* money. The credit card company is paying *your* bill with *their* money. If you pay off your $50 debt by the due date, you don't pay any interest… so that $50 will only cost you $50. But . . . if you make only the minimum payment, you will be charged interest on the balance. Let's go back to that $50 electric bill. If the minimum payment is $10, and you borrow $50, how much is your balance after you pay the minimum?
Man:	$40.
Woman:	Yes. And if your interest rate is 15%, and your balance is $40, how much will you pay that month in interest? 15% of $40—so $6, right?
Man:	Yes . . .
Woman:	So now how much do you owe the credit card company?
Man:	$46?
Woman:	And how much have you already paid?
Man:	$10.
Woman:	Exactly. If you add the $46 you owe to the $10 you've already paid, how much is that?
Man:	$56.
Woman:	And how much was the electric bill?
Man:	$50.
Woman:	Exactly.

Dictation, page 248

1. When you go to the bank tomorrow, ask about a loan.
2. Will the bank give us a loan if we don't have any money in our savings account?
3. If we agree to pay off the loan in two years, they might give us one.
4. But if we get a two-year loan, our monthly payments will be really high.
5. You're right. We might have trouble if you don't get that raise.

Listening, A and B, page 249

Reporter: Most people need to borrow money sometime in their lives. But how do banks decide who to give loans to? Just as teachers look at test scores when they decide who should pass a class, lenders look at credit scores when they decide who should get a loan. Now students can improve their test scores by studying. But how can you improve your credit score?

At school, you get a score when you take a test. But where does your credit score come from? Every time you pay a bill—your telephone bill, for example—you're taking a credit test—even though you might not know it. If you pay the bill on time, you get points. If you're late, you lose points.

At school, you know what kinds of questions will be on the test, and who will give you your score. However, most people do not even know that they are taking these "credit tests". And they certainly don't know who is "correcting" the tests, or what their scores are.

So what kinds of questions are on the "credit" test? Here are a few: How much debt do you have? How many credit cards do you use? How many credit cards have you applied for?

Next, who is correcting the test, and how can you find out your score? The answer is different in different places. In the United States, there are several credit reporting companies. When you apply for a loan, the lender will ask one of these companies for your credit score. To find out your score, you have to ask for it. You can check our Web site for information about how to get your score. But don't ask for your score more than once a year. Why not? Because you'll lose points if you do!

Finally, how can you improve your score? First of all, pay your bills *before* the due date. If your payment is even one day late, you'll lose points.

Second, if you have several credit cards, use only one. However, do NOT cancel the other cards. Just stop using them. Why? You lose points when you cancel a credit card.

Third, if you do not have a credit card, apply for one. When you get it, pay off your balance every month—the balance, not just the minimum payment. If you pay only the minimum, you will lose points.

That's all for today. If you need more information about credit scores, go to our Web site at www . . .

Unit 19: Decisions and Dilemmas

Listening, A, B, and C, page 255

Jenny:	So, what happened? Did Evan propose? . . . Ana? Are you OK? Have you been crying?
Ana:	Oh Jenny, why did I ever meet Evan? If we'd never met, I wouldn't have broken up with Mark. And

Mark would never have broken my heart, I'm sure of it! I should have listened to my mother. If I'd listened to her, none of this would have happened. And Mark and I would be married right now . . . I wish Mark were here. If I had another chance with him, I'd never let him go.

Jenny: Oh, please Ana, calm down and tell me what happened.

Ana: OK, so Evan picked me up. He looked really serious, but I thought he was just nervous—you know, about proposing.

Jenny: Oh, honey . . .

Ana: We drove to the park—you know, the park where we met . . .

Jenny: Honey, what happened?

Ana: He broke my heart. He stopped the car—I thought he was getting ready to propose—Oh, what an idiot I am! And then he said it—I wish that I could forget what he said next . . .

Jenny: What? What did he say?

Ana: He told me that he wished it weren't true, but . . .

Jenny: But what?

Ana: But he couldn't marry me because he didn't love me. And then he said "I hope you understand."

Jenny: I hope you understand? Understand what? Has he met someone else?

Ana: I didn't ask. I couldn't think straight. I just got out of the car and came here. But even if I knew the answer to that question, it wouldn't change anything, would it? It's out of my hands. If he doesn't love me, he doesn't love me . . .

Grammar to Communicate 1, A, page 256

1. We're Harry and Paul Hong. We like it here. All of our friends are here. We don't want to move.
2. I don't like raising kids in the city. I think they need fresh air.
3. Right now, it takes me only 10 minutes to get to work. I don't want to spend a lot of time in traffic.
4. The Hongs are great neighbors. We're going to miss them.
5. We don't get to see our grandchildren enough. We have a big house with a lot of extra room.
6. I'm getting older and I need my son's help, but he lives so far away.

Grammar to Communicate 3, B, page 260

1. I went out with the same guy for ten years. I wanted to get married, but he didn't. My mother told me he would

never marry me, but I didn't listen to her. If I'd listened to my mother, I wouldn't have wasted ten years of my life.
2. She went out with a co-worker. That was a big mistake. When they broke up, the situation was very difficult at work. Finally, she ended up quitting her job. If she hadn't gone out with a co-worker, she wouldn't have had to quit.
3. When we got married, my wife and I moved in with her parents. It wasn't easy. We had a lot of fights in the beginning. Finally, we got our own place, and things are much better. If we hadn't lived with my in-laws, we would've avoided a lot of arguments.
4. Several years ago, I met a wonderful girl, but my parents didn't approve of her. I listened to them and I broke up with her. That was the biggest mistake of my life. If I had listened to my heart, I wouldn't have broken up with her—I would have married her.
5. I went out with Jerry for about two years. Then he broke up with me. After about a year, I started going out with a really nice guy named Alex. But then Jerry wanted to get back together, and I broke up with Alex. That was a big mistake, because after a month, Jerry broke my heart again. If I'd been smart, I would've stayed with Alex.

Dictation, page 262

1. I wish I were still with Marta.
2. If you had proposed to her, she wouldn't have broken up with you.
3. If my parents had approved of her, I would have proposed to her.
4. If you weren't afraid of your parents, you wouldn't worry so much about their opinion.
5. I hope Marta and I get back together someday.

Listening, A and B, page 263

Host: Tonight's topic is regrets. If you had the chance, what would you change about your life? If you have a regret, we want to hear it. Let's go to our first caller. Roger? What would you change about your life?

Roger: I'd choose a different career. My father was a dentist. I went to dental school to make him happy. But in my heart, I knew I was making a mistake.

Host: If you had listened to your heart, what would you have done?

Roger: I would have become an architect. That was always my dream.

Host: And if you were an architect right now, would you be happy?

Roger: I can't say for sure, but at least it would have been my own decision.

Host: So if you could give our younger listeners some advice, what would it be?

Roger: I'd tell them that their happiness is in their own hands—that they need to listen to their hearts, and make up their own minds.

Host: Thanks for your call, Roger. OK, let's take another call. Beth? Go ahead.

Beth: I'm calling because I hope my story will help other parents. My husband and I have only one child—a son. We married young and never went to college, but we wanted our son's life to be different. We saved so that he could go to a good university. But after just one semester, he called and said he had met the girl of his dreams—he was going to propose to her. We were shocked, and refused to meet her. Even worse, we told him that if he continued seeing her, we would stop paying for college. We weren't thinking straight. We thought that if we said that, he'd stop seeing her.

Host: And did he?

Beth: No . . . But he stopped seeing *us* . . . Now we have three grandchildren that we've never met. I have tried many times to contact my son and apologize, but he won't take my calls.

Host: Beth, if Jerry were listening right now, what would you say to him?

Beth: Jerry, if you are listening, I want you to know how sorry your father and I are. I wish I could see you, meet my daughter-in-law, and hold my grandchildren in my arms. I wish you'd give us a second chance.

Host: Jerry? If you're listening, why don't you give your Mom a call? I don't think you'll regret it. Well, we have to take a break here. . .

Unit 20: Moving On

Listening, A, B, and C page 269

Dr. Johnson: Good afternoon, Hannah. I'm Dr. Johnson. Please, have a seat.

Hannah: Thank you.

Dr. Johnson: So, I see from your record that you're a freshman . . .

Hannah: Yes.

Dr. Johnson: And you're having trouble concentrating on your studies?

Hannah: Yes.

Dr. Johnson: Have you ever had this problem before . . . say, in high school?

Hannah: No, never. I never had any problems at school. I got *A*s in every subject. School work was always easy for me. I never had to do anything over. I always handed everything in on time, or even early. And I was very organized. I could always find what I needed on my desk. I put everything away after I used it, and threw away anything I didn't need. And I was never, ever late to class.

Dr. Johnson: And now?

Hannah: I finish my homework on time. But I never think it's good enough, so I do it over several times. So finally, I hand it in late. Even worse, I'm late for almost every class, because I can't get up in the morning. And when I do get up, I can't find anything because my room is such a mess. Every weekend, I tell myself that I'm going to clean out my closets and put things away… but I never do it.

Dr. Johnson: How about in class? Are you able to concentrate when you're in class?

Hannah: No, I'm not. I've given up taking notes.

Dr. Johnson: Why's that?

Hannah: Because I can't take notes and listen to the professor at the same time. That was never a problem in high school. And whenever a professor calls on me, I get so nervous that I can't think straight. Oh, doctor, what's going on? Am I going crazy?

Dr. Johnson: No, you're not going crazy. In fact, your experience is very common—especially for freshmen who were used to being the best students in their high schools. Don't worry. We'll figure this out together.

Hannah: Really?

Dr. Johnson: Really. First of all, you need to slow down and . . .

Grammar to Communicate 2, A, page 272

1. My children are grown up now. One is 28, and the other is 35. But I understand the problems single parents have today because it was hard to bring my kids up alone. They counted on me for everything.

2. I almost gave my job up because I was so busy and never had any free time. But of course I needed the money, so I couldn't stop working.

3. And even though I was working, we never had any money, so we had to cut down on a lot of things. My kids didn't get a lot of new clothes, and we never ate out.

4. By the end of each month we had usually run out of money. It was so hard to make ends meet on my salary.

5. I had to go over our budget all the time. I had to look at all the bills every month and my bank statement. Then I had to decide what we needed and what we didn't.

6. I really wanted to buy a house, but when I applied for a loan, the bank turned me down.

Grammar to Communicate 3, D, page 275

1. **A:** Are you going to start college in September?
   B: No, I'm going to put it off for a year. I need time to put more money aside.

2. **A:** What happened at your interview? Did you like the company?
   B: Yes, very much. If they offer me a job, I'm not going to turn them down.

3. **A:** What are you going to do with your books at the end of the course?
   B: I'm going to throw them away!

4. **A:** What are you going to do with *your* books at the end of the course?
   B: I'm going to put them away in a safe place.

5. **A:** Are you going to keep your job?
   B: No, I'm going to have to give it up. I don't have time to work and study.

6. **A:** Should we give the teacher a goodbye gift?
   B: No, let's take her out for a meal.

Dictation, page 276

1. Why did you show up late?
2. I ran into Tony and talked to him for a few minutes.
3. I thought you and Tony had broken up.
4. We made up after our fight and we're friends now.
5. You got over him quickly.

Listening, A, B, page 277

Writer: Congratulations on making it through this English course! We hope you have enjoyed using this book, and most importantly, we hope that it has helped you improve your English. Learning a language is never easy, and you should be proud of yourself for not giving up. Now, before you put away this book and move on to other challenges, we would like to leave you with some words of advice. This advice comes from our experience as both language teachers and language learners. We hope

that you will find it useful.

First, take responsibility for your own learning. For example, don't wait for the teacher to call on you. Raise your hand and volunteer to answer. And don't worry about making mistakes when you speak English. The only way to improve your speaking is by . . . speaking!

Second, understand that you will have good and bad days. You might wake up one day and feel wonderful about your English, but wake up the next day and feel like you can't speak a word. This is completely normal. Don't get frustrated, and don't give up.

Third, when you read something in English, don't look up every new word in your dictionary. Put your dictionary away, and practice figuring out the meaning of new words from the context. Over time, you will get better and better at it, and you will enjoy reading more.

Fourth, when you study vocabulary, it is better to study for short periods of time several times a day than to study for hours before a test. Try to go over new vocabulary for about 10 or 15 minutes before you go to sleep. Many students find that this method really helps them to remember vocabulary better.

Fifth, never hand in a first draft of a paper. Rewrite it several times before you hand it in. And when you finish your final draft, go over it one more time before you hand it in.

Sixth, don't put your work off to the last minute. If possible, finish your assignments early so that you have time to go over them before class.

Finally, use your English as much as possible. If you don't use it, you'll lose it! The work you do in the classroom is just the beginning. To really learn a language, you need to take what you learn in class, and use it in the real world.

Index

Listening

Reading

LIFESKILLS

Business and Employment

Community

Education

Environment and World

Health and Nutrition

Interpersonal Communication

Media

People

Resources

Safety and Security